Ghost Towns of Texas

Ghost Towns of Texas

By T. Lindsay Baker

University of Oklahoma Press : NORMAN AND LONDON

By T. Lindsay Baker

Water for the Southwest: Historical Survey and Guide to Historic Sites (New York, 1973)
The Early History of Panna Maria, Texas (Lubbock, Texas, 1975)
Poles in Texas: Resource Guide, Texas Heritage Unit (Austin, Texas, 1975)
The First Polish Americans: Silesian Settlements in Texas (College Station, Texas, 1979)
Historia najstarszych polskich osad w Ameryce (Wroclaw, Poland, 1981)
The Polish Texans (San Antonio, Texas, 1982)
A Field Guide to American Windmills (Norman, Oklahoma, 1985)
The Survey of the Headwaters of the Red River, 1876 (Canyon, Texas, 1985)
Adobe Walls: The History and Archeology of the 1874 Trading Post (College Station, Texas, 1986)
Ghost Towns of Texas (Norman, 1986)

Library of Congress Cataloging-in-Publication Data

Baker, T. Lindsay.
  Ghost towns of Texas.

  Bibliography: p. 177
  Includes index.
  1. Cities and towns, Ruined, extinct, etc.—Texas—Guidebooks. 2. Texas—History, Local. 3. Texas—
Description and travel—1981–   —Guidebooks. I. Title.
F387.B35   1986   917.64′0463   86–40067
ISBN 0–8061–1997–7 (alk. paper)

The paper in this book meets the guidelines for permanence and durability of the Committee on Production Guidelines for Book Longevity of the Council on Library Resources, Inc.

Contents

Preface

My interest in ghost towns goes back almost as far as my interest in history. As a small boy with my grandfather, George A. Baker, I visited Kimball, a ghost town on the Brazos River. My grandfather had come to the area as a boy and knew Kimball when it was still alive and had an operating ferry. Dr. U. D. Ezell, of Kimball, in fact, had ridden on horseback across high water in the Brazos (too high for his buggy) in 1919 to attend to my father, who as an infant had contracted the dreaded influenza during the great epidemic in 1919. As my grandfather and I later walked through the deserted streets of the town, we looked into the ruins of buildings, and he remarked that this was so-and-so's house and that was this-and-such's store. I was amazed at the size and height of the stone walls from the Kimball Academy, which even then stood roofless and windowless. With this childhood visit to Kimball, I was well on my way to becoming a ghost-town buff.

As a teenager attending Cleburne High School, I was fortunate enough to study Texas history under Joe P. Ross. In his class each pupil was required to prepare a research paper—the first I had ever written. Automatically I chose Kimball, and my grandfather took me to interview an old-timer who had lived in the area north of Kimball almost all of his life. The core around which his house had been built was indeed a log cabin erected by his father. I interviewed the elderly gentleman, learning little about Kimball but much about daily life in nineteenth-century Texas. It left a strong impression. Back at school my teacher submitted the best of the research papers from his class for publication in the *Junior Historian* magazine, but mine entitled "From Kent to Kimball to Oblivion" was not good enough, and it was not even sent down to Austin for consideration. Maybe it is just as well, for this book contains my version of the story, though it is reaching print over two decades after my unsuccessful first attempt.

During the preparation of this book I have driven over 25,000 miles in all parts of Texas to locate and document abandoned towns. As I told my friends, it was a magnificent excuse to visit scores of places that I had heard about but never seen. During these five years I have averaged about one month out of every twelve camping as I sought out ghost towns. While conducting the fieldwork I visited over three hundred abandoned towns throughout Texas. They ranged from virtually intact but empty towns to bare sites in cultivated fields indistinguishable from any others nearby. Some have been surrounded by urban growth, while others have been miles from even the nearest ranch house. The variety of sites, as demonstrated in the book, is difficult even to imagine until one has begun visiting them.

In preparing the book I identified well over one thousand abandoned towns in Texas. From this multitude I selected approximately three hundred for actual site documentation. Unless they were complete "washouts" with no visible remains or were impossible to locate, I prepared detailed photographic and written documentation, creating a morgue of photographs numbering in the thousands. At the same time I conducted research in regional libraries and archives, interviewed remaining residents, copied historic photographs, and sought the advice of local historians, librarians, and museum curators. Work began in more distant areas and I gradually worked back toward my home base in the Panhandle, completing the last fieldwork in early 1985. By this time I had chosen from the hundreds of places most of the sites which eventually ended up in the book.

My most frequent questions during the past five years have been, "Do you know about ———?" and "Did you go to ———?" With the work now in print, these questions will probably become "Why didn't you put ——— in the book?"

In response to the expected queries, I would like to say that I used three criteria for selecting the ghost towns which are found in the book. The first requirement was that the site had to offer something for visitors to see—ruins, abandoned buildings, cemetery, interpretive markers—something tangible. My second criterion was that the sites necessarily would have to have public access. Though most of the abandoned towns are located on private property, they do have access on public roads. Readers must be cautioned, however, that they must seek permission from private landowners if they wish to walk onto the actual site unless it is one of the handful that are found on public property. The third criterion that I employed was to give the entire state of Texas equal treatment geographically. In this way there are ghost towns in the book that are within a day's drive from any point in the state.

By following these self-imposed guidelines I have necessarily eliminated some of the best and most interesting abandoned towns in Texas. The decision was wholly mine. Upland and Frio Town, both fascinating, are located on private land without public access and thus do not appear. Because Nashville-on-the-Brazos and San Luis are obliterated, they were omitted. Similarly it was impossible to include the scores of interesting abandoned towns that are scattered through the area roughly between Fort Worth and San Angelo, one of the richest hunting grounds for ghost towns in Texas. Perhaps another volume in the future will permit the addition of more sites which conform to the first two criteria but which for the sake of even geographical distribution were not included in this work.

A book of this nature must rely heavily on the work of others. Since the Texas Centennial in 1936 numerous individuals have become fascinated by the stories of abandoned towns in the state, and their articles and small books provided invaluable aids to me in identifying potential sites for inclusion in this study. I would like to give particular credit to Grover Cleveland Ramsey, Ed Bartholomew, Dick King, Jim Wheat, R. D. Crane, Stuart McGregor, and Samuel Wood Geiser for their books, articles, and manuscripts. Without their pioneer efforts my job would have been immeasurably more difficult.

Librarians and archivists have provided magnificent assistance and encouragement. Among the repositories that have contributed the most to this book have been the Research Center at the Panhandle-Plains Historical Museum, Southwest Collection at Texas Tech University, Barker Texas History Center and Perry-Castañeda Library at the University of Texas, Texas State Library and Archives, Special Collections at Stephen F. Austin State University, Library and Photographic Collections at the Institute of Texan Cultures, Library of the Daughters of the Republic of Texas at the Alamo, Cornette Library at West Texas State University, Main Library at Texas A&M University, Southwest Collection at the El Paso Public Library, Archives of the Big Bend at Sul Ross State University, and the public libraries in Fort Worth, Amarillo, Cleburne, El Paso, Gonzales, Houston, Austin, Lufkin, and Galveston. Special thanks go to Louise Addington of the Nocona Public Library.

Numerous individuals opened personal files and gave "tours" of sites in their areas, providing me with insights that otherwise I would never have had. Among these many people I would like to single out for particular mention Louise Addington, Nocona; Bob Edwards, Dallas; Mr. and Mrs. Tom Rutherford, Whon; Bill Hatchett, Callahan City; Ed Hammack, Salt Flat; Mary Glover Henson, Pine Spring; Skipper Steely, Paris; George C. Werner and William C. Griggs, Houston; Roy Sylvan Dunn, Nixon; James McReynolds, Chireno; C. E. Harlow, Jr., Van Horn; Barbara Neal Ledbetter, Fort Belknap; Jack Skiles, Langtry; W. P. Winn, Sher-Han; Donaly E. Brice, Austin; Don Abbe and Ernest Wallace, Lubbock; the Reverend Jess Bigbee, Independence; Morris Britton, Sherman; Robert H. Thonhoff, Fashing; Kenneth D. Perry, Alpine; Don Hofsommer, Plainview; the Reverend William L. Watson, O.M.I., San Antonio; Oscar B. Betsill, Doole; Hattie M. Coffee, Peyton Colony; Robert B. Finney, Bartlesville, Oklahoma; J. S. Martucci, Detroit, Michigan; Dianna Everett, Bobby Weaver, and H. Allen Anderson, Canyon; and the staff of the Bullard Community Library.

After completing the texts on the various sites listed in the book, I sent preliminary drafts to local experts for their review. Among these many people whose assistance I would like to acknowledge are C. E. Harlow, Jr., Van Horn; Alline Rutherford, Whon; Robert H. Thonhoff, Fashing; Jan Blodgett, Lubbock; Rebecca D. Radde, Meridian; Verna Anne Wheeler, Crosbyton; C. Richard King, Stephenville; Robert A. Huggins, Big Bend National Park; Mrs. R. P. Jones, Quanah; Kenneth D. Perry, Alpine; Vic Lindley, Mertzon; Luther Moore, Livingston; Rodgers Symm, The Grove; Bob Edwards and James Pratt, Dallas; Brenda Hines, Bronte; Bonnie McDowell and Mrs. Lee Smith, Aspermont; Jack Skiles, Langtry; Dorothy L. Harrington, Sherman; Jack Whitmeyer, Colmesneil; Darrell Debo, Burnet; Sallie B. Harris, Mobeetie; Robert L. Flournoy, Lufkin; Jane Hoerster, Mason; Kenneth A. Wolfe, Laredo; Public Relations Department, Lajitas on the Rio Grande, Lajitas; Lucille Bullard, Jefferson; Mr. and Mrs. Clifton Caldwell, Albany; Bue Euridge, Comanche; Mark A. Geeslin, Jayton; Virginia S. Schuhsler, Cameron; Henri Elizabeth Pepper, Sweetwater; Barbara Neal Ledbetter, Fort Belknap; Okla A. McKee and James M. Day, El Paso; Maurice C. Shelby, Edna; Mrs. Hollis Blackwell, Goldthwaite; Skipper Steely, Paris; Louise Addington, Nocona; Bill Hatchett, Callahan City; Donna Bennett, Camp Verde; the Reverend Jess Bigbee, Independence; Hattie M. Coffee, Peyton Colony; Robert W. Peters, Carlsbad, New Mexico; Mary Glover Henson, Pine Spring; Isabel Hammack Gilmore, Salt Flat; Sherman Harriman, Amarillo; staff of the Bullard Community Library, Bullard; B. Byron Price, Billy R. Harrison, and Dianna Everett, Canyon; the Reverend Bob Wright, O.M.I., San Antonio; David B. Gracy, Donaly E. Brice, and Jerry Sullivan, Austin; John Allen Templeton, Jacksonville.

The purpose of this book is to get people out of their easy chairs and into the field where they can see, smell, and touch Texas history where it was made. If readers find that the status of sites has changed since my writing about them, I would be very much obliged if you would drop me a line and let me know. In addition, if you discover places which you feel merit inclusion in a subsequent volume on Texas ghost towns, I would be most grateful for your suggestions.

I hope that everyone has as much fun going to these places as I did.

Canyon, Texas

T. LINDSAY BAKER

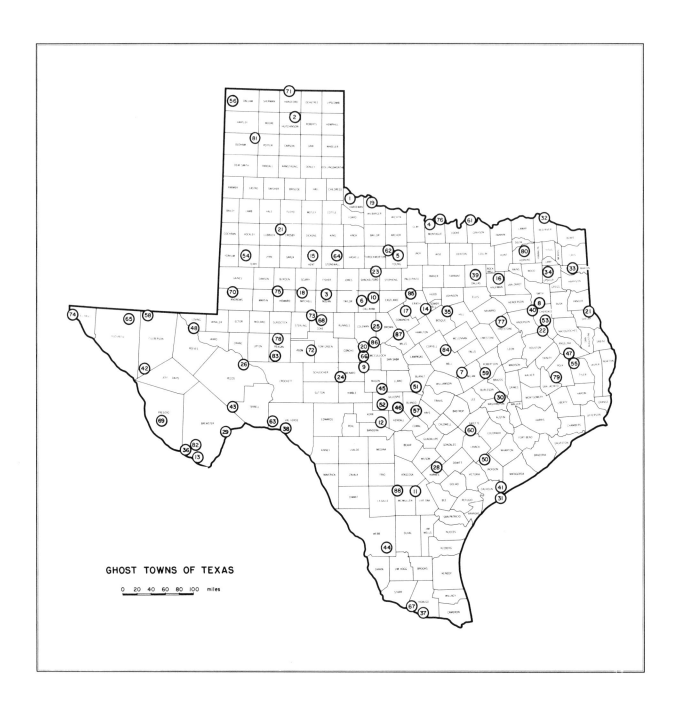

GHOST TOWNS OF TEXAS

0 20 40 60 80 100 miles

Ghost Towns of Texas

Gypsum plant at Acme about 1908. Courtesy Georgia Pacific Corporation, Acme, Texas.

Acme

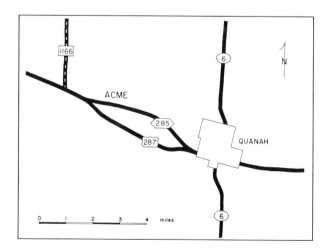

In Texas "Acme" means gypsum, for the town of Acme served one of the largest gypsum mining and processing centers in the United States. The discoverer of the commercial gypsum deposits at Acme was James Sickler, who in the 1880s near Gypsum City, Kansas, had operated a small gypsum processing plant which produced plaster. When the mineral deposit he exploited became exhausted, he turned his eyes southward to Texas in search of another source of supply.

In 1890, Sickler located a large gypsum bed on Groesbeck Creek just west of Quanah in Hardeman County. He reestablished his gypsum milling plant at the site which later became known as Acme. Sickler and others founded the Lone Star Cement Plaster Company and were followed in the gypsum business near Quanah by other Kansans who established the Agatite gypsum mill on Groesbeck Creek about a mile downstream from the earlier plant. For years the two gypsum enterprises competed bitterly, giving rise to one of Texas's most interesting railroad stories.

The Acme Tap Railroad was the shortest common carrier in all Texas, being only one and a half miles long. It began and ended at Acme. One of the two gypsum plants had railway loading facilities, but the second could not be reached by rail service without crossing the property of the first. Quite naturally the former refused to give its competitor rail access, so in 1909 the isolated firm organized the Acme Tap Railroad as a common carrier. This accomplished, it condemned a right-of-way for tracks and built across the com-

Collapsing building near Acme. Photograph by the author, 1980.

petitor's property in order to gain rail service. The short-line railway operated until the plant closed in 1938.

Acme grew to become a considerable town along Groesbeck Creek adjacent to the gypsum plants. Although it never was incorporated as a municipality, it had a post office as early as 1892, and by the turn of the century it boasted numerous residences, a hotel, railway depot, general store, and school. The Fort Worth and Denver Railway passenger trains regularly stopped at Acme about six o'clock each evening so that the crew and passengers could walk across to the hotel for their dinner. The hostelry had so much trade that it had to use two dining rooms to handle all its customers. Much of the housing at Acme was constructed by the plaster companies for their employees who rented the residences.

Gypsum production at Acme began with crude excavations from shallow pits, but within a short time it shifted to underground mining. Then, after the passage of years, the operations changed back to large-scale open pit mining, which con-

tinues to this day. Through the decades a number of curiosities were unearthed by the excavations, including the remains of several prehistoric mastodons, which reputedly were sent to museums in St. Louis. Today the old Acme gypsum plant is owned and operated by Georgia Pacific Corporation. Formerly making plaster products, today it produces primarily gypsum wallboard for the construction industry. It is shipped throughout the United States.

The town of Acme has virtually faded into the past. There are ruins of several commercial and residential buildings, the concrete foundations from the former company store, and vast surface refuse left behind by the former residents. The area contains several scattered rural residences, two of which are surviving examples of former gypsum company houses built for employees years ago.

LOCATION: *Acme is located immediately east of the Georgia Pacific plant on Spur 285 about 4.3 miles northwest of Quanah in Hardeman County.*

Adobe Walls

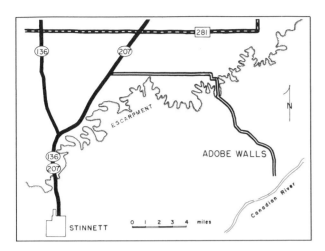

Adobe Walls was a community of merchants, clerks, cooks, and laborers, which prospered for a few months on the north side of the Canadian River in the Panhandle during the days of the great buffalo hunt. Its purpose was to serve the crews of buffalo hunters and skinners who were operating in the area. Today it is best known as the site of the 27 June 1874 Battle of Adobe Walls between the occupants of the post and about two hundred Plains Indians.

After the hide hunters in 1872–73 had decimated the western Kansas buffalo herds, they began shifting their operations southward across the Arkansas and Cimarron rivers into the Texas Panhandle. They had killed so many bison in Kansas that it became difficult for them to make a living taking hides. Consequently in the winter of 1873–74 hunting crews moved southward into an area that had been exclusively the hunting grounds of the Comanche, Kiowa, Cheyenne, and Arapaho Indians.

When the hunters began shifting south, merchants in Dodge City, Kansas, fearing the loss of their trade, also began planning branch stores to operate in the midst of the new buffalo range. Because of its railway connections, Dodge City had been the center of the hunt in Kansas, and it remained the most important shipping point for hides, even when the hunters moved south, since its railroad was the closest to the Texas Panhandle at that time.

The first party of Dodge City merchants entered Texas in March 1874, choosing a site for their store about two miles north of the Canadian River on a broad grassy meadow area already known as Adobe Walls. The name came from the gaunt ruins of a much earlier trading post which had been built there thirty years before by the firm of Bent, St. Vrain and Company, owners of Bent's Fort on the Santa Fe Trail. These ruins were the site of an unsuccessful attempt by the Bent enterprise to establish a trading post among the Comanche and Kiowa Indians.

The Kansas merchants built a large complex known as the Myers and Leonard Store, complete with a cottonwood picket corral enclosing a large hide yard, a picket-walled store, and even a restaurant. In April a second party of merchants representing Charles Rath and Company arrived at Adobe Walls and built a separate sod store about two hundred fifty yards south of Myers and Leonard. Before long the merchants were joined by James N. Hanrahan, who with Charles Rath built a sod saloon, and Tom O'Keefe, who erected a picket blacksmith shop.

By summer 1874 between two and three hundred hide men were in the Texas Panhandle killing bison by the thousands, and trade boomed at Adobe Walls. The hide men sold their dried hides at the stores and in turn bought their supplies from the merchants. Traders contracted with teamsters to haul their hides to the railroad in Dodge City. All went well until late June, when an Indian uprising broke out.

Comanche and Kiowa warriors attacked several of the outlying hide men's camps, where at least four men were killed and gruesomely mutilated. This was only a foretaste of what was coming, for at dawn on the morning of 27 June 1874 approximately two hundred Comanche, Kiowa, and Cheyenne warriors descended on the trading post. The thirty merchants, employees, and hide men who happened to be there ran for safety in the two stores and the saloon and fought for their lives much of the day.

The Indians had been told by their medicine man that they would be able to club the white men to death in their sleep and that even if they awakened, the bullets from their guns would pass through the warriors harmlessly. Undoubtedly the attackers were disheartened to see their friends fall one after the other before the buffalo hunters' big game rifles. The fight continued until the middle of the afternoon, when the warriors retreated to the surrounding hills. Three whites had been killed, while thirteen Indians were left on

John Thomson Jones, alias "Antelope Jack" and "Cheyenne Jack," a buffalo skinner killed and mutilated by hostile Indians shortly before the 1874 Battle of Adobe Walls. Courtesy Panhandle-Plains Historical Museum, Canyon, Texas.

1975 the Panhandle-Plains Historical Society, with assistance from several other agencies and foundations, excavated the site during a five-season archeological investigation. Today visitors see several historical markers which were erected forty to sixty years ago, the graves of men killed during the fight, and slight mounds marking the outlines of some of the former buildings. Adobe Walls is a registered Texas Archeological Landmark and nothing may be removed from the site.

LOCATION: *Adobe Walls is located about 17 miles southeast of a point on Texas Highway 207 about half-way between Spearman and Stinnett in Hutchinson County. The best route to the site is via a paved and graded county road which leaves the state highway 3.7 miles southwest of its intersection with Farm to Market Road 281 and 6.3 miles northeast of its intersection with Texas Highway 136. From this point, which is marked by a highway department sign, drive due east 7.5 miles on the county road, which at this point begins winding and twisting down the side of the Canadian River escarpment, finally ending up 9.5 miles farther at the archeological site, which is identified by several granite historical markers.*

the field of battle. The fight was a standoff.

All the white men's horses, mules, and oxen had been either killed or stolen, so the men were unable to depart the post. Two runners on foot left to warn the hunters in the outlying camps of the danger, and within a week two hundred men had ridden into the stores at Adobe Walls for safety. Messengers requesting aid were sent on horseback to Dodge City, but a month passed before the Kansas merchants sent a relief column. At that time the traders loaded onto freight wagons the most valuable merchandise and most of the accumulated hides, leaving behind what they could not haul away. A handful of hunters lingered around the post into August, but as the hunting was not as good as they had expected, they too left the site, abandoning it completely. In autumn the Indians returned to loot and burn the vacant buildings.

For over a century the trading post site remained abandoned. There was a short-lived Adobe Walls post office beginning in 1887, but it was housed at the headquarters of a nearby ranch. Finally in

Avenger Field

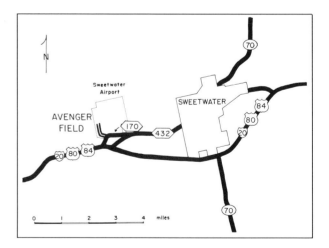

Avenger Field, which is marked today by the Sweetwater Airport and the Sweetwater branch of Texas State Technical Institute, over forty years ago earned the distinction of having been the largest all-woman air base in American history.

The story of Avenger Field and its all-female trainee corps goes back to the months immediately

WASP trainees receiving instruction at Avenger Field. Courtesy National Air and Space Museum, Smithsonian Institution, Washington, D.C.

Sunbathing during free time at Avenger Field. Courtesy National Air and Space Museum, Smithsonian Institution, Washington, D.C.

following American entry into World War II. With conversion to war production, aircraft manufacturers in America were successfully producing war planes faster than the army could train men to pilot them. In order to release male fliers for combat duty, the Pentagon approved a plan to use women as ferry pilots to transport aircraft within the United States.

The women chosen to become what later were known as Women's Airforce Service Pilots, or WASPs, already were certified civilian pilots. Their flying experience for the most part, however, had been confined to light, single-engine private planes. After passing physical examinations and proving their basic flying abilities, they assembled at Avenger Field, west of Sweetwater, for their formal military training. The instructional program for women pilots actually began in November 1942 at Howard Hughes Field in Houston, but by early 1943 most of the training had shifted to Avenger Field.

The site of the base for thirteen years had been the Sweetwater municipal airport. After the attack on Pearl Harbor, its operation was assumed by the U.S. Army and for several months the base trained first British and then American male pilots. The first contingent of women trainees arrived in February 1943, and shortly thereafter Avenger Field became an all-woman installation. The only men regularly employed at the base were service personnel and a handful of instructors and army officers.

During the operation of Avenger Field, the Army Air Corps successfully trained 1,074 women pilots. Upon graduation they served in all parts of the United States ferrying every type of aircraft that the Air Forces had. At least thirty-seven WASPs gave their lives for their country in accidents as they logged an amazing sixty million miles in operational hours.

Day-to-day life for the women at Avenger Field was very confining, with flying and aviation training taking precedence over all other activities. The base, as might be expected, was "off limits" to male trainees from surrounding military facilities, but remarkable numbers of them found themselves having to make "emergency landings" at Avenger Field.

According to an often-told story, a now unidentified woman flier from Avenger Field one summer day decided that she would try sunbathing in the open cockpit of her PT-19 plane. After reaching a comfortable altitude and finding all quiet around her, she slipped off her shirt and lay back in the pilot's seat to soak up the West Texas sunshine. A few minutes later her solitude was broken by an unexpected roar from other planes. The WASP turned around to be greeted by the grins and waves of male cadets from nearby bases.

Ducking into her open cockpit as far as she could retreat, the WASP trainee banked her plane away from the others and began fumbling with her clothes. At this point the wind pulled her shirt out of her hands, letting it sail through the air to the Texas plains below. When she landed in front of the long wooden buildings at Avenger Field, the embarrassed trainee called out from the plane for someone to bring her a blanket!

Avenger Field remained a WASP training base until 20 December 1944, when it closed. For several months a few male pilots trained there, but then the base was abandoned by the War Department. It remained dormant, serving as a municipal airport, until 1955, when the U.S. Air Force placed a sophisticated radar station there. This facility operated until 1969, when the military abandoned the site entirely. Since that time it has continued to be used as a private airport and since 1970 has been the home for the Sweetwater branch of the Texas State Technical Institute. The site, however, has never seen such intense human activity as that which took place during the twenty-three months when it was the national center of training for the Women's Airforce Service Pilots.

LOCATION: *Avenger Field existed on the site of the present-day Sweetwater Airport. To reach the former base take exit 240 from Interstate Highway 20 on the extreme west side of Sweetwater, and follow Loop 170 a short distance north to a turnoff marked for the Sweetwater Airport. Follow the signs 0.5 mile to the airport proper, where several World War II–vintage hangars and other structures have survived. A historical marker for Avenger Field stands on the north side of Interstate Highway 20 at its intersection with Loop 170.*

Belcherville

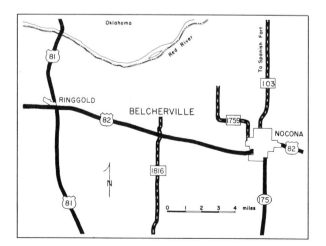

Belcherville, in the 1950s reputedly the least populated incorporated city in Texas, boomed as

a trade center in the Red River Valley around the turn of the century. At one time it claimed as many as two thousand inhabitants, but today it is virtually deserted.

Belcherville came into existence as a result of land promotion during the late 1880s. In 1886 John and Alex S. Belcher laid out the townsite one mile square containing 170 blocks, 20 of which were reserved for business purposes. The two Belchers had purchased a ranch in the area but not for cattle raising. They intended to divide the property into acreages and sell it to farmers at an average price of ten dollars an acre. Belcherville was planned as the commercial heart of the Belcher land colonization scheme. On 13 July 1887 they sold the first lots, and within less than a decade their town reached its zenith. Lots in the townsite initially sold at prices ranging from twenty-five to one hundred fifty dollars apiece.

A post office was established at Belcherville on 27 August 1887 originally intended to be called Belcher. Since there already was a post office by that name in Texas, postal authorities changed the post office name for the community into Belcherville. The community retained its post office until 1954.

Folklore states that Belcherville's decline came because the town refused to give the Gainesville, Henrietta and Western Railway a bounty of a thousand dollars to build through the community, but in reality the railroad preceded the town and was the reason it was built at its present site. In fact, for a while the railway had Belcherville as its terminus, greatly stimulating the initial growth of the town.

The decline of Belcherville was prompted in part by the extension of the railway line farther westward toward Henrietta. On 6 February 1893 the town suffered a fire which destroyed much of its business district. According to stories still told to visitors, one side of the town was burned by residents from the other side. Then, the oral informants declare, the inhabitants of the burned side the next night took revenge by starting fires on the still-standing side. Only a few of the destroyed structures were ever rebuilt.

Whatever the cause for the fires, they definitely prompted the demise of Belcherville. The townsite seemed jinxed by newcomers, and many of them chose to settle elsewhere. The population began shrinking, a process which has continued

Loungers sitting in the band stand on the public square at Belcherville about 1917. Courtesy Louise Addington.

Customers and their automobiles outside the drugstore in Belcherville about 1918. Courtesy Louise Addington.

Sheet music and Sunday school materials strewn on the floor of the Belcherville Baptist Church. Photograph by the author, 1981.

throughout this century. The official census tabulation showed 305 inhabitants in 1900, 181 in 1910, 85 in 1930, and only 51 in 1950, the last year that the town was enumerated as a municipality. Even in 1950, though it was still legally incorporated and boasted two churches and one store, Belcherville had no mayor, no school, and no telephone exchange. During the 1950s the second Tuesday of each month was the occasion for a community supper. Every person who had a birthday during the previous month was honored by being a special guest at the dinner.

Today the town has only about a dozen residences, two abandoned churches, and numerous stone foundations marking the sites of former buildings. Even the railroad is gone. The playground swings at the old Belcherville school stand like sentinels on the hill southwest of the townsite, where classes used to be held in a now long-departed three-story building.

LOCATION: *Belcherville lies on the side of a slight hill at an "S" bend in Farm to Market Road 1816 about a quarter mile north of its intersection with U.S. Highway 82 about 6.5 miles east of Ringgold and 6.2 miles west of Nocona in Montague County.*

Belknap

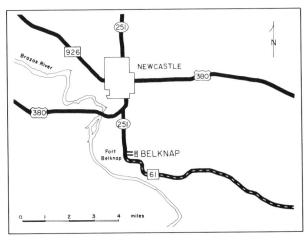

Belknap, a town which sprang up on the east side of the military post of Fort Belknap, had an existence very closely tied with that of the fort. Though many of the fort structures were restored and reconstructed during the Texas Centennial in 1936, little remains of the town other than its interesting graveyard.

The military post at Fort Belknap originated in 1851, when it was established by General William G. Belknap. Originally located two miles higher on the Brazos River, it moved downstream a few months later to a point that it occupied for the next twenty-five years. The post was one of a series of forts stretching from the Rio Grande to the Red River, which were constructed in the early 1850s to protect the Texas frontier from marauding bands of Indians.

The town of Belknap was built about half a mile east of the fort, just off the military reservation, and in 1856 it became the first seat of Young County. Its businesses did a healthy trade with the officers and men from the fort, as well as with travelers. The town became a regular stop on the Butterfield Overland Mail in 1858, being described by a passenger on the first westbound stagecoach on that route as containing 150 residents, several stores, a saloon with a billiard parlor, and a post office. The post office had been established on 14 August 1856 under the name of Fort Belknap, and it operated until 5 November 1866.

Belknap was the nearest large white settlement to the Brazos River Indian Reservation about fifteen miles to the southeast. It had been begun by the state of Texas as a reserve for the peaceful

The covered well at Fort Belknap. Photograph by the author, 1984.

Indians who remained in the state. Tribes represented by the almost two thousand Native Americans located there included the Caddo, Anadarko, Tonkawa, Waco, and small groups from other tribes. Though the Indians were not warlike, the hostility of the white settlers who were moving into the general area verged on open warfare, and Indian agent Robert S. Neighbors was forced five years later to lead his wards for their own safety to federal reserves in the Indian Territory. Neighbors, who had served both the republic and state of Texas as an Indian agent, was assassinated on a street in Belknap on 14 September 1859 by a newcomer to Texas, Edward Cornett. He probably did not even know the man who killed him.

The town of Belknap lost much of its population during the Civil War, when the fort was

abandoned by regular army troops and the danger from Indian attacks increased. The community came back to life when the fort was reoccupied by federal troops in 1867. A soldier who arrived at the time noted that "the village adjacent to the fort had been a station on the overland mail route, and when it was occupied by settlers and the fort filled with troops I have no doubt it was, as I was informed it had been, the prettiest frontier post in Texas." The post office was reestablished under the name of Belknap on 20 January 1874, but in that very year the county seat moved to Graham. Two years later the military post was closed as no longer needed. The town had been declining, for in 1870 only about seventy inhabitants still resided in Belknap, and only forty-four remained in 1880. The town became a virtual ghost, though it kept its post office until 1908, and today the townsite is marked only by its cemetery and a few scattered rural residences. The nearby fort, rebuilt half a century ago, contains a museum and presents to the public not only its own history but also that of the town.

LOCATION: *Belknap and Fort Belknap are found on Texas Highway 251 about 3.0 miles south of Newcastle in Young County. The fort and surrounding park are on the west side of the road, while the civilian cemetery, with the marked grave of Robert S. Neighbors, may be reached by taking an unimproved sandy field road 0.3 mile east from the highway over two cattleguards and through an arched cemetery gate.*

The 1884 Belle Plain College building slowly succumbing to the elements. Photograph by the author, 1984.

Belle Plain

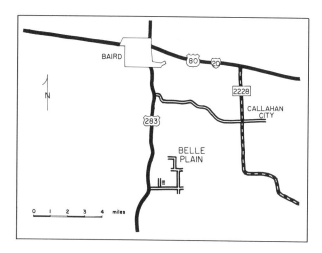

Mesquite clogs former streets once filled with horses and carriages, while cattle browse in the ruined basement of a college building that once rang with music at Belle Plain, one of the most promising towns in West Texas during the 1870s.

After 1874, when U.S. Army troops under Colonel Ranald S. Mackenzie defeated the Comanches in the Palo Duro Canyon, large numbers of settlers began moving into central West Texas. Freed for the first time from imminent danger of Indian attacks, the inviting, inexpensive lands proved to be a magnet to stock raisers. One of the many individuals who entered the area was Nelson M. Smith, a land promoter who in 1875 purchased a section of land just north of the Callahan Divide in present-day Callahan County.

By 1876, Nelson Smith had platted a townsite in the southwest corner of his section of land and had begun selling lots to prospective residents and businessmen. Growth at the beginning was slow, with only three places of business operating in the summer of 1876, one of them a saloon. At that time B. F. Austin came to the town as a boy and in later years he had distinct recollections of the saloon, operated by J. W. Cheatham, which was housed in a picket structure with mud chinking to keep the wind from blowing between its vertical log pickets. He recalled that "the whisky was served in mugs, drawn from faucets in ends of barrels," adding that "the barrels were placed on end and on split-log scaffolds about 18 inches from the floor, next to the back wall of the room."

Belle Plain began growing more quickly, reaching a total population of about three hundred inhabitants by 1880. At one time it had not only the

The T. H. Floyd residence at Belle Plain, with its former flower beds still marked by carefully placed stone borders. Photograph by the author, 1984.

seat of Callahan County, organized in 1877, but also several mercantile stores, three saloons, a hotel, a newspaper entitled the *Callahan County Clarendon*, stonemasons, building contractors, blacksmiths, and even a carriage builder. There was a very active Methodist congregation and both Masonic and Odd Fellows lodges. Numerous lawyers and physicians resided in the town. In August 1879, Captain G. W. Robson visited Belle Plain and described it for his readers in the *Fort Griffin Echo*, reporting that "we do not know of a more pleasant or beautiful place or one with brighter prospects for a prosperous future than Belle Plain."

The crowning glory of Belle Plain was its college, one of the first such institutions in West Texas. As early as 1878 local Methodist leaders had considered founding a school of higher learning in central West Texas, but it was 1880 before they began active efforts to raise funds for the establishment of a college. John Day donated ten acres south of the business district in Belle Plain for the site, and twenty-two students enrolled in the autumn of 1881. The next year enrollment jumped to eighty-five and soon a dormitory was built for female students. By 1887 church authorities provided $10,000 for the construction of an imposing three-story college administration and classroom building, the stone walls of which are still partially standing.

Belle Plain College offered the full classical course of studies including Latin, Greek, French, and German languages as well as mental and moral philosophy, history, algebra, trigonometry, astronomy, physics, and chemistry. The reputation of the college, however, rested on its music department, the school reportedly having over a dozen grand pianos. The Texas Military Institute operated as an adjunct to the school to provide military training for the young men. Belle Plain College flourished for a few years, but the severe West Texas drought of 1886–87 dealt it a blow from which it never fully recovered. As the fields and pastures seared from the heat, many residents of the area were forced to leave just to find employment. Already facing financial problems, the school floundered though it did not close its doors until 1892.

Belle Plain College, however, outlived the town of Belle Plain. In 1880 the Texas and Pacific Railway built westward from Fort Worth into Callahan County and beyond. Residents of Belle Plain had expected the line to run through their town, but instead it went six miles to the north. The railroad company began a new town, Baird, which grew at the expense of the older community. Most of the businesses from Belle Plain moved north to the railway, as did the *Callahan County Clarendon* in 1883. Also in that year a countywide election was held at the behest of Baird residents to determine whether the county seat would stay at Belle Plain or move to the newer community. Baird won the contest and the county seat moved. The county commissioners even decided to disassemble the new stone jail at Belle Plain, and it stands to this day in Baird. The town declined so quickly that only four families were left there in 1897, and today it is an absolute ghost.

LOCATION: *Belle Plain is located only about a mile east of U.S. Highway 283 about 6.5 miles south of Baird, but reaching the site requires a circuitous route via graded county roads. Leave U.S. Highway 283 on County Road 218 at a point 7.5 miles south of Baird (4.5 miles north of the U.S. Highway 283 junction with Texas Highway 36) and drive 1.6 miles east to a four-way intersection. This passes near the beautifully maintained Belle Plain cemetery just north of the county road 0.6 mile east of the highway. From the four-way intersection drive north on County Road 220 about 1.0 mile to a jog 0.1 mile to the west on County Road 293 and then north an additional 0.6 mile on County Road 294 to an "L" turn to the west, placing you in the heart of Belle Plain. None of these graded roads is recommended after wet weather.*

Bryant Station

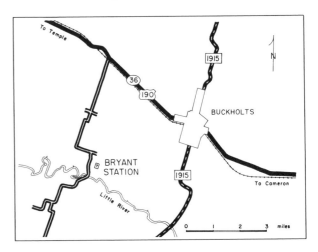

Bryant Station, initially an Indian trading post, was founded by and named for one of the heroes of San Jacinto, Benjamin Franklin Bryant. He was a native of Georgia who had come to Texas with his wife in 1834, settling first in Shelby County. Bryant organized a company for the Texan army during the revolution against Mexico, joining the main body of troops under Sam Houston at the Bernardo Plantation on 29 March 1836. His unit remained with the forces until after the Battle of San Jacinto.

Sam Houston, a friend of Bryant, later as president of the Republic of Texas appointed him a representative of the republic in dealing with the Indians and requested that he establish a trading post on the Little River about seventy-five miles northwest of Washington-on-the-Brazos. One of its purposes was to serve as a buffer between the Indians on the west and the white settlements farther to the east.

The land granted by the republic to Bryant consisted of about three thousand acres fronting on the north bank of the Little River. Bryant himself served as a "blazer" in the party headed by George B. Erath that surveyed the property. Soon Bryant built for himself and his family a fortified cabin from which he traded with the Indians and engaged in some limited agriculture. With the passage of time a community grew up around Bryant's cabin, taking the name of Bryant Station. In 1858, Jacob DeCordova described the community as "a large and flourishing settlement," as indeed it was. In the years preceding the Civil War it possessed not only Bryant's store but also blacksmith shops, other mercantile estab-

Graves in the Bryant Station cemetery. Photograph by the author, 1984.

lishments, and even a Masonic lodge. On 5 January 1848 it received a post office, with John C. Reid as its master, and it kept direct mail service with only brief interruptions until 1876.

Many travelers stopped at Bryant Station because it was near a point that became an important crossing on the Little River. A representative visitor was A. W. Moore, who noted in his diary for 27 May 1847 that he had "traveled up the prairie to Briants [sic] 14 miles . . . timber mean . . . and worthless for anything but firewood. In the evening went with Bryant up the river five miles. . . . Staid all night at Briants [and] left on the 28th for falls of the brassos [sic] 35 miles."

Occasionally Benjamin F. Bryant was called upon to lead local men against bands of warlike Indians that raided the vicinity. This occurred in 1839 when he commanded fifty-two settlers in a hand-to-hand fight with members of a war party who already had killed and scalped two families

in the neighborhood. The Texans followed the band and attacked an encampment of approximately sixty warriors. At first the assault seemed successful, but the Indians counterattacked and drove the white men into retreat. Bryant himself was wounded during the first charge, and ten of his men were killed outright, with five more suffering wounds.

During the Civil War, Captain G. R. Freeman raised a company for the Confederate Army at Bryant Station. Each man provided his own horse, gun, and equipment. The men were mustered into service at Hempstead as Company D of Colonel D. C. Gidding's regiment, serving until the end of the conflict. Afterward many of the men returned to their former homes in the area. The community around the former trading post prospered for several more years, but when the Gulf, Colorado and Santa Fe Railway built north of the settlement in 1881 and the railroad town of Buckholts was established only four miles away, Bryant Station

Iron truss bridge carrying traffic across the Little River near Bryant Station. Photograph by the author, 1984.

began a decline which by the turn of the century was nearly complete, even though a school continued to operate at Bryant Station into this century. In 1931 the bodies of Benjamin Bryant and his wife were moved from the townsite to the State Cemetery in Austin.

LOCATION: *Bryant Station has all but disappeared, leaving only its graveyard for visitors to see. To reach the site, drive south on an unmarked good gravel county road from U.S. Highway 190/Texas Highway 36 about 4.2 miles west of Buckholts in Milam County, immediately crossing the tracks of the Santa Fe Railway. Proceed south on the county road 3.5 miles to a distinct bend to the east. Continue an additional 0.7 mile, crossing two wooden bridges to a "T" intersection, a total distance of 4.2 miles. At the "T" make a sharp right turn to the south and proceed 0.2 mile to a gate and sign for the Bryant Station cemetery. The graveyard is located about a quarter mile east down a rough road through a pasture, and there one finds numerous interesting burial markers and a guest register inside a metal mailbox. The 1936 granite historical marker which originally stood at the site has been relocated to a roadside park on the main highway between Buckholts and Rogers.*

Burning Bush

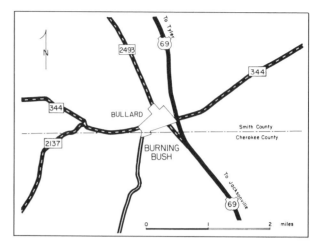

Burning Bush, on the Smith-Cherokee county line just southeast of Bullard, was an unsuccessful Methodist communistic colony. Established in 1913, it existed for six years, when it disbanded as a result of financial difficulties.

During the early years of this century, many Methodists in the northern states felt that their church was becoming too formal. Some of these "Free Methodists" banded together to form the Metropolitan Church Association, with its headquarters in Waukesha, Wisconsin, on the western outskirts of Milwaukee. The organization gained considerable momentum when two wealthy capitalists joined the venture: Duke M. Farson, a bond broker from Chicago, and Edwin T. Harvey, a millionaire hotel keeper.

Early in the century the Metropolitan Church Association, popularly called the Society of the Burning Bush, established several communal colonies in Virginia, West Virginia, Louisiana, and Texas. The year 1912 saw the formation of plans for the creation of a Texas community, when a real estate firm informed bond broker Farson that 1,520 acres were available to the organization near Bullard. The land was fertile, was watered by springs, and was well drained—ideal for an agricultural colony. Much of the land had been part of the William Pitt Douglas plantation before the Civil War, and his old plantation house and outbuildings still stood on the property, a further inducement for the potential northern purchasers. Five years earlier, in 1907, the plantation had been purchased by Charles E. Palmer, and he had planted part of the acreage in pecan, peach, and plum trees, though they had not yet begun bearing fruit and nuts by 1912.

The Society of the Burning Bush offered to trade for the plantation in Texas a section of land in Idaho, a tract only twelve miles from Chicago, and a hotel and brickyard in Las Vegas, New Mexico. The offer seemed too good for Palmer to resist, so he transferred title to the plantation in February 1912.

Soon representatives of the Metropolitan Church arrived in Bullard and set up headquarters in the old Douglas mansion. A year later a chartered train brought 375 church members from the North. Temporarily billeting in the mansion, the new residents quickly started erecting a sixty- by eighty-foot wooden tabernacle, small clapboard residences, and two large dormitories for unmarried male and female colonists. Construction continued for almost the entire history of Burning Bush, with work on sewage system, waterworks, electric powerhouse, and school, not to mention the erection of a two-story building to house visitors and a communal kitchen.

Members gave all their earthly possessions to the Metropolitan Church Association when they joined. Upon arrival at Burning Bush, they withdrew all their needs from a communal storehouse. lived in church-built houses, and ate in the community dining hall. All the business of the colony was conducted in the name of the Metropolitan

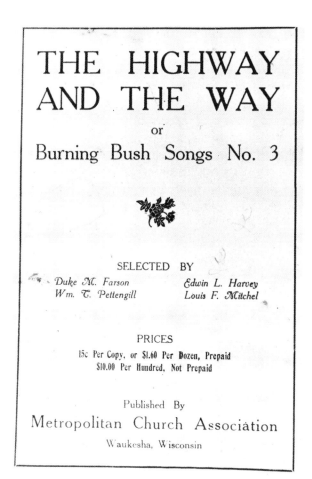

THE HIGHWAY AND THE WAY

or

Burning Bush Songs No. 3

SELECTED BY

Duke M. Farson   Edwin L. Harvey
Wm. T. Pettengill   Louis F. Mitchel

PRICES

15c Per Copy, or $1.60 Per Dozen, Prepaid
$10.00 Per Hundred, Not Prepaid

Published By

Metropolitan Church Association

Waukesha, Wisconsin

Special hymnbook used in religious services at the tabernacle by residents of Burning Bush. Courtesy Bullard Community Library, Bullard, Texas.

Aged barn standing at the site of the Burning Bush colony. Photograph by the author, 1981.

Church Association. Most of the revenue generated by the colonists came from the sale of agricultural products, principally the nuts and fruit from the trees that had been planted before their coming. Being unfamiliar with Southern agricultural practices, the colonists often raised less bountiful crops than those produced by their neighbors, even though the newcomers used advanced tractors, binders, and threshing machines then uncommon in the region. Truck crops became such an important part of the agricultural operation that the church even built a cannery, at one time purchasing an entire boxcar load of empty tin cans for use there.

Religious services at Burning Bush were very emotional experiences. One local resident in later years remembered that the "Bushers would even turn back flips [sic] in church and roll around on the sawdust floor of the tabernacle." Some of the special song books used in the services may be viewed today in the Bullard Community Library.

Financial problems caused the failure of Burning Bush. The colony, unable to support itself from the proceeds of its agriculture, was a constant drain on the treasury of the Metropolitan Church Association. Revenue from Duke Farson's bond brokerage business helped subsidize the settlement during much of its history, but when his business began to suffer, the problems in Texas grew worse. Many community members sought work outside the colony, giving their salaries to the church for the communal good. Even so the society had to purchase groceries on credit from a local merchant, J. L. Vanderver. When the bill amounted to over $12,000, the grocer brought suit on the unpaid notes and won a court judgment against the Metropolitan Church. The county sheriff seized the lands and sold them at auction on the steps of the courthouse in Tyler on 15 April 1919. The residents of Burning Bush dispersed, most of them returning to the North, but a handful remained in Texas to rent and later to buy their own farms and homes. Over the years the buildings that stood at Burning Bush were demolished, even the big Douglas mansion in 1957. Today the community is marked by only a few foundations and the beautiful pecan orchard across the street from the present-day Bullard High School.

LOCATION: *The site of Burning Bush may be viewed from the extension of Main Street 0.3 mile south of Farm to Market Road 344 in Bullard. The town stood east of the road beyond the Bullard High School across the road from the Douglas family cemetery.*

Calf Creek

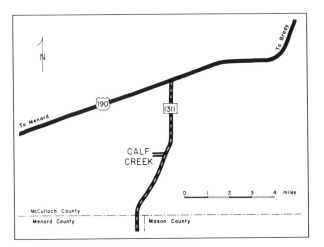

Calf Creek is known today for events that occurred seventy years before its establishment as a town. This rural community, which had a substantial population during the early years of this century, retained its school into the 1940s and its post office into the 1950s. It is just north of the site where Jim Bowie and ten other men bested an overwhelming number of Indians in an 1831 fight.

Ranchers began settling the area around Calf Creek in the 1870s and 1880s. The community takes its name from a stream where the early settlers erected a corral in which to pen calves during weaning. The town began at its present site shortly after the turn of the century, when Mr. and Mrs. Willis Huey sold part of their ranch to the Milton Land Company. This firm divided the acreage into parcels and sold it to farmers, many of whom came to the area to buy fertile agricultural land. The first church at Calf Creek, organized by the Presbyterians, was followed in 1903 by the Baptists and later by an independent Protestant group. For many years local residents attended a union Sunday school.

The location of the Calf Creek community changed two times. Initially it was known as Deland, for it was established on a ranch owned

Long silent piano in a classroom at the Calf Creek school. Photograph by the author, 1984.

Stone walls marking a building site at Calf Creek. Photograph by the author, 1984.

by the Deland family. Then in 1900 Lem Tucker moved to the vicinity from Blanket, Texas, and built a store about a mile north of the first community. The town center remained here until after the start of land colonization activity by the Milton Land Company, when it shifted another mile to the north, to its current location. At each site the town had a different post office name: Deland, Tucker, and finally Calf Creek. In its final location the town had its post office, a store, a dry goods and millinery shop, two cotton gins, a seven-grade school, a large cemetery, and even a telephone exchange.

During the early years at Calf Creek, its families generally went by wagon to the county seat at Brady only twice a year, to buy clothes for winter and for summer. The men in the community took turns traveling into town for supplies, someone going about every two weeks and bringing back staple groceries and other goods for himself and everyone else. Sometimes during the summer the supplies included a big block of ice that could be used by all the residents for a community ice-cream supper.

Calf Creek is best known today for its proximity to the reputed site of Jim Bowie's battle with Indians in 1831. In November of that year Bowie set out from San Antonio to visit the silver mine which he supposedly had found in the area of the eighteenth-century San Saba Spanish mission. During the course of their travel north of the mission, Bowie and ten companions were attacked by a large party of hostile Waco, Caddo, and Tawakoni Indians. In the fight and subsequent siege the Bowie party purportedly killed more than fifty of their assailants while suffering only one casualty themselves.

Today Calf Creek is an absolute ghost town. The site is marked by an abandoned four-room concrete block school erected in 1921, a large cemetery, several abandoned rural residences, and foundations from a number of former buildings.

LOCATION: *Calf Creek in southern McCulloch County is comparatively easy to find. Drive south 3.3 miles on Farm to Market Road 1311 from its intersection with U.S. Highway 190 about 11.4 miles southwest of Brady. Turn west down a gravel road at a sign for the Calf Creek cemetery and drive an additional 0.2 mile to the school and cemetery. The fifty-year-old granite historical marker for Jim Bowie's Calf Creek fight with the Indians stands at the east side of the farm to market road just 1.0 mile south of the townsite.*

Callahan City

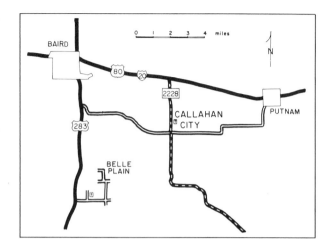

Callahan City owed its existence to the Western Cattle Trail, which led from Texas northward across the Indian Territory to Dodge City, Kansas. The community prospered during the 1870s and 1880s, but virtually every trace has disappeared, except for its cemetery and a very large oak tree which stood at the town center.

The Western Trail was opened in 1874, and by 1876 it had begun assuming much of the cattle traffic which earlier had been driven northward on the Chisholm Trail. By the late 1870s tens of thousands of Texas cattle were being driven along the new route to Kansas markets. One of the main feeders into the trail began in the San Antonio area and led northward to Fort Griffin, where other feeders merged with it to form the main trail. The feeder trail from San Antonio included a waterhole known as the Deep Hole on Deep Creek, and it was just southwest of this watering place that the town of Callahan City sprang to life in the mid-1870s. The community was built on a low rise overlooking the trail as it led to the waterhole.

Callahan City never had a large population, though at one time it possessed two stores, a school, and several residences. It received its post office under the name of Deep Creek on 8 May 1878, and it kept direct mail service until 11 November 1881, its post office name having changed to Callahan in 1880. At the center of the town stood a large oak tree just a few feet north of the two stores. The school was built across an open area to the north, facing the stores, while houses were erected west along the main street. For rec-

Oak tree standing at what once was the center of Callahan City. Photograph by the author, 1984.

reation the citizens enjoyed a horse race track on the creek flats just north of the townsite.

The residents of Callahan City fought bitterly to secure the seat of Callahan County when it was formally organized in 1877. As early as November 1876 local citizens had canvassed the area on horseback, soliciting signatures on a petition for the separation of their county from Eastland County, to which it had been attached earlier for administrative and judicial purposes. On 17 November they presented their petition with 190 signatures to the Eastland County commissioners, who ordered an election for Callahan County officials on 23 December 1876. The election was never held, however, because the legally mandated thirty days notice was three days short.

Area residents waited five months, through the winter of 1876–77, before again petitioning for an election of county officials. This time the voting took place and the first officials of Callahan County were elected. In July 1877 the county

judge called a meeting of the new officials at Callahan City to be held on 30 July for the purpose of organizing the county government. They met in the Merchant, McCoy, and Company store, but because of the heat they moved to the cool shade of the large oak tree. At this session most of the officials gathered and posted the required bonds for their positions. The court then adjourned, planning to meet next at Belle Plain, about six miles to the southwest. Belle Plain (also discussed in this book), became the chief competitor with Callahan City for the county seat, and a desperate fight ensued between the two towns. By late August and early September public sentiment caused the county commissions to act on the important question of selecting a permanent county seat. As stipulated by state law, the commissioners petitioned the governor to set the date for an election.

The balloting was held on 13 October 1877, and Belle Plain won by a margin of fifty-one

Neglected grave in the Callahan City cemetery. Photograph by the author, 1984.

22
c

votes. Disgruntled by their defeat, the Callahan City promoters filed suit that insufficient time had passed between the posting of the election notice and the balloting, and the election was ruled invalid. Consequently the county commissioners requested that the governor set another election, which took place on 8 December. Intense interest followed this election as well, with residents in the northeastern, eastern, and southeastern areas of the county strongly favoring Callahan City, but again the overwhelming vote went for Belle Plain.

Callahan City lost its chance to become the seat of the county, though it remained an active town for a few years as a result of its nearness to the Western Trail. By the time of the great West Texas drought of 1886–87, the community had fallen into a decline from which it never recovered. Today the site is absolutely abandoned, marked only by the big oak tree in the right-of-way at the side of a county road.

LOCATION: *The site of Callahan City can be reached easily. Drive south on Farm to Market Road 2228 a distance of 3.1 miles from its intersection with Interstate Highway 20 at a point about 4.5 miles east of Baird and 6.3 miles west of Putnam. At a four-way intersection with a gravel county road, turn east and drive 0.1 mile up a slight rise to the large oak tree growing on the south side of the right-of-way. This old tree marks the center of Callahan City, the county road being the former main street. The Western Trail crossed the present-day gravel road at a depression marked by a culvert 0.15 mile farther west of the oak. The very interesting Callahan City cemetery, with graves dating from the 1870s, may be seen at the east side of Farm to Market Road 2228 about 2.7 miles south of the interstate highway.*

Calliham

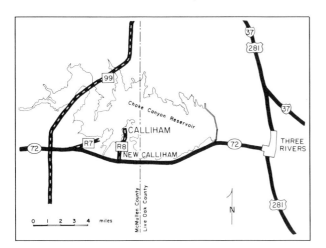

Calliham, an absolute ghost town just south of the Frio River between Tilden and Three Rivers, suffered its demise only in the 1970s. It was killed by the construction of the Choke Canyon dam and the concurrent purchase of all surrounding land by the U.S. Army Corps of Engineers.

The area along the Frio River in the Calliham vicinity was first settled by ranchers in the years following the Civil War, but the site of the town remained unoccupied until 1918, at which time petroleum had been discovered in the area. The first recorded indications of petroleum were found in 1908, when rancher Charles Byrne drilled a water well on his ranch in the Frio Valley. He struck not only water but also high-pressure natural gas, which shot a stream of water over one hundred feet into the air, creating an artificial lake which for a time became a resort for local young people on outings.

Byrne took a sample of oil from a seep in the bed of the Frio together with a photograph of his new well to investors in an effort to develop what he hoped would become a major oil field. Soon he met W. M. Stephenson, who was sufficiently impressed with the evidence to lease three hundred thousand acres of mineral rights in Live Oak and McMullen counties. Within a short time, under the name of the Grubstake Investment Company, Stephenson had begun drilling an exploratory well on the J. T. Brown ranch, which in November 1917 blew in with a capacity of sixty-two million cubic feet of gas from a depth of just over eight hundred feet.

With this drilling activity in the neighborhood, in 1918 J. T. Calliham built a store on his nearby

Entry to an abandoned Calliham home. Photograph by the author, 1981.

Lawn chairs in the shade awaiting their departed owners at Calliham. Photograph by the author, 1981.

Study of an abandoned Calliham residence. Photograph by the author, 1981.

ranch. H. H. McGuffey of Wentz, Texas, occupied the building, calling the store "Guffyola." Two years later McGuffey moved away and the store name changed to Calliham, in honor of the ranch owner. In 1922 another test well struck a rich flow of oil on Calliham's ranch, and the area around the store sprang to life as an oil field boomtown. For the next half dozen years the community boasted a population ranging between four and five hundred residents, most of whom first lived in tents and later in frame "shotgun" houses. The Grubstake Investment Company controlled most of the development at the townsite. Promoter Stephenson and his agents held land auctions from a small wooden platform in the town square, where they sold lots at prices from one hundred to three hundred dollars apiece.

During the days of the boom, Calliham contained a large number of business establishments, among them four grocery stores, two restaurants, two service station/garages, two boardinghouses, a dance hall, barbershop, school, and two two-story hotels, one of which even had a rooftop garden. The investment company installed both a waterworks and a gas street-lighting system. Residents kept in touch with news of the outside world

through the pages of the weekly Calliham *Caller*. During the heyday of the boom, which coincided with national prohibition, the town was served by a moonshiner known to the locals as "Jitney Jake."

Oil production from the Calliham field grew so large that a pipeline was laid from the town to Three Rivers, where a refinery was constructed. About the same time a twelve-inch pipeline was laid to connect the field with San Antonio, giving the Alamo City its first supply of natural gas. Substantial petroleum production continued from the Calliham area for the next two decades, but the late 1920s saw the end of the boom. By 1933 the town population had declined to 150, though it increased again during the World War II years. Immediately after the war Calliham reportedly occupied about a third of its former area.

By the mid-1960s Calliham had become a sleepy little town with only a general store, post office, service station, Baptist church, and rock shop. Hopes for its revival were fanned by talk of the construction of a new dam on the Frio River to provide water to growing Corpus Christi, but these expectations were dashed when the residents learned ten years later that their town would not become a lakeside Mecca. The engineers' calculations showed that when the reservoir was filled to capacity at flood level, five feet of water would cover Calliham. The U.S. Army Corps of Engineers, builders of the dam, purchased the entire town of Calliham through the right of eminent domain, evicting the inhabitants, some of whom had spent their entire lives there. Many of the residents complained bitterly that they had been given only two years' warning that they would have to leave their homes even though the dam had been planned for over a decade. Some departed for a hastily built "New Calliham" a mile south of the original townsite; others left completely.

Today old Calliham is utterly abandoned. Some of its empty buildings still stand, but most of them have been razed by government crews, leaving only their foundations and surface debris scattered about the site of the former town.

LOCATION: *Calliham stands in what today is the Choke Canyon State Park 10 miles west of Three Rivers and 13 miles east of Tilden. At the latest report the site still had public access on paved roads inside the park, but its future status is uncertain.*

Camp Verde

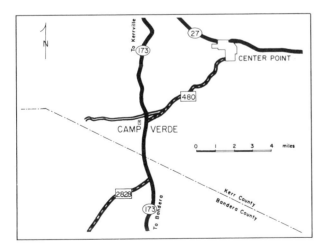

The town of Camp Verde came into existence shortly after the establishment of the U.S. Army post of Camp Verde in 1855. It existed initially to serve the needs of the military post and then later as a rural community near the Bandera Pass.

The army founded Camp Verde on 8 July 1855 as one of a string of forts to defend the Texas frontier. The next year it became the center of a U.S. government experiment in the use of camels as beasts of burden for the army in the desert Southwest. The idea for the project came from Secretary of War Jefferson Davis, who knew first-hand the problems of transportation in the West from his experience during the Mexican War. At his insistence Congress appropriated $30,000 to purchase a number of camels in the Middle East, ship them to Texas, and then experiment in their use. For the next decade the army tested the animals throughout the Southwest, but Camp Verde remained the center for the trials except during the Civil War years. During the conflict the post was occupied by Confederate militia, but it returned to federal jurisdiction in 1865. The camp remained occupied until 1869, when it was no longer needed. The post had outlived the camel experiment, which had been abandoned in 1866.

The civilian community of Camp Verde was located half a mile east of the military post. Known at the time as the Williams community, it began with the establishment of a store in 1857. Initially it was located south of the post, but within a few years it changed to its present site. Because the town was off the military reservation, the merchants could legally sell intoxicants otherwise unobtainable by the soldiers and officers.

Charles Schreiner, a twenty-one-year-old immigrant newly arrived from Germany, purchased the Camp Verde store early in 1858, when the health of its founder began to fail. Schreiner and his partner, Caspar Real, built up the business through contracts to provide beef and other supplies to the nearby military camp. Because the population in the area was so sparse at the time, however, the two entrepreneurs operated the store only on army paydays. A post office for the Camp Verde community opened in 1858, and it continues to operate at the store today.

Indians raided the Camp Verde area until after the close of the Civil War, and most descendants of old settlers still tell stories of the attacks. In a typical incident, warriors raided the horse barn and corrals on the Tedford ranch on Verde Creek not far from the fort. By the light of the moon, John M. Tedford went out to investigate noise that he had heard from inside the house. A warrior in hiding shot him in the arm with an arrow,

Turn-of-the-century store, post office, and saddle shop at Camp Verde. Courtesy LLL Sawmill, Camp Verde, Texas.

Cypress timber being cut into lumber near Camp Verde early in the twentieth century. Courtesy LLL Sawmill, Camp Verde, Texas.

but Tedford's family managed to get him to the military post to seek medical attention. The effects of the wound, combined with inexpert treatment from the army surgeon, left Tedford's arm crippled for the rest of his life but did not prevent him from serving as the Kerr County sheriff from 1870 to 1876.

Today the Camp Verde community consists of the Camp Verde store, a cemetery, and remnants from the 1850s military post. The last semi-intact structure from the camp serves as a residence on private property.

LOCATION: *Camp Verde is located in Kerr County at the intersection of Texas Highway 173 and Farm to Market Road 480 about 12 miles south of Kerrville. The cemetery is on the south side of a county road 0.5 mile west of the state highway, and the site of the military camp is on the north side of the same county road 0.4 mile farther to the west.*

Castolon

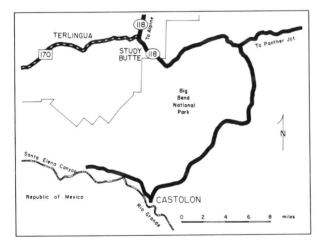

Originally known as Santa Helena, Castolon stands just above the floodplain of the Rio Grande near the Santa Elena Canyon in Big Bend National Park. Fifty years ago it was the center of an irrigated agriculture- and ranching-based community consisting of at least fifty families on the American side of the river as well as a number of families living on the other side in Mexico.

The first known resident of the Castolon area was Cipriano Hernández, a native of Camargo in the state of Chihuahua, Mexico. He had settled at Shafter, Texas, in the mid-1890s before moving to the Big Bend country below the Santa Elena Canyon in 1903. He occupied two sections of land on the American side of the river about five or six miles downstream from the mouth of the canyon, where he irrigated fertile bottomland and operated a small supply store out of his home. Soon he was joined in the mercantile activity by Patricio Marquez, who opened a second store. In time more and more Mexican-American families settled in the area.

The land ownership in the valley changed hands several times until most of the property came into the possession of Wayne Cartledge, who for many years managed the mining interests at Terlingua for Howard E. Perry. After Cartledge purchased the irrigated acreage and nearby range country about 1919, he began introducing scientific agriculture to the valley, at the same time beginning commercial cotton production. He also opened a new and larger trading post, which served customers from both sides of the river. In the meantime several additional agricultural communities sprang up in various locations both upstream and downstream.

While the population of the Castolon area was growing, events were taking place in Mexico which would influence those on the Texas side of the border. In 1910 the Madero Revolution broke out, and within months Mexican unrest caused Castolon residents to request protection from the United States Army. The calls for aid grew louder when bandits began attacking isolated ranches and settlements on the American side of the international boundary.

By 1911 a troop of U.S. Cavalry was stationed at Castolon, later to be supplemented by infantry units. These soldiers established a subcamp there which operated from their actual base at Marfa. During most of their stay in the Castolon area, the men lived in a bivouac consisting of tents, but in 1919 the War Department approved the construction of a permanent camp consisting of barracks, lavatory/latrine, officers' quarters, noncommissioned officers' quarters, barn, and corral with stables. By early 1920 they were ready for occupancy, but on 1 April 1920 the army pulled out from Castolon because of decreased border troubles. The new buildings were hardly used at all. For a time Wayne Cartledge used the vacant government buildings, and then in 1925 he pur-

Granary and tack room at the corrals used by the army during its stay at Castolon. Photograph by the author, 1981.

Portable steam engine and boiler, manufactured in 1915, which was used to pump water from the Rio Grande for irrigation and to power machinery at the Castolon cotton gin. Photograph by the author, 1981.

chased them. He and his employees lived in some of the structures, while he placed his general store in the former barracks.

The most impressive agricultural development in the Castolon area took place in the years following the departure of the U.S. troops and the restoration of order along the border. Wayne Cartledge introduced not only cotton cultivation, but also the raising of fruit trees, hogs, turkeys, and bees, not to mention such enlightened practices as crop rotation and seeding of rangeland with permanent grasses. In order to process the cotton crop more efficiently, in 1923 he constructed a cotton gin which operated until 1942.

The end came for the Castolon community with the establishment of the Big Bend National Park in 1944 and the subsequent federal government acquisition of private land within its bounds. Already the Mexican population of the area had been declining because of reductions in quicksilver mining in nearby Terlingua. After several years of negotiations, in 1957 Cartledge signed a deed transferring his holdings at Castolon to the

Chalk Mountain Masonic Lodge. Photograph by the author, 1984.

National Park Service, though he retained the right to operate the Castolon store for an additional three years. About this time the last of the other private holdings in the area came under federal ownership. With the government acquisition of the lands around Castolon, the community withered away, its only permanent residents becoming park service employees. The town ceased to be a center for farming and ranching and instead became an attraction for visitors to the national park. The Castolon store in the former barracks building, however, remains open for business and still serves many customers from the Mexican side of the Rio Grande. Many of the buildings from the former town remain intact to this day.

LOCATION: *Castolon is located near the Rio Grande on a paved National Park Service road which leads 35 miles south from the main east-west road through the park. The townsite lies about 8 miles east from the mouth of the Santa Elena Canyon.*

Chalk Mountain

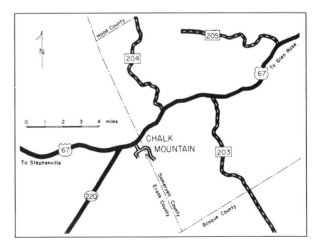

Established as a trading center before the Civil War, Chalk Mountain barely clings to life, with one operating filling station and a Masonic lodge.

Although settlement came to the Chalk Mountain area in the 1850s, the town came into being

Ox teams in Snyder drawing wagons loaded with building materials for the Kent County courthouse at Clairemont in 1893. Courtesy Mr. and Mrs. Riley Miller.

in the 1870s. As early as 1876 the community had a post office, with Elisha D. McCoy as postmaster, and by 1890 it had two active churches, a cotton gin, and a school. Pupils from across the county line in Somervell County also attended the Chalk Mountain school in Erath County. At the turn of the century the community numbered eighty-one residents, but this figure fell to fifty by 1910. The population continued to decline so that today the town has only about half a dozen occupied residences. All the others have been abandoned, most of them leaving visible only foundations to mark where they formerly stood.

The most prominent landmark in Chalk Mountain is its two-story frame Masonic lodge. The chapter received its charter in 1904 and occupied the upper floor of a newly built commercial building, a store operating on the ground level. The lower story has been vacant for years, but the lodge still meets monthly on the Saturdays on or just after the full moon. Nowadays the thirty or so local members are sometimes outnumbered by visitors from other lodges, a Chalk Mountain member remarking recently, "I guess they get a kick out of the antiquity."

LOCATION: *Chalk Mountain is located on U.S. Highway 67 about 19 miles east of Stephenville and 13 miles west of Glen Rose in extreme southeastern Erath County. Its cemetery, with grave markers dating back to the 1870s, is a mile and a half southeast of the town just across the line in Somervell County.*

Clairemont

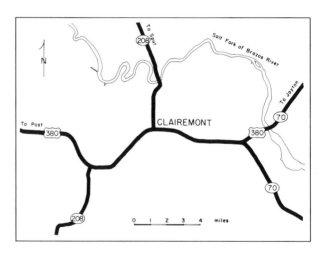

Clairemont, the first seat of Kent County, was established in ranch country on the rolling plains by R. L. Rhomberg in 1888. The founder named the townsite after his daughter, Claire.

When Clairemont sprang to life, ranching was the principal economic activity in its region, and to this day it remains very important. When the population of the area surrounding Clairemont became sufficiently large, the residents petitioned the state in 1892 for permission to organize their own county government, and Clairemont was chosen as the county seat. Also in 1892 the town received its first post office. The next year lumber was hauled from Snyder, and stone was quarried from Butte Knob east of the town for the con-

Street scene in Clairemont. Photograph by the author, 1980.

struction of a two-story red rock courthouse, which soon was followed by a matching stone jail just to the east.

By the turn of the century the town boasted not only of being the county seat but also of having a church, school, several commercial enterprises, and a population of sixty-five. Within a decade the population had grown to two hundred, the level it kept until World War II, and the town became known to the outside world from the pages of its Clairemont *Reporter*.

Clairemont suffered competition from several newer towns, particularly from Jayton and Girard, and after World War II its population dropped considerably. A mild oil boom in the early 1950s temporarily boosted the town, but in 1954 Jayton replaced Clairemont as the seat of Kent County. Since then the decline has been nearly complete. On the last visit by the author, there was not a single operating business. The abandoned wood frame post office building was slowly deteriorating, while rodents made dens in stacks of old mail strewn on its floor. The former courthouse, its upper floor removed, still stands, as does the well-preserved but abandoned red stone jailhouse. The entire townsite is covered with abandoned structures, foundations, and vast surface debris.

LOCATION: *Clairemont is found at the intersection of U.S. Highway 380 and State Highway 208 in central Kent County.*

Undelivered mail littering the floor of the abandoned Clairemont post office. Photograph by the author, 1980.

Through the cemetery toward the nineteenth-century Methodist church at College Mound. Photograph by the author, 1984.

College Mound

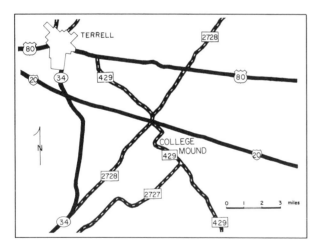

College Mound, one of the earliest permanent settlements in Kaufman County, is older than most of the communities that surround it today. It had its origin in the 1840s, when several families from Indiana and Tennessee chose it for their new home in Texas.

The first post office at College Mound opened on 18 May 1850, with John J. Beck, one of the original settlers, serving as its master. With the passage of time College Mound acquired stores, a cotton gin, a public school, and a Methodist church. The church was established in a log house in 1845 as a union church to serve all denominations, but in time it became Methodist, and in 1865 a wooden frame building replaced the log church. In 1897 the congregation erected the present sanctuary.

Soon after the beginning of settlement, a cemetery was started at College Mound. The oldest known burial in the graveyard is that of Annie, the wife of John J. Beck, who died on 5 May 1846, though there are several other graves nearly as old. The cemetery is a fascinating place filled with scores of intricate nineteenth-century memorials, many of them hand carved by self-trained craftsmen.

The story of how College Mound received its name is an interesting one. According to traditions still related by the residents, in the early days of the settlement an educated man from the East appeared searching for a location where he might build a "college." At this time a college meant almost any school that taught more than the most basic subjects. He selected as the site a prominent hill just north of the present-day church, now topped by an unpainted farmhouse. The Easterner then departed, promising to return with the money to build his school. After he left, the man died, and his plan never came to fruition, but the name College Mound caught on and the community adopted it.

Though College Mound is peaceful today, it has not always been that way. On one occasion two saloonkeepers from nearby Elmo, then a town larger than Terrell, reputedly appeared in the settlement intent on breaking up church services. Sitting with the congregation, the two barkeepers began heckling the minister, who interrupted the service and asked for silence. Once again they began their raucous behavior, but they stopped when an unknown man appeared in the sanctuary. Having an appearance somewhat resembling that of Abraham Lincoln, the stranger removed his hat and coat and then escorted one of the saloonkeepers outside to give him a sound thrashing. Having beaten one of the tavernkeepers, the man then invited both of them to join in the service. They declined the invitation, but they never again gave the minister any trouble.

LOCATION: *College Mound and its beautiful church and cemetery are easily accessible on Farm to Market Road 429 about 0.6 mile southwest of its intersection with Interstate Highway 20 about 8.0 miles southeast of Terrell.*

Comyn

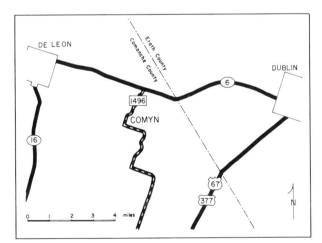

Though known as a twentieth-century oil town, Comyn is much older than the West Texas petroleum boom of this century. Its area was first settled in the mid-1870s after the threat of Indian raids had been removed by the final expulsion of the Plains Indians from western Texas to Oklahoma.

The first store at Comyn was a trading post established by W. M. Catheney after the first settlers had occupied the area. The entrepreneur shortened the name of his store to "Theney," and the community for several years bore that name. Then in 1881 the Texas Central Railway built through the region, placing a track siding and station in the community. The railroad named its station after M. T. Comyn, a company official, and for a number of years the town was known as Theney, Comyn, and Comyn-Theney.

By the early twentieth century Comyn had become a thriving country town with such enterprises as a post office, lumberyard, blacksmith shop, drugstore, mercantile stores, cotton gin, cafe, barbershop, and even a Woodmen of the World lodge. Its history changed dramatically, however, in 1918 because of events miles away.

In 1917 strong oil wells were discovered near Ranger, thirty miles to the northwest, and within weeks an oil boom had begun. More wells soon were brought in at towns like Desdemona and Breckenridge, both also north of Comyn, but there were only limited means available for transporting the vast amounts of newly found oil to markets. Consequently the Humble Pipe Line Company, a major buyer of petroleum from the West Texas field, in 1918–19 constructed a pipeline to connect Comyn (and thus the nearby Ranger field) with its terminal at Webster, near Houston. The company built a huge tank farm at Comyn to hold petroleum from the Ranger area until it could be pumped through the pipeline to southeast Texas. With all the construction at Comyn, a large tent city temporarily sprang up in and around the town, but when the work abated most of the transient population moved to other places.

Major pipeline construction returned to Comyn in 1924, when the Humble Pipe Line Company extended the Comyn pipeline westward to Kemper near Big Lake after the discovery of large oil reserves in the Permian Basin. Workers laid a double pipeline from Comyn westward between 1924 and 1926, and at the same time they expanded the trunk line between Comyn and Webster. Even more storage tanks were erected.

Once bustling industrial building now quiet at Comyn. Photograph by the author, 1984.

Declining production from the West Texas oil field later in this century decreased the Humble activity at Comyn with a resulting decline in its population. Although a large school complex had been built at the town in 1924, the dwindling number of pupils in attendance forced the school to close in 1952. After Humble reduced its tank farm to a skeleton operation, even more people moved away to find jobs elsewhere.

Today there is not a single store left in Comyn, virtually all the old oil tanks are empty, Humble has only an office and pipeline pumping station, and some of the old tanks have been converted into peanut storage. The old store and post office were torn down in 1969 and even the railway station is gone.

LOCATION: *Comyn is located at a sharp bend in Farm to Market Road 1496 about 2 miles south of its intersection with Texas Highway 6 approximately 5 miles east of De Leon in Comanche County.*

Cuthbert

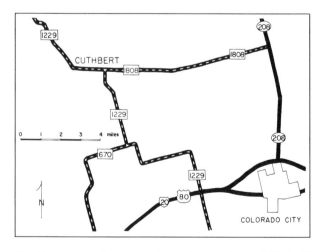

Cuthbert, an absolute ghost in northern Mitchell County, came into existence in 1890. In March of that year Mr. and Mrs. D. T. Bozeman purchased a half section of land at the site and constructed a dugout home in which they lived for several months.

Bozeman had secured employment as a teacher in a country school serving the vicinity, and he bought his land on the wagon road that led north from the railroad at Colorado City to the ranch country on the Llano Estacado. The site was about fifteen miles northwest of Colorado City, a decent day's travel by freight wagon. As soon as he could buy the lumber and have it hauled to his property, Bozeman built a store and wagon yard to serve the teamsters and to provide for their needs. A year after he had arrived, Bozeman secured a post office named Cuthbert after one of his friends, Thomas Cuthbertson, and Ellen, Bozeman's wife, assumed duties as the first postmistress.

In time more people started buying land around the Cuthbert post office and a true community began to develop. Most of the residents engaged in agriculture and stock raising. In 1904 Mr. Bozeman resigned his teaching job to devote himself exclusively to his business interests. In that same year he secured a switchboard from the local telephone company and installed it in his home, Mrs. Bozeman serving as the operator for the local subscribers. Early in this century the community included not only two stores, a post office, and a telephone exchange, but also a blacksmith shop, a school, a cotton gin, and a community church.

The Cuthbert school, located on land provided by D. T. Bozeman, was an unusual structure. Built from lumber, it stood two stories tall, one classroom directly above the other. Resting on large rocks for its foundation, the building had to be guy-wired to anchors on each side to prevent its blowing over in high winds. A woman who attended classes there later in life reminisced that "when the wind blew hard . . . the building would sway back and forth," adding "I am sure it was not conducive to the best study situations as we pupils tried to brace ourselves if it did go over with the next gust of wind."

Cuthbert witnessed some of the excitement when the T. and P.-Abrams No. 1 oil well was drilled just over a mile north of the town in 1920. Though it was never an impressive well, it had the distinction of inaugurating commercial oil production in the Permian Basin, which within a few years became one of the largest oil fields in the United States.

Quiet reigns supreme in Cuthbert. Photograph by the author, 1984.

Debris from once thriving Cuthbert. Photograph by the author, 1984.

With the improvement of rural roads through its area after World War II, Cuthbert withered away. No longer was it necessary for local residents to drive over dirt roads which became muddy wallows after rains to buy groceries or pick up mail at Cuthbert, for the village lay only about fifteen minutes away from Colorado City via paved highways. Today even the last filling station has closed, and not a soul lives in the former town.

LOCATION: *Cuthbert lies on Farm to Market Road 1229 about 1.5 miles west of its intersection with Farm to Market Road 1808 approximately 15 miles northwest of Colorado City. A historical marker for the T. and P.-Abrams No. 1 oil well stands at the side of Farm to Market Road 1229 about 1.3 miles northwest of the townsite.*

Doan's Crossing

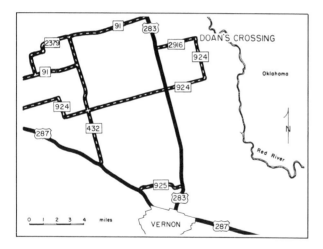

Although millions of Texas cattle crossed the Red River at Doan's Crossing a century ago, today it is difficult to find the spot without a detailed map. The site was known to thousands of cattlemen as "the jumping-off place," as it contained the last store on the Western Trail before drovers crossed their herds from Texas into the Indian Territory on their way north to the Dodge City markets. Virtually every trail herd stopped for supplies in the store operated by Corwin F. Doan.

Doan first came west from his Ohio home in 1874, when he and his uncle, Jonathan Doan, ran a trading post at the Comanche and Kiowa Indian Agency near Fort Sill in Indian Territory. Returning home in 1875 suffering the effects of illness contracted when he nearly froze to death, Doan again came back to the West in September 1878. Bringing with him his wife, two adolescent girls, an infant, and an elderly uncle, Corwin and his party traveled by rail to Sherman, Texas, and then they trekked westward by wagon to the point where the newly opened Western Trail crossed the Red River. There Jonathan Doan had already built a picket building to house a store.

The building was bare when Corwin Doan and his group arrived, for Jonathan had departed for the winter, leaving in the otherwise empty store a lone jar of stale mustard, a keg of powder, and large quantities of strychnine used for killing wolves. Not knowing what to do in the situation but being sorely disappointed at not finding the beehive of commercial activity they had expected, the party set about making the dirt-floored hut livable. Once this was accomplished, Corwin spent the winter months shooting and poisoning wild game for its hides. The next spring he shipped the skins to St. Louis dealers, and from the proceeds paid his freight bill and ordered a full stock of groceries and supplies for the store. Finally about the time that the goods arrived, Jonathan Doan reappeared, asking to be made part of the business. Thus the trading company was styled C. F. Doan and Company.

Doan's adobe store about 1940. Courtesy Panhandle-Plains Historical Museum, Canyon, Texas.

1931 cattle drivers' monument with the 1881 adobe store in the background. Photograph by the author, 1984.

Having come to the store in the autumn, Corwin Doan missed seeing the cattle that had passed by the site in 1878 on their way north to Kansas, but vast herds appeared the next year. Doan himself estimated the number in 1879 to have been one hundred thousand head. Describing his trade as brisk would be an understatement, for the store did an incredible business. Corwin Doan later recalled that he thought nothing of selling bacon and flour in carload lots. The goods were shipped by rail to places like Denison, Sherman, and Gainesville and then transferred to freight wagons for the final leg of their trip westward to Doan's Crossing.

The first post office was established at Doan's on 13 November 1879 with Corwin Doan serving as postmaster. From that time the store became the northernmost point in Texas to which mail could be directed for drovers on their way either to or from Kansas. Doan reminisced that "many a sweetheart down the trail received her letter bearing the postmark of Doan's and many a cowboy asked self-consciously if there was any mail for him while his face turned a beet red when a dainty missive was handed him."

Because of its strategic location at the Red River crossing, Doan's store became a meeting place for an amazing variety of people. Before his warm fire sat not only cowboys but also European noblemen, Indian chiefs, buffalo hunters, and the handful of "drummers" who would venture that far from civilization to sell their goods. Doan recalled that one night in his store, while a crowd sat around the fire listening to music from a French harp, the door opened and in sailed a hat through the air across the room. Close behind followed a huge black cowboy, who commenced to dance around the floor to the tune of the music. "It was one of Ab Blocker's niggers who had been sent up for the mail, giving the first notice of the herd's arrival," Doan later recounted.

The first building at the Doan's community was the picket store built in 1878, but others soon appeared. In 1881 the merchant, while still living in the picket structure, erected an adobe store and then built log cabins for the various family groups. In 1887 he built a large frame building for the store from lumber which was hauled overland from Gainesville, after which time the adobe structure became the family residence. With the passage of time, more people settled around Doan's store, and the community once contained over a dozen structures, among them McBride's Hotel, the Bat Cave Cafe (housed in a dugout and thus its name), the Cowboy Saloon, Doan's Store, the headquarters of the Bar-X Ranch, and several residences. In 1889 Doan with others had the village surveyed and platted into a townsite, but the projections for growth proved too ambitious and never materialized.

The real boom at Doan's Crossing lasted only a short time, for the Fort Worth and Denver Railroad built tracks south of the community in 1885. From this time towns like Harrold and Vernon became shipping points for cattle, and the number of animals being driven northward overland dwindled. Doan's Crossing remained a healthy community until about World War I, but competition from the towns on the railroad finally forced Doan's into obscurity. Even its post office was removed in 1919.

The one event which kept Doan's Crossing in the public eye was its annual picnic. The celebration first took place in late spring 1884, when all the cowmen were either up the trail or out for spring roundups, and, as Doan recalled, "The women of course were playing the role of 'the girl I left behind me.'" Corwin and the five women in the village organized an outdoor picnic for the ladies' entertainment. Over the years the event swelled from a family outing into a sumptuous feast, entertainment, and old settlers' reunion for thousands of residents from the Red River Valley each year.

Today Doan's Crossing consists of the original 1881 adobe store, a handful of occupied and abandoned rural residences, and a beautiful grey gran-

ite historical marker with bronze relief sculpture erected by the old trail drivers in 1931.

LOCATION: *Doan's Crossing may be found at the juncture of Farm to Market Road 2916 with Farm to Market Road 924 about 3.1 miles east northeast of U.S. Highway 283 in northern Wilbarger County.*

Doole

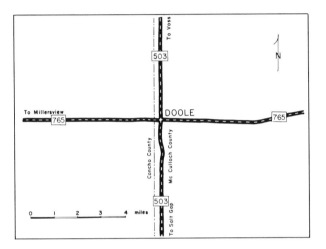

Doole, an intriguing town in western McCulloch County, has had a comparatively short history. It was established about 1908, reached its peak of population during the 1930s and 1940s, and since then has declined to become a virtual ghost of its former self.

The origin of Doole came with the establishment of a school at the site in 1908. Known as the Crossroads School, the institution came to be one of the most important institutions in the town, which initially was called Gansel. Surrounding the community were large ranches, notably those of the Bryson, Middleton, Taylor, and Gansel families. From miles around children came on horses and mules and in buggies and spring wagons to attend classes.

The first stores were built about 1910 by Logan L. Deen and J. M. Pate, with a cotton gin being opened by Tom Cobb. By this time farmers were beginning to purchase acreages from the ranchers, and the gin was needed to prepare their cotton for marketing. About 1911 the local residents began to feel the need for their own post

Concrete bleachers that accommodated crowds at the Doole athletic field. Photograph by the author, 1984.

office, so they went to David Doole, Jr., the post-master in Brady, for advice on how to apply for one. Postal authorities in Washington denied their request to name the new post office Gansel, so in appreciation for assistance from the Brady postmaster they named it in his honor. The name caught on and the community has gone by the name of Doole since that time.

The school was the dominant feature of Doole, both socially and physically. The building stood atop a prominent hill on the west side of the town, enclosed by a rock wall and towering over everything else in the community. In the flat valley between the school complex and the town was a combined football and baseball playing field, itself also enclosed by another high stone wall. Facing east on the hill beneath the school, bleachers were built from concrete so that fans could view athletic contests from permanent seating. Though the classroom buildings are now gone, the rock walls and the bleachers remain, giving visitors the impression of ruins from a Roman amphitheater of antiquity.

During World War I, Doole had only about twenty-five residents, but by 1930 its population

Tools and furniture long forgotten in a Doole work-shop. Photograph by the author, 1984.

had grown to 250, a figure that it kept for over a decade. After the close of World War II, however, the town began losing its inhabitants. The main cause for the decline was the consolidation of agriculture and consequent reduction in the number of small family farms. A local resident recently remarked to the author that forty years ago "it wasn't anything to see a hundred people in Doole on a Saturday night, but not any more." The statement is true, for today the town has only about two dozen residents, two stores, a post office, a church, and a remarkable number of abandoned houses and commercial buildings. Its days as an inhabited place seem to be numbered.

LOCATION: *Doole may be found at the intersection of Farm to Market Road 503 with Farm to Market Road 765 in extreme western McCulloch County.*

Estacado

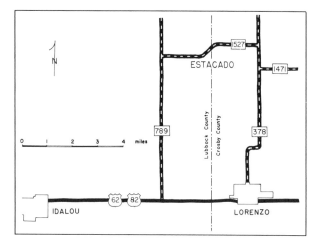

Founded by Quaker farmers, Estacado was the first agricultural settlement on the Staked Plains of Texas. Though the colony fell apart in 1893, its members proved that farming could be conducted successfully in a region that before had been considered fit only for cattle raising.

Paris Cox founded the Estacado colony. He was the treasurer for a group of Quakers originally from North Carolina, who had moved to Indiana in search of a permanent home. They sought a place where they could farm and practice their religion without being molested. Conse-

quently Cox began investigating land in the West that might be appropriate for such a settlement.

In 1877 and 1878, Cox purchased for twenty-five cents an acre several thousand acres of railroad land in western Crosby and eastern Lubbock counties. Then in 1878 he traveled from Indiana to inspect the land that his group had bought. Arriving in the area, having traveled there with a party of buffalo hunters, he met H. C. ("Hank") Smith, who the year before had established the first ranch on the South Plains only a few miles away from the land the Quakers had purchased. Cox made an agreement with Smith to dig a well and with a plow to break out twenty-three acres of land from the native sod. At Cox's request Smith planted part of the acreage and sent samples of the grain and vegetables grown back to Cox and the Quakers in Indiana during the summer of 1879.

Being impressed with the results of the test, Paris Cox and his family together with three other Quaker families moved to the new land in the autumn of 1879. Cox built a sod house for his family, but the others lived in tents. The winter was especially severe, and all the families except that of Cox gave up and left in disgust. Determined that the site would prove well chosen, Cox remained and planted crops in the spring of 1880. Dr. William Hunt visited the Cox farm later that

Paris Cox, the founder of the Estacado Quaker colony. Courtesy Panhandle-Plains Historical Museum, Canyon, Texas.

The A. R. Michaels family at the original Paris Cox farmstead in Estacado. Courtesy Southwest Collection, Texas Tech University, Lubbock, Texas.

year and described what he saw in these words: "I visited the colony (Estacado) in August and September, 1880. The first crops ever planted on the Staked Plains were then growing. I saw corn, oats, millet, sorghum, melons, Irish potatoes, (fair) sweet potatoes, and garden vegetables—all did well."

Since evidence of sufficient moisture and soil fertility had been proved by Cox's harvest, other Quakers began coming to Texas in autumn 1880. Within two years ten families had settled at the community, which Cox named Marietta in honor of his wife, Mary. Later the name was changed to Estacado when it was learned that there was already a post office named Marietta in Texas. The settlement continued to grow, so that by 1890 it had approximately two hundred residents. Most of the new arrivals built themselves dugouts as their first shelter, then sod houses, and finally if they were successful enough, they erected wood frame houses made from lumber shipped in by freight wagon.

In 1886, Crosby County was organized and the citizens chose Estacado to be its seat. At the time they did not know that about half of the town actually lay in Lubbock County. Until a courthouse was erected, the officials kept their offices and records in dugouts and shacks around the town. Finally in 1888 bonds were issued in the amount of $10,000 for the construction of a courthouse and jail. To demonstrate their low opinion for law in the range country, some of the local cowboys openly defied the sheriff by gambling at poker as they sat on the piles of lumber intended for the new courthouse. The officers paid only passing notice to most of them, and Estacado in time gained a reputation for law and order.

The pioneer agricultural settlement also has the distinction of having provided the first organized education on the South Plains. Miss Emma Hunt initiated the efforts at teaching in the fall and winter of 1882 in a dugout classroom. Two years later the classes shifted to the Quaker meetinghouse. By 1888 the school had thirty-two pupils

Historical marker at the edge of a cultivated field commemorating Estacado, the first agricultural settlement on the South Plains. Photograph by the author, 1985.

taught by two public school teachers who received a salary of $45 monthly. For two years starting in 1890 the community also had a school of higher education, the Central Plains Academy, which offered two years of schooling beyond secondary level and was the first college on the Llano Estacado.

After its initial hardships, the town of Estacado prospered for a decade, but in 1891 a rapid decline began. In that year the citizens of Crosby County voted to remove the seat of government from Estacado and place it in Emma, a newer town closer to the center of the county. After this occurred most of the Quaker farmers abandoned the town, many of them going back to the eastern states. They had already lost the leadership of Paris Cox; he had died in 1888 at a comparatively early age. By 1893 all the Quakers except two families had left the community, though some of their places were taken by other settlers. During the 1920s all that was left of Estacado was a couple of general stores, two churches, a country school, and about half a dozen residences. Today the population is about the same, but the stores, churches, and school have gone, and a cotton gin has been added.

LOCATION: *Estacado is located at the Lubbock-Crosby county line on Farm to Market Road 1527 about 2 miles west from its intersection with Farm to Market Road 378 approximately 6.5 miles north of Lorenzo.*

Fastrill

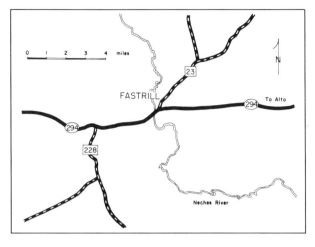

A logging camp on the east side of the Neches River in Cherokee County, Fastrill in the late 1920s and early 1930s had a population of six hundred. Today its site is nearly obliterated and serves as an experimental tree farm.

The Southern Pine Lumber Company established Fastrill in 1922 as the center of its logging operations in Cherokee and Anderson counties. A company town, Fastrill had an artificially contrived name: FA came from the name of F. F. Farrington, a former postmaster in Diboll, while STR and ILL came from the names of P. H. Strauss and Will Hill, both company officials. The Texas Southeastern Railroad built a line to connect the logging camp with the lumber company sawmill at Diboll, about forty miles to the southeast.

Though most of its buildings were of a temporary nature, constructed from inexpensive planks and timbers from the company mill, Fastrill's residents considered it to be a good town. "Oh, it was a fine place to live," a former resident reminisced, "All the people had a lot of pride." Serving its estimated six hundred inhabitants were rows of wooden houses, many of them fronting on a main street lined with planted sycamore trees. It also had a four-teacher school with as many as a hundred pupils, two churches, a company commissary, and a post office established on 11 December 1922.

Although work for the loggers was hard, life was pleasant at Fastrill. The lumber company permitted its employees to raise substantial gardens in the town, even providing them with implements and mules to aid their efforts. The firm

Crumbling remains at Fastrill. Photograph by the author, 1981.

erected and equipped a canning plant to encourage its employees to use their free time constructively. During the hot, humid summertime, however, many of the families preferred to spend their free time on Sundays down on the Neches fishing, swimming, and visiting. Some of them tended a huge wooden fish trap that caught many of the larger fish as they swam downstream. Others walked to the riverside on account of its local institution known as the Gouge-Eye Saloon, which sat on a bluff overlooking the stream where the railroad curved downriver from the town. Many years later a local resident remembered that the road from the saloon ran by his home and that "young men from up-country would go riding down as night fell; in the middle of the night they'd come whooping and racing their horses in maudlin manner on the way home."

Although Fastrill was generally peaceable, sometimes its residents vented their anger violently. On such an occasion in 1926, a Mexican from the town who worked on a road gang for the Texas Southeastern Railroad was attacked by a tall Spaniard, who began shooting at him with an automatic pistol beside the tracks in Fastrill. The Mexican, who was short in stature, quickly ran for his house, where he too grabbed a pistol. He emerged from the house with the gun firing, and the Spaniard, who had started the affray, turned to run for his life. A man on the same railway crew as the Mexican, who witnessed the incident later recalled that "our foreman, Robert Red, yelled for us to get down behind piles of crossties beside the track. The Spaniard was running down that road straight for us. Bullets were whining all around us." The Spaniard raced past the track-laying crew, the Mexican still firing at him. "He kept running . . . on down that road. And nobody there ever saw or heard of him again."

Logging camps by their nature were temporary. By the late 1930s the trees in the area served by the Fastrill crews had been largely cut out and the Southern Pine Lumber Company began transferring its men to other camps. From its former hundreds of residents, Fastrill by 1940 had only thirty. Soon most of the last had moved away, the company salvaging the majority of its buildings so that their materials could be used elsewhere.

Today the straight lines of pine trees in the Arthur Temple, Sr., Research Area operated by the Texas Forest Service occupy the site of Fastrill. Scattered about the perimeter of the research area one can still find a few dilapidated sheds, a tiny wooden icehouse, and a few wire fences around former yards. The earthen embankments from the Texas Southeastern tracks are still visible in places, and crepe myrtle bushes even yet grow at the site of the former school. Otherwise Fastrill has virtually disappeared.

LOCATION: *The Texas Forest Service Arthur Temple, Sr., Research Area occupies most of the site of Fastrill. It is located on the west side of Farm to Market Road 23 about 0.5 mile northeast of its intersection with Texas Highway 294 about 12 miles west of Alto. Most of the surviving remains of the town may be seen from the farm-to-market road.*

Fort Griffin

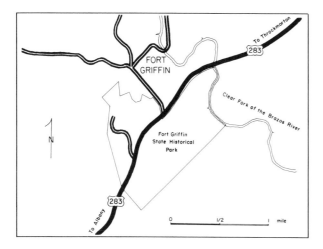

Taking its name from the military post which stood on the hill overlooking it, the town of Fort Griffin was one of the roughest and most violent places ever to exist on the Texas frontier. During its heyday in the late 1870s, its saloons, dance halls, gambling dens, and bordellos hosted thousands of transient cattle drovers, soldiers, and buffalo hunters as its unsavory reputation spread through the entire American West.

The town of Fort Griffin was situated on the northern edge of a military reservation established by the U.S. Army on 31 July 1867. During its early years the town lived as a parasite, satisfying the desires of the soldiers for alcohol, diversion, and female companionship. The fort had been started as one in a chain of posts either begun or reoccupied after the close of the Civil War to protect the white settlements farther east from attacks by marauding bands of Plains Indians. Service at the post was dreaded by soldiers and officers alike, for virtually every building was of a temporary nature, most of them made from roughly sawed lumber. The enlisted men's barracks, for instance, were huts measuring eight by fourteen feet with five feet ten inches up to their roofs; there were so few of the huts that six soldiers were quartered in each of them.

Beneath the fort lay a meadow about half a mile wide bordered on the west by Collins Creek. The flat led northward into a big bend in the Clear Fork of the Brazos River. From the fort ran a road almost due north across the flat to a natural rock crossing of the river, and on either side of the road sprawled the town, built without any order whatever.

The town of Fort Griffin, called The Flat from its location on the meadow, became known far and wide for its violent reputation. Even Collins Creek, which flowed along its west side, took its name from a tragedy. Before the Civil War a man by the name of Collins settled beside the stream. While walking to a spring one morning to fetch water, he was shot by unknown assailants who had concealed themselves in the brush. As a chronicler noted, "the operation proved so fatal that Collins died before he could get out of his tracks." The killers undoubtedly had heard the rumors that the man supposedly had buried a large sum of money, as he "usually did his banking business with a hole in the ground," but it is not known whether they found the horde.

Within a short time after the founding of the fort, The Flat had become a bustling town with three to four hundred inhabitants, most of them representing the lowest classes of society. They were predominately gamblers, saloonkeepers, prostitutes, con men, and fugitives from justice, with just enough law-abiding citizens to conduct the legitimate business necessary to keep the town going. By 1874 a "crime wave" had engulfed

The main street of The Flat today. Photograph by the author, 1981.

Fort Griffin residents posed for a picture outside a store in August 1909. Courtesy Southwest Collection, Texas Tech University, Lubbock, Texas.

Griffin, and to protect his men the commander at the fort declared the town under government control, expelling many of the undesirable residents. Later in the year Shackelford County was organized and the commander had to relinquish his control. Soon the beginning of the buffalo hunt in the area and the opening of the Western Trail to Dodge City brought hundreds of transient hunters, skinners, and drovers to the Clear Fork, and the population of The Flat more than doubled its former number. The saloons thrived and the gamblers prospered.

The commercial slaughter of bison for their hides entered Texas in the winter of 1873–74, coming from Kansas, where Dodge City had been its center. The Kansas herds had been decimated by that winter, and hide men moved their operations southward into the Texas Panhandle. In late 1874 the combination of Indian hostility with reduced herds prompted some of the hunters to transfer their operations from a base in Kansas to one on the southern fringe of the herds, and they chose Fort Griffin. At the time it was the westernmost outfitting point on the Clear Fork of the Brazos, being located about 125 miles west of railway connections in Denison, Sherman, and Fort Worth. The hunting continued, based primarily at Fort Griffin, for the next five years, and thousands upon thousands of dried buffalo hides passed through the town on heavy freight wagons bound for the railheads farther east, while the hide men bought most of their supplies, guns, and ammunition at The Flat.

Purely because of its geographical location, Fort Griffin similarly profited from the Western Cattle Trail which led from Texas to Dodge City. Opened in 1875, this trail routed millions of cattle northward over the next half dozen years. With the trail passing just west of The Flat, the town became a natural stopping point for drovers in need of supplies, relaxation, and entertainment. Many of them found it ideal to stop for a day or two there to let off steam after the work and tension of trail driving. This they did all day and all night.

Another group of people at The Flat were the Tonkawa Indians, for the U.S. Army had located the camp for its Tonkawa scouts at the military post of Fort Griffin. The post surgeon later complained that on the streets of the town it became

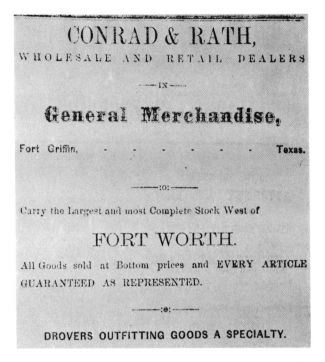

Advertisement for Fort Griffin merchants from the *Fort Griffin Echo*, 8 March 1879. Courtesy Southwest Collection, Texas Tech University, Lubbock, Texas.

"a frequent sight to see the Indians with men and women in a state of beastly intoxication."

It is an understatement to say that the revolver settled more differences at The Flat than did the law, for good marksmanship and quick wits could promise a longer life than clean living and fresh air. A man who knew Griffin at its height later wrote that within twelve years thirty-five men were "publicly killed," while eight or ten more were found dead with no questions asked, and probably a dozen were executed by lawmen or an extralegal vigilance committee. Among the gunmen who frequented the town were "Doc" Holliday, "Hurricane Bill" Martin, Wyatt Earp, and Pat Garrett.

In a representative incident from the period, a retired soldier named Scotty had a quarrel with one of the town toughs. After the man returned home, he saw the ruffian coming after him and ran around to the back side of his house, where his wife was washing clothes in a washtub by the fire. Despite pleas from the wife, who fell on her knees begging, the badman deliberately shot Scotty to death before her very eyes.

1870s Masonic lodge hall, which later served as a school until 1937, standing in ruins at Fort Griffin. Photograph by the author, 1981.

On another occasion an inoffensive local musician became the rival of one of the hooligans for the heart of a young lady in The Flat. The innocuous lover won out, but the rowdy suitor thirsted for revenge. One day they happened to be in the same saloon, the musician playing billiards, when the ruffian put himself in the way and the gentleman accidentally stepped on the toe of his boot. Though he politely apologized, the discarded lover turned, drew his pistol, and after taking careful aim fired into the musician, killing him instantly. No questions were ever asked.

Finally a vigilance committee was formed by more substantial members of the Griffin population to control some of the illegal acts. Most of its efforts, however, were aimed at punishing crimes against property. One of their victims was Charley McBride, a known horse thief. The Griffin correspondent of the Dallas *Daily Record* reported in April 1876 that McBride was "caught in the very act of taking what wasn't 'his'n,'" and

hanged from the branch of a convenient pecan tree. He added: "A pick and shovel may be seen underneath the rotting body, a silent hint, I presume, to the sympathetic spectator to cut down, if he wishes, and inter the blackened and hideous corpse." Another observer of the same incident noted that pinned to the man's shirt was a piece of paper on which were written the words: "He said his name was McBride, but he was a liar as well as a thief."

In its heyday The Flat had a permanent population of about a thousand residents and an estimated floating population of transients numbering about twice that. In addition to its palaces of pleasure, it also had several large general stores and outfitters, a tannery, hide yards, several hotels, boardinghouses, livery stables, wagon yards, a stationery shop, the *Fort Griffin Echo* newspaper, a bakery, a barbershop, and a drugstore. To educate the town's youth an academy operated for several years.

The most famous of the many saloons in The Flat was the Beehive, the site of numerous bloody encounters. Above its door hung a painted wooden sign with these words inscribed before a picture of a hive of bees:

Within this hive we are alive.
Good whiskey makes us funny.
So if you're dry come in and try
The flavor of our honey.

Several events converged in the early 1880s to spell the doom of The Flat. First, the commercial buffalo hide hunt effectively came to a close by 1880. Then in 1881 the adjacent military post was abandoned as no longer needed for frontier defense. At the same time railroads were building westward toward Fort Griffin, but none of the builders chose routes through the town. One of these lines, however, passed through Albany, the county seat, in 1881, sealing the fate of Griffin. Soon the last of the remaining Griffin merchants shifted their operations to Albany to supply the needs of the few cattlemen who were still driving their livestock overland to the Kansas markets rather than shipping it by rail. Within a couple of years the streets of Fort Griffin were quiet and most of its buildings stood empty. The town survived as a rural community with school and country store into this century, but today it is an absolute ghost.

48
F

LOCATION: *Most visitors are disappointed when they see The Flat, one of the most notorious towns in all the American West, for not a single intact building survives at the site. To reach the former town, turn northwest onto a graded county road from U.S. Highway 283 approximately 0.6 mile northeast of the entrance to the Fort Griffin State Historical Park in northern Shackelford County. Proceed down the gravel road over a cattle guard 0.5 mile to a four-way graded road intersection. At this point, turn right (northeast) onto a gravel road leading down to the Clear Fork of the Brazos. This country lane with fields and pastures on either side a century ago was the main street of The Flat that led from the fort down to the river crossing. There are neither signs nor markers to identify the site of the famous ghost town. The abandoned stone Griffin school stands northwest of the intersection, while a fine 1887 iron truss bridge carries the county road over the Clear Fork. Historical interpretation of local history, as well as preserved and reconstructed fort buildings, may be viewed in the state park which encompasses the area of the former military post on the hill south of the townsite.*

Fort McKavett

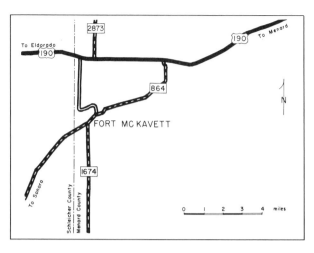

The town of Fort McKavett was born when the fort died, and then in turn the town died so that the historic fort might survive.

As a military post Fort McKavett was established near the headsprings of the San Saba River by five companies of the Eighth Infantry under Colonel Thomas Staniford on 14 March 1852. It remained in this location for only a few weeks before it moved two miles downstream to a high hill on the south bank of the river. The post took its name from Captain Henry McKavett, who had been killed fighting in the Mexican War in 1846. The site finally chosen was indeed well selected, for the post gained a reputation for being one of the most attractive as well as one of the healthiest forts on the Texas frontier.

Fort McKavett had two periods of military occupancy. It was garrisoned from its establishment in 1852 until 1859, after which time it lay abandoned until 1868. It was closed because Indian hostilities were temporarily concentrated at more northerly points, and then the Civil War began. During the war civilians lived in some of the post buildings, but most of them fell into disrepair. After federal troops returned to Texas following the war, orders were given in 1867 for the reoccupation of McKavett as one of a series of forts reaching from the Red River to the Rio Grande and protecting overland trails. The Fourth Cavalry reactivated the post on 1 April 1868, but the soldiers found the fort to be, in the words of the post surgeon, "one mass of ruins, only one house . . . habitable."

The job of reconstructing the fort fell to Colonel Ranald Slidell Mackenzie, who arrived in

March 1869 to assume command of the newly formed Twenty-fourth Infantry, a black unit. Mackenzie revitalized the troops, transforming them into one of the most efficient regiments in the frontier army, and at the same time building the fort into an establishment which surpassed the preceding post in both design and comfort. Using native limestone, locally burned lime for mortar, native timber, and cut lumber hauled in by freight wagon, Mackenzie supervised the construction of a post which eventually included forty rock buildings and half again that many built from wood.

As the years passed, the need for Fort McKavett as a military garrison diminished, and on 30 June 1883 it was formally abandoned by the army. The site had been leased by the War Department, so the possession of the land reverted to its actual owners. Even before this time a civilian church and school had been erected at the fort, and as soon as the soldiers departed local residents moved into the former barracks, officers' quarters, and other buildings. For the next eighty years Fort McKavett lived as an ordinary town averaging over a hundred residents who served the surrounding ranch country. The main difference between it and the other communities in the region

Cast-off electric range from the 1920s rusting away at Fort McKavett. Photograph by the author, 1981.

Abandoned ranch house just outside Fort McKavett. Photograph by the author, 1981.

was that Fort McKavett families lived and worked in former military buildings or in structures built from stone taken from abandoned army buildings.

By the 1960s, Fort McKavett was still an active community with just under a hundred people. In 1967, however, events took place in Austin which forever changed the history of the community. The Texas legislature passed a bill which permitted the State Parks Department to purchase all or parts of several frontier forts so that they might be preserved for the future. At Fort McKavett the department began by acquiring three buildings, but by 1980 the agency had obtained most of the surviving buildings in the former community. The residents had to find homes elsewhere, converting the town into a virtual ghost. Though the town of Fort McKavett no longer exists as a community, visitors today may see the military post much as it appeared over a century ago. Interpretive exhibits telling not only the story of the fort but also that of the town may be viewed in the restored hospital building.

LOCATION: *The Fort McKavett State Historical Site is located 5.7 miles southwest of U.S. Highway 190 on Farm to Market Road 864 approximately 22 miles west of Menard and 37 miles northeast of Sonora. The grounds are open to the public seven days a week.*

Fry

Fry was an oil boom town, but not where it would ordinarily be expected. The town stood near the Brown-Coleman county line on the old road between Brownwood and Coleman.

The origin of Fry came with the discovery of the short-lived Fry oil field in extreme western Brown County. Although there had been petroleum activity in the county intermittently for over two decades, no producing wells had ever been drilled in the area of Jim Ned Creek. James W. Quinn, a rancher in the vicinity, is credited with the discovery, but his two partners were equally important. In 1925, Quinn chanced to meet Bert Ehorn, a wealthy Wisconsin farmer who had come to Texas to speculate in petroleum. After Quinn had interested Ehorn in the possibilities of finding oil on Jim Ned Creek, Ehorn got in touch with William V. Lester, a promoter he had met earlier in Dallas. They formed a three-way partnership and set out to buy leases in the locality suggested by Quinn.

Concrete sidewalk leading to nowhere at Fry. Photograph by the author, 1984.

Concrete footings for refinery equipment at the Amerada gasoline plant. Photograph by the author, 1984.

In April 1926 the three men purchased leases for 876 acres from local farmers and ranchers, most of them members of the Fry family. On 1 June drillers began a well. Their effort attracted considerable attention since it was located fifteen miles from the nearest producing wells. Only twenty days later genuine excitement spread through the neighborhood, for the drillers struck oil at a depth of 1,276 feet, the black gold gushing into the air. The Quinn-Ehorn-Lester wildcat against odds of fifty-one to one had come in as a producing oil well. Soon thereafter another wildcat a mile away also came in as a producer. The boom was on.

Within weeks hundreds of new wells were being drilled in the vicinity of Jim Ned Creek. Brown County oil production skyrocketed from only 89,807 barrels in January 1926 to 516,570 barrels in December of the same year. The true boom came in 1927, with 7,519,647 barrels being produced. The drilling activity was phenomenal. Brown County had 188 producing wells at the beginning of 1926, but before the end of the year an additional 1,044 wells were drilled. Almost all of these were in the Fry field.

Along with the boom came people—thousands of them—to work in the oil field or to live from those who worked there. A local resident reminisced that "there is no way in the world for me to tell you how many people were there. . . . There were just people, people, people. Every kind you could think of." All these workers and hangers on needed places to live, eat, and sleep, and almost overnight the town of Fry sprang up along the old road from Brownwood through Thrifty to Coleman. From a bare pasture in June 1926 it became an entire town in only six months, complete with post office, grocery stores, drugstores, dry goods stores, meat markets, restaurants, filling stations, garages, barbershops, and cold drink stands, not to mention the places of business for its boot-leggers, gamblers, and prostitutes, most of whom set up shop near Jim Ned Creek. Some of the local landowners preferred not to sell land in the town, so they leased small plots of ground for about ten dollars a month. One enterprising rancher built wooden shacks measuring about eighteen by thirty feet and rented them monthly for forty to sixty dollars. Outside the town Claude Robertson operated a dance hall where music played until late almost every night. The ballroom was the scene of numerous knifings and shootings, most of them brought on by patrons' imbibing the boot-leg liquor that flowed as long as customers had money to pay.

Production in the Fry field was so great that oil transportation became a critical problem. Conse-quently several pipelines were laid to the field, among them lines carrying petroleum to other pipeline connections at Cross Cut and to the rail-road at Bangs. So much natural gas was produced along with the oil that the Amerada Petroleum Corporation set up a gasoline refinery using gas as fuel on the north side of Jim Ned Creek in March 1927. The plant was wholly inadequate for the volume of petroleum available, so the firm constructed a second gasoline refinery on the south side of the creek that had a capacity of 26,000 gallons daily. A pipeline to Bangs carried the refined gasoline to a tank car loading facility on the railroad.

Because of the unrestrained drilling and pro-duction, the Fry oil field declined almost as quickly as it had grown. By 1934, only eight years after the discovery, the annual production had declined so greatly that it equalled only that of a single month in 1927. With the slowdown in drilling and production came the demise of Fry. By 1940 it had only one country store and about a hundred inhabitants. Now they are all gone. To-day it is utterly abandoned and marked primarily by the concrete footings and sidewalks from the Amerada gasoline plant and scattered detritus of the oil field activity of sixty years ago.

LOCATION: *The remains of Fry may be seen from an unmarked paved county road about 1.4 mile west from its intersection with Farm to Market Road 585 approxi-mately 6.2 miles north of U.S. Highway 67/84 in west-ern Brown County.*

Girvin

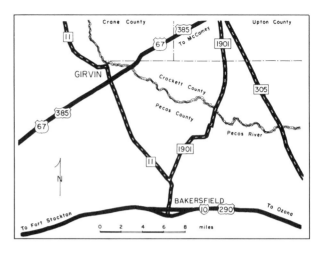

Girvin gives visitors the appearance of the stereo-typed ghost town from Western films. It stands in semiarid northern Pecos County beside the tracks of the former Orient Railroad, almost all of its buildings abandoned and most of them in ruins or caving in.

Permanent white settlement came to the Girvin area in the 1890s, when stock raisers entered the region to establish ranches. Several attempts were made to found towns in the area, as shown by the short-lived post offices at Adams and Phoenix, but none was successful until the Kansas City, Mexico and Orient Railroad built through in 1911 and crossed the Pecos near what became Girvin. The town took its name from the Girvin ranch where it was located, and it received a post office by that name on 31 January 1913. In 1912 the rail-road built a combined wooden passenger and freight station at the site, and soon other busi-nesses joined the post office and depot to give Girvin a general store, a hotel, a saloon, and a lumberyard. For many years Girvin's shipping pens beside the tracks held thousands of cattle in transit to markets.

The first school at Girvin met in a sixteen-by sixteen-foot wooden building. By the late twenties or early thirties the Girvin Independent School District built a new brick school, but even then it was inadequate in size for the classes. During the 1930–31 school year Girvin had 110 pupils, so many that one of the three teachers had to hold classes in a nearby lumberyard.

The economic base for Girvin was the ranch-ing industry, for it served a broad area as a supply center and shipping point. When oil production

Girvin as seen from the railway. Photograph by the author, 1981.

Abandoned store in Girvin preserved principally because of the aridity of the region. Photograph by the author, 1981.

Farm equipment slowly being covered by blowing sand at Girvin. Photograph by the author, 1981.

began in the Yates and Trans-Pecos oil fields in the late 1920s, the town also became a rail delivery point for petroleum equipment and supplies. The oil fields created an immediate demand for electrical power, and the Pecos Valley Power and Light Company erected a generating plant on the Pecos River across from Girvin in the extreme northwest corner of Crockett County. Consequently Girvin received electricity in 1929. About 1931 a saltworks was built about a mile west of the town.

The demise of Girvin began in 1933. In that year a new highway was built to connect Fort Stockton with McCamey, and it passed one mile south of Girvin. Already people had started leaving the neighborhood, seeking employment elsewhere, so that in the 1933–34 school year Girvin had only thirty-four pupils. The school closed in 1939. The census of 1940 showed only seventy-five people left in the town. Then in 1944 the Santa Fe Railway, successor to the Orient, razed

the half of the Girvin depot which had been devoted to freight, later closing the passenger station in 1955. The post office left the town in 1956, being transferred to a store at the new crossroads a mile south.

Today Girvin is nearly a ghost. The old town has no places of business whatever, only a couple of residents, and numerous abandoned buildings, perhaps the most impressive being a two-story concrete filling station/garage complex. The brick schoolhouse is maintained as a community center and polling place, but the cemetery has grown up in prickly pears, mesquite trees, and weeds, as has most of the town.

LOCATION: *Girvin lies beside the Santa Fe Railway tracks at Farm to Market Road 11 about 1.0 mile north of its intersection with U.S. Highway 67/385 about 34 miles northeast of Fort Stockton. A confusing sign for "Girvin" stands beside the commercial buildings at the crossroads a mile south of the original townsite.*

Grove, The

(See The Grove)

Haslam

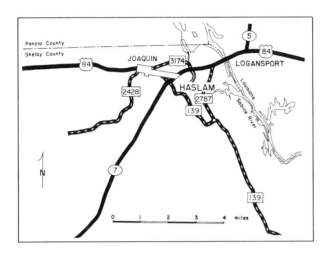

Inside one of the "concrete castles" at Haslam. Photograph by the author, 1981.

Today perhaps the most impressive of all the East Texas ghost towns, Haslam was the center of the Pickering Lumber Company activities in the state. It is remembered for its towering hulks of reinforced concrete—remnants of a mill complex which produced as much as 300,000 board feet of lumber daily.

The Pickering Lumber Company, builder of Haslam, began with the activities of W. R. Pickering, an entrepreneur from Missouri. The son of English immigrants, he started his career with lead mining near Joplin, Missouri, but in 1894 he organized the Pickering Lumber Company. By the early years of this century, his son, William Alfred Pickering, had taken over the company because of the father's ill health. In 1898 the firm began purchasing timberland in Louisiana and then in Texas three years later. By 1906 the company had purchased 100,000 acres in Shelby County and was planning the construction of a major sawmill complex to process the lumber cut from the reserves.

Originally the Pickering firm had planned to locate its sawmill in the town of Center, but city officials seemingly were unable to waive local taxes enough to induce the firm to place the mill in the town. Accordingly the company purchased land near the Sabine River in northeastern Shelby County and from 1903–15 built a completely new company town. At the time the general manager of the company was a school friend of W. A. Pickering named Haslam, and Pickering named the town for his old chum.

Haslam and its mills were built to last for decades. Not only were there such industrial installations as sawmills, planing mills, lumber curing sheds, power plant, waterworks, fire department, and twenty-five acres of log ponds, but also company housing for three to four hundred families, a company commissary, and even a hotel. Haslam became a completely self-sufficient community. Dominating everything were the huge concrete buildings which housed the major components of the industrial complex.

Haslam provided housing for many Pickering loggers who spent only their weekends at home. Six days a week they worked in the forests, living in temporary housing or tents, and then they came into Haslam riding on the last logging train to come to the mill on Saturday. They spent about thirty-six hours or so with their families before catching a ride back to the logging camp on the empty train returning early Monday morning.

In 1931 the Pickering Lumber Company closed

Old office desk from the Pickering sawmill rotting away from age and moisture. Photograph by the author, 1981.

down its East Texas lumber operations. Its timber resources in Texas had been consumed. It sold the Haslam mill complex to W. C. Garrett of the Haslam Lumber Company and to the May brothers of Beaumont, who operated a hardwood mill there for a while. These smaller mills ran for a few years, but Haslam became a ghost as soon as they closed. Just after World War II the community still had six places of business and about two hundred fifty people, but today it is completely abandoned. The shells of many of the big concrete buildings still stand, some of them covered with poison ivy, and throughout the former town one can see the debris left behind when the mills closed—from heavy footings for machinery to fancy office desks—all slowly deteriorating in the humid East Texas climate.

LOCATION: *Haslam may be reached by taking a gravel county road that leads south from U.S. Highway 84 opposite the highway junction with Farm to Market Road 3174 approximately 1.2 miles west of the Sabine River bridge across from Logansport, Louisiana.*

Gasoline pump which once fueled cars at Haslam. Photograph by the author, 1981.

Helena

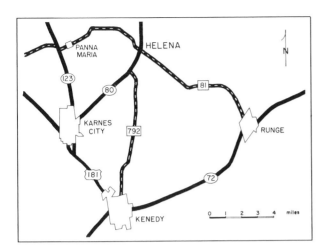

Helena was a tough town, but not too tough to die. A number of years the seat of Karnes County, this mercantile center of the county began its decline after it was bypassed by railways and its courthouse moved to one of the new railroad towns.

Situated near the Alamita Crossing of the San Antonio River, Helena developed at the intersection of two major South Texas trails: the Ox Cart Road, which joined San Antonio with Indianola on the Gulf of Mexico, and the trail connecting Gonzales with San Patricio and Brownsville. It was a natural place for a town to appear. For a number of years there had been a Hispanic trading post at the site, but in 1852 two Anglo-Americans, Thomas Ruckman and Dr. Lewis S. Owings, established a general mercantile store there and soon afterward founded a town. Hiring a surveyor, they laid off a townsite, which they named Helena after Owings's wife.

In the eight years between the establishment of the town and the outbreak of the Civil War, Helena grew to become an important South Texas town. It received a post office on 7 November 1853, and on 27 February 1854 it became the seat of the newly organized Karnes County. The voting for the election of the first county officials took place under the porch of the Ruckman and Owings store, the merchants providing the pens, ink, paper, and tables. By the time of the Civil War, Helena had two hotels, a courthouse, jail, four general mercantile stores, a drugstore, two blacksmiths, boardinghouses, a number of taverns, a public school, and Masonic lodge.

Helena residents suffered comparatively less than many Texans during the Civil War by reason of their location on main overland freight routes and the consequent availability of goods frequently nonexistent elsewhere in the state. In the years immediately following the conflict, however, the Karnes County area on the fringe of settlement became a haven for hundreds of outlaws. A writer in the *San Antonio Express* in 1868 described Helena as "a mean little Confed town, with 4 stores, 4 whisky mills, and any

Helena during its heyday. Courtesy Karnes County Library, Karnes City, Texas.

The iron box that was the Karnes County jail sitting behind the old courthouse at Helena. Photograph by the author, 1982.

amount of lazy vagabonds laying around, living by their wits." He added that these inhabitants "own nothing, but have money enough for whisky, tobacco, and occasionally a game of monte."

The unsavory reputation of Helena in the post-war years is illustrated by the Helena duel, which took its name from duels by the lawless element in the town. In this duel the combatants' left hands were tied together with a deerskin thong, while each of them was provided with a short-bladed knife. The men were given a spin and told to begin their duel. The blades of the knives intentionally were short so that neither of the combatants would strike any vital organs, but would fight until one or the other bled to death. With the passage of time, most of the lawless element moved away from Helena, but the town retained its violent reputation through occasional killings which took place there over the next two decades.

Helena remained the commercial center of Karnes County until the arrival of the San Antonio and Aransas Railroad during the mid-1880s. After Helena failed to subscribe the funds for the bonus requested by the railway company, its president chose to route the line between San Antonio and the gulf coast via Beeville, skirting west of Helena. Along the railway new towns like Kenedy, Runge, and Karnes City sprang to life, drawing trade away from the older county seat. All these towns grew to considerable size during the next years, and on 21 December 1893 an election was held to determine whether the county seat would remain in Helena or be moved elsewhere. By an overwhelming vote the citizens of the county chose to move the courthouse to newly built Karnes City, where it remains today. Just a few days later, on 7 January 1894, the San Antonio *Daily Express* reported that "the old town of Helena looks like a tree without any leaves on it since the county seat left. Scarcely a person from outside the town is seen on the streets. The boys have taken possession of the old courthouse building and last night they held a big kangaroo court."

Over the next three decades Helena became a sleepy little backwater community and finally the virtual ghost which it is today. The present day visitor finds about twenty scattered rural residences, a couple of combined grocery store/filling stations, several historical markers, general and Masonic cemeteries, and the ruins and foundations of numerous former buildings. At the center of the old Jefferson Square in the former town stands the 1872 Karnes County courthouse, which together with the post office and jail are preserved as historical monuments housing the local museum.

LOCATION: *Helena is found at the intersection of Texas Highway 80 and Farm to Market Road 81 in north central Karnes County.*

Hot Springs

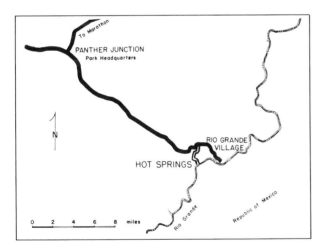

Hot Springs, also known as Boquillas Hot Springs, has been the site of medicinal use of natural hot spring water since Indian times. During the twentieth century the springs were developed commercially and a small community grew up around them, but now the site is uninhabited in the Big Bend National Park.

The first people to discover the curative properties of the hot springs were Indians living along the Rio Grande. They not only left their picto-

graphs on the rocks near the springs, but they even carved out a coffin-shaped "bath tub" by chipping away the limestone where the hot water flows to the surface on the banks of the river.

The site of the hot springs was purchased in 1909 by J. O. Langford, a native of Mississippi. Most of his life Langford had suffered the deleterious effects of malaria which he had contracted as a youth, and he found no treatments for it effective. In an effort to improve his health, he moved to a drier climate in Texas. By chance he heard of a section of state-owned land on the Rio Grande containing the medicinal springs, and he successfully filed for its purchase with a bid of $1.61 per acre.

By 27 May 1909, Langford, his wife, and daughter had arrived at the site which they had bought without seeing. There they set up a tent where Tornillo Creek flows into the Rio Grande almost adjacent to the springs. Finding a Mexican family already living on his property, Langford made an agreement to rent them the land for their farm in exchange for their labor when needed. Langford, his health improved by daily bathing in the spring, set about improving the property by constructing a stone bathhouse over the spring and by erecting a store and post office. The location was ideal for a border trading post, for it was on the wagon road connecting San Vicente, four or five miles upstream, with Boquillas, about the same distance downstream. Soon Langford began advertising the hot springs for invalids, and in time he developed a considerable clientele, with individuals traveling many miles to his remote location in search of cures for a variety of ailments.

Langford's trade slowed down with increased bandit and revolutionary activities across the river in Mexico after 1910, though his store and spa never were molested. For security reasons, however, the Langford family departed Hot Springs in 1916, moving first to Marathon and then to El Paso. During Langford's absence many people traveled by automobile to the springs in order to bathe in the hot waters, but they found neither accommodations nor store available.

In 1927, J. O. Langford returned to Hot Springs, and over the next fifteen years he developed the site into a complete facility for invalids seeking treatment in the curative waters. Not only did he erect a new stone store, but he also

Tourists enjoying the hot spring water which still flows at the ruins of J. O. Langford's bathhouse on the banks of the Rio Grande. Photograph by the author, 1982.

Baylor college students posed for a photograph on the campus at Independence in 1884. Courtesy Texas State Library, Austin, Texas.

built a new home and even a tourist court to provide accommodations for increasing numbers of guests. In time Hot Springs became widely known for its medicinal properties. The Langford family remained at the springs until 1942, when they sold the property to the state of Texas so that it might become part of the Big Bend National Park. For another decade Maggy and H. Baylor Smith operated the store and post office as a concession from the state, but since 1952 no one has resided at Hot Springs. The buildings and the springs, however, are preserved and protected by the National Park Service and are accessible to the public.

LOCATION: *Hot Springs is located at the end of a 1.9-mile semimaintained graded road leading from the paved National Park Service road about 3.5 miles west from the Rio Grande Village campground in the Big Bend National Park. The rough, narrow road is not recommended after rains and is not suitable for large truck campers or for vehicles pulling trailers. Visitors may still bathe in the hot spring waters and many bring their swimsuits for that purpose.*

Independence

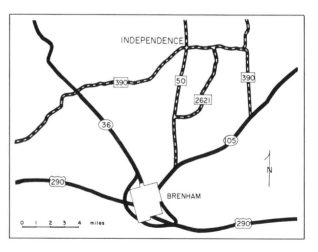

Today only a rural community, Independence over a century ago was known from its educational and cultural institutions. It became the home of many famous early Texans.

John P. Coles located first at Independence, which initially was known as Coles Settlement. His home, built in 1824, still stands and is the

Former building from Baylor Female College about 1907, two decades after the school had been moved from Independence. Courtesy Mrs. Evelyn Streng Collection, Institute of Texan Cultures, San Antonio, Texas.

oldest house in Washington County. The vicinity attracted numerous settlers because of its fertile soil, and about 1833 it received its first school. In 1839 a Baptist church was established which remains active to this day, being one of the oldest Baptist congregations in all of Texas.

In 1836, only shortly after the Texas Declaration of Independence was signed in nearby Washington-on-the-Brazos, the city fathers of Cole's Settlement at the suggestion of Dr. Asa Hoxie changed the name of their town to Independence in honor of the event. Many prominent citizens of the Republic of Texas knew Independence, but by far its most famous resident was Sam Houston, who lived there from 1853 to 1858. It was here that Houston joined the Baptist church in 1854 and was baptized in the waters of Rocky Creek. After his death in 1863, his widow, Margaret Lea Houston, moved back to the town to be near her mother and to give her children the opportunity to attend good schools.

Independence was the birthplace of Baylor University. The Congress of the Republic of Texas on 1 February 1845 granted a charter to the fledgling institution, which during its first year of operation in 1846 offered only a preparatory school in a building formerly occupied by a local acad-

emy. Beginning actual upper-level studies in 1847, Baylor originally was a coeducational institution. When its second president, Rufus C. Burleson, assumed duties in 1851, it was decided to separate the school into male and female departments. They operated as individual parts of the school until 1866, when Baylor University was designated for men and Baylor Female College was created for women, both functioning under the same board of directors. The two schools existed for another two decades in Independence, but in 1886 their location was moved to Waco for Baylor University and to Belton for the Baylor Female College, which today is the University of Mary Hardin–Baylor.

The reason for the departure of Baylor from Independence was the same as that for its general economic decline. Railway lines were built almost every direction from the town but none passed through it. Consequently trade went to competing towns that had the advantage of rail connections. Because it was sometimes difficult for the college students to find transportation to the Independence schools, they too often chose to attend classes elsewhere. After the departure of Baylor from Independence, the town began a decline which continued for a century. It now is

Mrs. Sam Houston's home still standing in Independence. Photograph by the author, 1981.

a rural community with about thirty occupied dwellings. Visitors find Independence a fascinating place because of its many historic nineteenth-century homes, the ruins of old Baylor University, exhibits in the Texas Baptist Historical Center, and an intriguing cemetery.

LOCATION: *Independence is located at the juncture of Farm to Market Road 50 with Farm to Market Road 390 in northern Washington County approximately 11 miles north of Brenham.*

Indianola

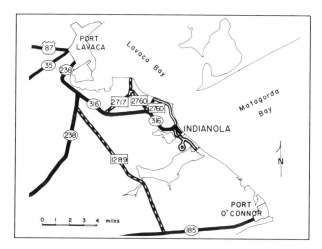

Indianola, once second only to Galveston as a Texas port city, today has virtually disappeared, leaving only its cemetery and a few ruined foundations. It boomed as a seaport during the middle years of the nineteenth century only to fall victim to two devastating hurricanes in 1875 and 1886.

German immigrants founded Indianola as Karlshaven. In 1844 the site became the point of arrival for immigrants brought to Texas by a society of German noblemen which in that year began the organized movement of thousands of German peasants to Texas. The society was not pleased with Galveston as a port of entry, so it selected an undeveloped site on the west side of Matagorda Bay to serve that purpose. Since there was not a single building to shelter the newly arrived immigrants, many of them died from illness or exposure before they could trek inland to the areas where they expected to settle.

One of the immigrants, Johann Schwartz, in 1845 built the first house in what later became the town of Indianola. Anglo-American landowners in the area saw the potential for a port town at the site, so in 1846 they had it surveyed and began selling lots to merchants and others. The start of the Mexican War enhanced the prospects for the new town, and it became a depot for munitions and military supplies for the army. The future of Indianola was assumed to be assured in 1849, when Charles Morgan made it the port on Matagorda Bay for his line of steamships serving the Gulf and Atlantic coasts, and soon Indianola could claim the arrival and departure of ships every day. By 1860 it had over a thousand people, and by 1870 over two thousand.

Indianola grew to importance because of the volume and diversity of its trade. It remained a major port of arrival for immigrants; it was a major export point for hides and tallow and later for refrigerated beef; it was a military depot; it was the seaport nearest to San Antonio and western Texas; and by the early 1870s it had railway connections with other towns along the Gulf coastal plain. As early as 1852 Indianola became the seat of Calhoun County. Although the town was occupied by Union forces during the Civil War, it suffered little destruction as a consequence.

One of the finest descriptions of Indianola came from Cora Montgomery, a visitor from the North. In her book, *Eagle Pass; or, Life on the Border*, published in 1852, she remembered seeing Indianola in this way:

Every body was disappointed in Indianola; it was so different from their ideas, but nobody found serious room for complaint. A belt of white sand separated the ocean of green prairies from the ocean of blue water, and along this belt was arranged a line of wooden buildings, unrelieved by trees or enclosures, like a string of overgrown packing boxes set out on the beach to dry.

Built beside Matagorda Bay at sea level, Indianola was vulnerable to any and all tropical storms along the Gulf coast, and it fell to destruction before two "once-in-a-century" hurricanes just over a decade apart. The first of these storms struck on 16 September 1875, and it devastated the town. Everything was flooded, and homes and businesses were battered by winds reaching 110 miles an hour. Virtually no buildings survived intact, and the deaths were estimated be-

Steamship moored at the Indianola wharf in the 1870s. Courtesy Texas State Library, Austin, Texas.

East on the main street of Indianola toward Powderhorn Bayou in 1873. Courtesy DeWitt County Historical Museum, Cuero, Texas.

Indianola business district in its heyday before the 1875 hurricane. Courtesy Texas State Library, Austin, Texas.

The devastation left in the wake of the 1886 Indianola hurricane. Courtesy Texas State Library, Austin, Texas.

Jonesboro

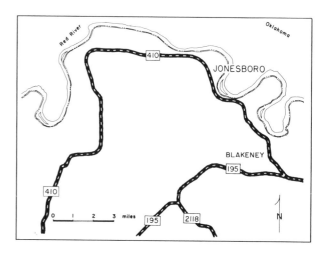

Bathing beauties on the Indianola beach in 1918. Courtesy Addie Lee Koenig.

tween one hundred and three hundred. The surviving Indianolans cleared the debris and rebuilt their town, but it never reached the vitality that it had enjoyed before the storm. By 1880 the population had declined to fewer than a thousand people. Then on 19 August 1886 a second even more destructive hurricane descended on Indianola. What wind and water failed to destroy a subsequent fire engulfed, and Indianola ceased to exist. As one writer noted, "Of the many ghost towns in Texas, none died as tragic a death as Indianola."

LOCATION: *The site of Indianola may be found at the extreme southeast end of Texas Highway 316 about 12.5 miles by road southeast from Port Lavaca in Calhoun County. At the townsite one sees a few fishing camps and bait shops, the foundations and buried cisterns from a handful of former buildings, the interesting Indianola cemetery, and an imposing pink granite statue of French explorer Robert Cavelier, Sieur de la Salle, who had landed nearby in 1685.*

Jonesboro is noted in the annals of Texas as having been the oldest Anglo-American settlement in the state. For a number of years the community had a ferry crossing on the Red River, and it was in this area that both Sam Houston and David Crockett entered Texas.

The story of Jonesboro goes back to the earliest settlement in the Red River country. Sometime about 1815 the vicinity was hunted by Henry Jones, who later operated the ferry at Jonesboro and gave it its name. The first settlers to occupy farms near the crossing were probably Adam Lawrence and William Hensley, who arrived about the same time that Jones appeared, and by 1817 there were at least five households settled in the vicinity. Before 1820 at least another five families had established farmsteads at or near Jonesboro.

Events on the north side of the Red River contributed to settlement at the new community, for in the mid-1820s the United States government expelled several families of squatters from the American side of the river, while in 1826, Miller County, Arkansas Territory, on the north side dissolved and prompted more Americans to move south of the river. Not all the newcomers, however, remained in the Jonesboro neighborhood; a number of them moved farther south to settle in a new colony around San Felipe on the lower Brazos River that Stephen F. Austin had founded in 1823.

By the 1830s Jonesboro had become a flourishing community. Since it was located at the head of steam navigation on the Red River, numerous traders and merchants based their firms in the town. Though the residents settled on the border

Old Jonesboro Crossing on the Red River. Courtesy Sue Flanagan.

with the United States, many of them considered themselves Texans and organized a company of riflemen for service in the Texas Revolution. The men reached San Jacinto only days after the battle that won Texas independence, and since they did not have the extreme hatred for Mexicans exhibited by the troops who had lost friends at the Alamo and Goliad, General Sam Houston made the Red River volunteers responsible for guarding and protecting captured Mexican General Santa Anna, whose life had been threatened by many of the more vengeful Texan soldiers.

The Texas Congress in 1837 chartered the town of Jonesboro, which about this time was described as having about fifty houses and a growing population. Soon, however, the growth ceased, for

Jonesboro was eclipsed by Clarksville, the new seat of Red River County. Contributing to its decline was the further movement of the frontier westward, drawing away many of the trading firms which had made it their headquarters. Other Jonesboro merchants moved their trade to towns toward the southeast. A Red River flood in 1843 heavily damaged the buildings at Jonesboro and shifted the river channel about a mile to the north, leaving the town landlocked. Soon it withered away completely.

LOCATION: *The historical markers for the site of Jonesboro stand on the north side of Farm to Market Road 410 about 6 miles northwest of Blakeney at Salt Well Slough in extreme northern Red River County.*

Kellyville

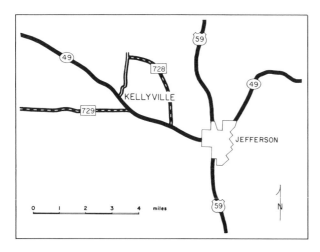

Although it is difficult for visitors today to imagine, Kellyville just over a century ago was a center of iron smelting and heavy industry. Today it is marked by an extensive roadside park amid the pine trees of rural Marion County.

Kellyville was founded as a manufacturing center in 1848 by Zachariah Lockett and John A. Stewart. The site they chose for their enterprise was known as Four-Mile Branch, and it was a popular camping place for teamsters about four miles west of Jefferson, then the commercial center of northeast Texas. Freight wagons were constantly coming into Jefferson loaded with agricultural products from settlements to the west and then returning filled with goods that had come to Jefferson by steamboat. Lockett and Stewart decided that the teamsters' camping place would be the ideal spot for a general wagon repair shop, as indeed it turned out to be. The business grew from wagon repair to include a small iron foundry producing such goods as plows and agricultural tools. For these products the two men smelted small amounts of iron from locally mined hematite ore.

In 1852, George Addison Kelly joined the firm as foreman. Kelly had been born in Tennessee in 1832, but he had come west first to Natchitoches Parish, Louisiana, and then to Texas. Learning that the teamsters and stock raisers constituted a market for cowbells, Kelly traveled to Kentucky

The Kelly family burial plot in the Kellyville cemetery. Photograph by the author, 1981.

in 1854 to study the manufacture not only of bells but also of other iron products. Four years later he became a partner with Lockett and Stewart in their foundry west of Jefferson, and in 1860 he bought out their shares completely. In the next year he introduced the "Kelly Blue" plows, which over the next decades were used by thousands, the term "Kelly Blue" becoming synonymous with plow for many Texas farmers.

The Civil War interrupted growth at Kelly's ironworks, which he named the Kelly Plow Company. Traditions state that he raised a company for the Confederate Army but that when they gathered to be mustered into service he was rejected and told to return to his foundry to make cannonballs for the army and plows and stoves for the civilian population.

Already by the outbreak of the war a considerable community of employees and their families had grown up around the furnace. In time it contained an estimated one thousand inhabitants, two churches, a school, a hotel, and a post office, not to mention two cemeteries. At the end of the war, Kelly purchased the holdings at the old Nash Iron Furnace farther west in Marion County, which in 1847 had been the very first iron furnace in Texas, and with the added equipment Kelly began smelting more locally mined ore. Then in 1874 he rebuilt his blast furnace to increase his iron smelting capacity. Business boomed, with the *Engineering and Mining Journal* reporting that Kelly produced and sold ten thousand plows in 1877 alone. Then disaster struck.

In 1880 the Kelly Plow Company suffered a disastrous fire. The buildings and equipment were not insured, so the firm lost much of its investment. Since the nearby town of Jefferson had already declined as a trade center and at the time was not served by any railroads, George A. Kelly decided to move his entire manufacturing operation to Longview, which he saw as a much more promising location. There he abandoned iron smelting entirely, devoting his firm solely to the manufacture of agricultural implements.

As soon as the factory left Kellyville, the town withered away to nothing more than a rural community. Today the site of the former town is marked by a large roadside rest area with a historical monument erected by the state in 1936. In some areas of the park one still finds on the surface iron ore, slag, and pieces of iron that remain

from the days of the foundry. The two cemeteries, one for whites and the other for blacks, lie a short distance beyond the park. In one of the graveyards visitors may view the burial place of George A. Kelly, the man who so influenced the history of the town.

LOCATION: *The site of Kellyville centers on the roadside park at the northeast side of Texas Highway 49 about 4.0 miles west of Jefferson.*

Kelsey

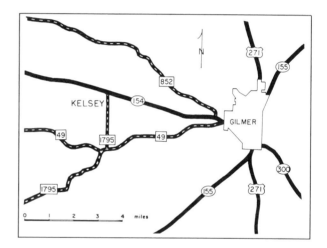

Kelsey, in Upshur County near Gilmer, is a one-of-a-kind town, for it became the mother colony of all the Mormon communities in Texas. Today a rural community, it is a ghost of its former self.

Two brothers, John and Jim Edgar, of Andalusia, Alabama, founded the Mormon settlement at Kelsey in 1898. Eight years earlier missionaries had converted them with their families to become members of the Church of Jesus Christ of Latter-day Saints. In order to be with others of their new faith, they had moved to the Mormon settlement at Mesa, Arizona, but had become dissatisfied with the desert climate and began to miss their homes in the South. Jim returned to Alabama, and John also packed up his belongings in 1897 and headed that way. By the end of the year, he had reached Upshur County, Texas, but because of financial need he stopped to rent a farm for a season to make enough money to continue his journey home. John made an abundant

The last commercial store to operate at Kelsey, standing vacant behind the historical marker for the town. Photograph by the author, 1981.

Crumbling remains of a Kelsey home. Photograph by the author, 1981.

harvest and wrote to his brother suggesting that he join him in East Texas, which he did.

In late 1898 the two brothers purchased 140 acres of farmland, followed in 1900 by the purchase of another like amount of land. Although it was not their purpose to found any religious colony, their activities soon attracted the attention of church authorities in Salt Lake City. The religious leaders concluded that Upshur County might provide a good location for the formation of a Mormon settlement, or gathering place, for converts to the church who were experiencing persecution elsewhere in the South. Accordingly missionaries were dispatched to the area, where in 1901 they began a Mormon Sunday School. By the end of the year nine Latter-day Saint families already had settled in the area and built a log chapel measuring twenty-four by thirty feet.

In 1902 a post office was established for the growing Mormon settlement, taking its name from Kelsey Creek which flows through the neighborhood. Two years later church authorities had the county surveyor lay out a town by that name on land belonging to Jim Edgar. More and more Mormons began moving in, most of them farming, but a few of them finding employment in nearby sawmills and shingle mills. By 1911, Kelsey had five stores, a brick kiln, three sawmills, one shingle mill, a cotton gin, two blacksmith shops, and a gristmill. In 1910 the Marshall and East Texas Railway was built through the town, erecting a wooden depot there. Although there had been a school at Kelsey as early as 1901, members of the community in 1911 erected the red brick Kelsey Academy, which operated as a public school through 1943 with Mormon missionaries serving as its state-salaried teachers.

Kelsey reached its height in population and importance about 1917. At this time it had about 750 inhabitants, with several hundred additional Mormons living just a few miles southeast at Enoch, and the town had a business district containing fourteen commercial enterprises. After 1917, however, the community began to deteriorate for two principal reasons. First, Kelsey had prospered early in the century because members of the Latter-day Saint church needed a haven in the South where they might escape religious persecution. With increasing tolerance in the region, the need for such a haven lessened. The second major factor contributing to the decline was the

abandonment of the Marshall and East Texas Railway. It had been built mainly as a logging line, and when the timber areas it served were depleted, its economic base disappeared. The last train ran through the area in September 1917, leaving the Kelsey farmers with no practical means for transporting their crops to market. The economic depression of the 1930s increased the problems for the Kelsey farmers, forcing more of them to seek employment elsewhere. Today Kelsey is a dispersed rural community populated principally by descendants of the original Mormon settlers, but it has no school, no church, and no places of business.

LOCATION: *Kelsey is scattered along either side of Farm to Market Road 1795 for about 1.5 miles south from its intersection with Texas Highway 154 about 6.2 miles west of Gilmer.*

Kimball

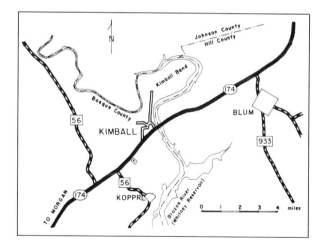

Kimball, where the Chisholm Trail crossed the Brazos River, today stands silent, for not a soul lives where a town once flourished and thousands of cattle crossed the river on their way north to Kansas markets.

Richard B. Kimball, a New York attorney, and Jacob DeCordova, a Jamaican-born land promoter, were responsible for the establishment of Kimball, but interestingly it was the second town to occupy the same general area. In 1847, Richard Kimball, through DeCordova as his agent, pur-

Ruined stone walls marking the site of a store in Kimball. Photograph by the author, 1980.

chased land script for several thousand acres in the area that became known as the Kimball Bend of the Brazos River. Although they bought the land in 1847, it was not until 1848 that George B. Erath and Neil McLennan surveyed the land and marked its boundaries. In that year the two speculators sold a portion of the property on credit to Sir Edward Belcher, representing the English Universal Land Company. This British firm in the fall of 1850 settled approximately 125 immigrants on the land, but the colony fell apart. The newcomers were mainly city folk, totally ignorant of agriculture in the new environment. In addition the winter of 1850–51 was wet and bitterly cold, so that by spring most of the English settlers had deserted the colony known as Kent. Land ownership reverted to lawyer Kimball.

In the meantime the New York lawyer had purchased an additional 60,000 acres in Erath County, and he needed money rather than land in order to meet his obligations. As a means of selling at least some of the property along the Brazos, Kimball and DeCordova decided to establish a town at a river crossing on the downstream side

Marker at the grave of a teenaged girl murdered in Kimball. Photograph by the author, 1980.

of the Kimball Bend. Much of the river in this section has steep banks and comparatively deep water, but the crossing on their property offered gentle slopes on both sides and a firm gravel bottom. It was the ideal location for a town to grow and thrive.

The townsite named in honor of the attorney was surveyed about 1854, and the developers began selling lots to businessmen and residents. By the mid-1850s the community included a public school, a blacksmith shop, a Baptist church, and four saloons. About this time lawyer Kimball moved to the area, building a home at the river bend, while about the same time DeCordova also erected a home in the vicinity. Both of them obviously expected the neighborhood to prosper.

It took ten years for the boom at Kimball to begin. It started after the end of the Civil War and lasted for about a decade. In 1865, Jesse Chisholm opened the central section of an overland route which took his name as the Chisholm Trail, and within a couple of years thousands of Texas longhorns were being driven northward over the route to Kansas markets at Abilene and Wichita. The trail began in South Texas and crossed the Brazos at the Kimball crossing; the adjacent town flourished. It was a peaceful stop for the drovers that was characterized by comparatively little violence. The cattlemen generally bedded down their stock on the south side of the river on the day they arrived at Kimball and then started moving the cattle across the river early the next morning. An enterprising Kimball citizen built a "swimming pen" for the cattle. Drovers would place a manageable number of cattle into this three-sided pen and then would "jump them" into the river and swim them across. In times of flooding, herds would build up several miles deep waiting for the water to subside so that they could cross safely.

By 1865, Kimball also had a ferry for transporting vehicles across the river. In 1868 a Masonic lodge was founded. The census enumerators in 1870 counted 219 people in the town. Though education had been conducted since the early days, in 1873 the Kimball Academy was built to house a private school.

The decline for the town began in 1875 with the shift of cattle drives westward. Within a couple of years the Western Trail to Dodge City had taken the place of the older Chisholm Trail, removing a valuable source of income for the Kimball merchants. Then in 1881 the Gulf, Colorado and Santa Fe Railway built through the area, passing downstream from Kimball and missing it by several miles. The place became little more than a country town. In the late 1940s the few residents left in Kimball were bought out by the U.S. Army Corps of Engineers to make way for the construction of the Whitney Dam on the Brazos, because the site of the community would be covered by water during times of extreme flooding after the dam was completed. The cemetery was moved down the highway two miles to the southwest, while the site of the former town was converted into a park, although the ruins of several buildings were permitted to stand.

LOCATION: *The Kimball townsite lies today in Kimball Bend Park at the south end of the Texas Highway 174 bridge across the Brazos River in Bosque County about 11 miles northeast of Morgan and 19 miles south of Cleburne.*

Lajitas

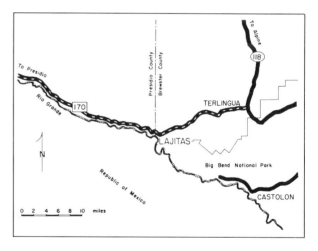

Lajitas is named after the flat rocks, the *lajitas*, that lie beneath the shallow water at the ford which for centuries has made it a natural crossing place on the Rio Grande.

For many years Mexican Indians farmed the narrow floodplain on either side of the river at Lajitas, but they were driven away from the area first by the Apaches and later by the Comanches as these nomadic tribes of Indians moved south-

Old and new Lajitas standing on the banks of the Rio Grande. Photograph by the author, 1982.

ward down the Great Plains in the eighteenth and nineteenth centuries. War parties from these two tribes frequently raided south into what is now Mexico, often crossing the Rio Grande at the ford with the flat rocks. Perhaps the first Anglo-American mention of the place came in 1852 from Lieutenant William H. Emory, a member of the Mexican-American Boundary Commission. Describing Lajitas, he noted that "here broad well-beaten trails lead to the river on both sides. A band of Indians . . . crossed the river at the time of our visit; they had come, by their own account, from the headwaters of the Red River, and they were on their way to Durango in Mexico. No doubt on a thieving expedition."

By the time the first Anglo-Americans came to settle in the vicinity of the crossing in the late 1890s, most of the Plains Indian raids had ended, and the Mexican farmers had returned to the area. The initial American landowner at Lajitas was H. W. McGuirk, who had been employed to maintain a telephone line leading from Marfa southward to the Mariposa quicksilver mine in the Big Bend country. For the next fifteen years McGuirk dominated the local scene. After clear-ing and leveling over a hundred acres of land along the river, he began raising irrigated cotton and opened a general store and saloon to serve the neighborhood on both sides of the river. Next he built an adobe school for the Mexican chil-dren, and about 1908 he erected an adobe Catho-lic chapel. It is interesting to note that McGuirk in 1903 married Josefa Navarro, a great grand-daughter of Texas patriot José Navarro, one of the signers of the Texas Declaration of Independence. McGuirk's activities were so successful that the *Alpine Avalanche* in 1902 was able to report that "Lajitas is becoming quite a town. It has one store, a beer saloon, a school house with 50 pupils, and a Customhouse for the sub-district port of entry." Though Lajitas had officially pos-sessed a post office as early as 1901, it never oper-ated until McGuirk petitioned in his wife's name for its reestablishment in 1904.

The nearest that Lajitas came to having a boom was during the border troubles that occurred dur-ing the Mexican Revolution in the years preced-ing American entry into World War I. At this time the U.S. Army established a cavalry encampment at Lajitas and the business at the store prospered.

Wagon beside the store in old Lajitas. Photograph by the author, 1982.

When the soldiers left, Lajitas returned to the doldrums of being a sleepy border trading-post community. The ownership of the store changed several times during the twentieth century, most of the time being the property of the Skaggs and Ivey families, but Lajitas remained a remote outpost occasionally visited by tourists either going to or coming from the Big Bend National Park. The community did not even receive its first electricity or telephones until the 1960s. The store remained the only place of business until the 1970s, but behind the scenes big changes had already begun.

In 1952 a Houston entrepreneur, Walter Mischer, started buying land around Lajitas, eventually ending up with about thirty thousand acres. In 1976 under the name of the Arrow Investment Company he began developing Lajitas into a tourist attraction. He restored the old adobe chapel, built a motel over the foundations of the former cavalry post, and constructed an entire block of wooden false-front commercial buildings "reconstructing" a wild West town that never existed at Lajitas in reality. Today the "Lajitas on the Rio Grande" complex of condominiums, motels, restaurants, and specialty shops stands along Farm to Market Road 170, while the old Lajitas, the true ghost town, lies down a graded road only a short distance away.

LOCATION: *Lajitas is found on Farm to Market Road 170 in extreme western Brewster County about 50 miles southeast of Presidio and 13 miles west of Terlingua.*

La Lomita

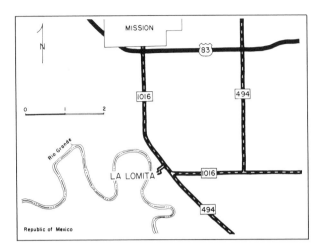

La Lomita, the predecessor of modern Mission, Texas, began with a grant of land from the king of Spain in 1767. After the middle of the nineteenth century the original grant came into the possession of the Catholic Missionary Society of the Oblate Fathers.

Priests from the order began using a little chapel at this place called La Lomita (meaning "the little hill"), which was about halfway between their mission stations at Roma and Brownsville. They also sought to develop it into a successful ranching and agricultural community. In 1899 the mission itself became a religious center when it received its own resident priest. The original chapel, built from adobe, had been unable to withstand the weather in the Lower Rio Grande valley, and in 1899 the present stone chapel was built. It was badly damaged by a tropical storm in 1933 but the next year was saved by local Catholics, who undertook major repairs.

A substantial community had grown up at La Lomita by the beginning of this century. At the time it had not only the church complex, including chapel, priest's house, dining hall, kitchen, bread oven, and guest cottage, but also Will McShane's general store, several frame homes, and a number of Mexican *jacal* huts. In 1908 the Oblate Fathers sold a considerable portion of their ranch acreage to a partnership of James W. Hoit and John J. Conway, who divided it into farms for sale to agriculturists from other regions of the country. Hoit and Conway also laid out the town of Mission, named for La Lomita Mission and just four miles north of the old community, and the new town boomed as irrigated agriculture spread through the valley. Soon the little ranch community around the old mission withered away, leaving only the chapel complex, which by the 1920s had been virtually abandoned.

LOCATION: *La Lomita Chapel, center of the former ranch community of La Lomita, today is beautifully maintained in a park area just off Farm to Market Road 1016. To reach the site, drive south on the farm to market road 4.3 miles from downtown Mission to a highway department sign for the chapel, turn southwest onto a gravel road leading over a bridge across an irrigation canal.*

La Lomita Chapel. Photograph by the author, 1981.

Langtry

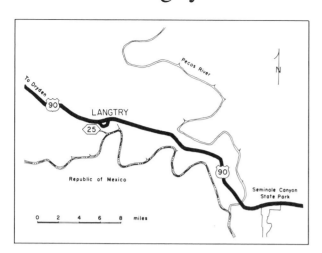

Langtry, originally called Eagle Nest, is known throughout America as having been where Judge Roy Bean held court as "the Law West of the Pecos." The town began as a grading camp during the construction of the Southern Pacific Railroad, which was built across the region in 1882 to link New Orleans and San Antonio on the east with Los Angeles and San Francisco on the west. As the crews worked from the east, Roy Bean

English singer Lily Langtry, for whom Roy Bean claimed to have named the town of Langtry. From *Frank Leslie's Illustrated Newspaper* (4 November 1882), p. 165.

Roy Bean (with white beard) and crowd in front of the first Jersey Lilly Saloon in Langtry at some date before it burned in 1897 and was replaced by the still standing building. Courtesy H. Leslie Evans.

Furniture in an abandoned Langtry residence. Photograph by the author, 1981.

operated a tent saloon that shifted location each time the camps of workers moved forward with the progress of the line. In the spring of 1882, he moved from a camp called Vinegaroon to a new one named Langtry in recognition of a foreman who had supervised a crew of Chinese laborers building through the area.

On 2 August 1882, Roy Bean was appointed justice of the peace for the precinct encompassing Langtry. He held the position by election for almost two decades, losing at the polls in 1886 and 1896. Bean is known from his superficially eccentric but sound judgments at court, which generally met in his saloon building. In one instance, for example, the judge held an inquest into the death of a man who had fallen from the Pecos River railway bridge. Finding that the man had a pistol and that his pockets contained forty dollars in cash, he fined the dead man the forty dollars for carrying a concealed weapon. On another occasion the judge released a railroad worker who had murdered a Chinese laborer purportedly because his law books did not specifically state that it was illegal to kill a Chinaman. In the former case the county needed the forty dollars to bury

Desolation in Langtry. Photograph by the author, 1981.

the dead man, while in the latter instance a mob composed of the accused killer's friends had assembled and threatened to riot if their comrade were not released.

Roy Bean claimed that he had named the town Langtry in honor of the popular English singer, Lily Langtry, but the Southern Pacific seems to have better evidence to the contrary. Bean in the 1880s had become enamored of the British singer from seeing her pictures, and he even called his saloon the "Jersey Lilly" in her honor. After his death the entertainer passed through the town on a passenger train, and she stepped from her Pullman car to view the dusty little sidetrack community which shared her name.

One of the most famous events in Langtry history was the 1896 world championship boxing match which took place there. Because Texas, New Mexico, Arizona, and Chihuahua had prohibited the fight (and the concurrent gambling), Bean and the fight promoters secretly scheduled it to take place on a sandbar on the Mexican side of the river near Langtry, which was beyond American jurisdiction and inaccessible to Mexican authorities. The spectators traveled to Langtry aboard a special chartered train, crossed the Rio Grande on a temporary catwalk, and on Mexican soil witnessed the defeat of Irish boxer Peter Mahar by Australian Bob Fitzsimmons in a brief one-minute thirty-five-second bout.

By the turn of the century, Langtry had become a substantial ranch community that supplied the needs for a widespread area along the Rio Grande and lower Pecos River. Forty years ago it still had a population of two hundred and contained two stores, a post office, school, restaurant, and several tourist courts as well as numerous homes. Today, however, it has just over a dozen occupied residences, about the same number of abandoned houses, several empty commercial buildings, and a now quiet school. It has one eating place and the Judge Roy Bean Visitor Center which preserves the second of two wooden buildings which housed Roy Bean's "Jersey Lilly" saloon, billiard parlor, and courtroom.

LOCATION: *Langtry stands on Loop 25 from U.S. Highway 90 about 60 miles northwest of Del Rio and about 40 miles east of Dryden. Approximately 20 miles east is the Seminole Canyon State Park, which contains magnificent Indian pictographs, many of which are an estimated eight thousand years old.*

Entry to an empty Langtry home. Photograph by the author, 1981.

La Reunion

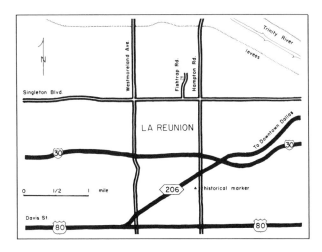

A French communal colony, La Reunion existed just west of the village of Dallas from the 1850s into the early 1860s, gradually melting away as the utopian settlement fell apart because of mismanagement.

La Reunion came into being as an indirect result of the economic and philosophical teachings of François Marie Charles Fourier, a French thinker during the early nineteenth century. Fourier, stressing what he interpreted as the natural order of society, believed that a utopia could be created by placing mankind into small cooperative communities in which all members worked for the good of the whole. The colonies were socialistic but not purely communistic, for Fourier did not prohibit the ownership of private property, but they were organized strictly for the benefit of the community.

During the nineteenth century several Fourieristic colonies were established in the United States, which the French founders saw as an unspoiled land for such experiments, and La Reunion was one of these settlements. Victor Prosper Considérant, leader of a French-based organization, traveled to Texas in 1853 to find the site for such a colony. Land was purchased in 1855 near the village of Dallas. The townsite chosen was on the slope of a limestone hill facing the Trinity River and its West Fork, about three miles west of the Anglo-American town. Though the hill in later years provided raw material for the manufacture of millions of dollars' worth of concrete, the site proved to be less than ideal for the French agriculturists.

Two hundred French-speaking immigrants arrived in Dallas in April 1855, having landed in Galveston and traveled overland from the coast. They were disappointed that more preparation had not been made for their arrival at the new colony. A lack of effective leadership and organization combined with unsuccessful agricultural production eventually caused the failure of the colony. Numerous settlers left La Reunion soon after coming, but during the first two years most of their places were taken by new arrivals.

Averaging an estimated two hundred residents for its first couple of years, after 1857 La Reunion began a steady decline. By the outbreak of the Civil War most of the former colonists had left the settlement, some of them returning to Europe, some moving to New Orleans, and others choosing homes elsewhere in Texas. A handful of their descendants still live in the Dallas area.

LOCATION: *The main tract of the La Reunion colony straddled the north-facing hill that lies on the south side of the Trinity River between Hampton Road and Westmoreland Avenue from Davis Street north three miles across the original bed of the Trinity River in present-day Dallas. Much of the area once occupied by the colonists has been completely excavated for lime used in the manufacture of concrete. La Reunion colony cemetery still may be seen across from a public housing complex and just northwest of L. G. Pinkston*

Historical monument for La Reunion in the corner of Stevens Park. Photograph by the author, 1984.

High School at 3345 Fishtrap Road, while a granite historical marker for La Reunion stands at the northeast corner of Stevens Park beside Hampton Road opposite its intersection with Old Orchard Drive. The Reunion Arena in downtown Dallas perpetuates the name of the old French colony.

Larissa

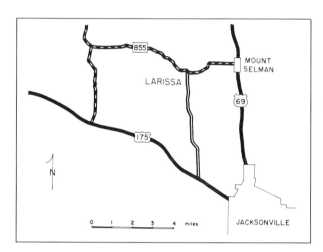

Larissa, famed in its day as "the Athens of Texas," today slumbers as a sparsely populated black community hidden in the red hills of Cherokee County. The first settlement in the vicinity came in 1837, when Isaac Killough with his wife and the families of his four sons and two daughters moved there from Taladega County, Alabama. They planted their first crops and erected log houses, forming a community consisting mainly of related family members.

Things went well for the Killough community until the summer of 1838. Fearing hostilities as a result of unrest among the Cherokees who occupied the same general area, the Killough family retreated from their new homes to a vicinity nearer to Nacogdoches and other white settlements. The Indians told them that they would be safe to harvest their maturing crops "until the first white frost." Together with their families, the Killoughs returned to bring in their corn. As they were completing the work in October, without warning a war party swept down on the settlement, killing or carrying away the majority

of its inhabitants—eighteen men, women, and children.

Although one member of the family returned after the Indian danger had subsided, real settlement did not come back to the vicinity until 1846. In that year a party of Tennesseans led by Thomas H. McKee moved into the neighborhood formerly occupied by the Killough family. They called their community McKee Colony, but the next year Thomas McKee had a townsite laid out on his land and named it Larissa after an ancient Greek center of learning.

In 1848, Thomas H. McKee erected a one-room log school, oral traditions relating that he sold a black slave at Shreveport, Louisiana, for $1,000 to raise the money needed to establish it. Two other local citizens contributed funds to raise the standards of the school, which became the Larissa Academy. In 1855 the Brazos Synod of the Cumberland Presbyterian Church assumed fiscal responsibility for the operation of the institution, which became Larissa College, and in 1856 the state legislature granted it a charter. Though its career was brief, Larissa College became one of the centers for higher education in Texas. Among the courses offered in its three-story classroom building were Latin, Spanish, and French, as well as natural philosophy, chemistry, physics, geology, mineralogy, animal physiology, botany, moral science, mental science, rhetoric, logic, and mathematics. The school also gave instruction in astronomy, claiming to have a telescope three times as powerful as the one at Yale University.

Larissa College operated until after the outbreak of the Civil War, when its male students left for military service. It reopened after the war but never regained its former vigor as an educational institution. In 1866 the Cumberland Presbyterians withdrew their support, leaving the college to function as an independent institution until its closing in 1870, when its assets were transferred to Trinity University at Tehuacana, the predecessor of present-day Trinity University in San Antonio.

The abandonment of the college was the first major blow to strike Larissa, but it was soon followed by a second. In 1872 the International–Great Northern Railroad built across Cherokee County through Jacksonville and missed Larissa by about eight miles. Less than a decade later an-

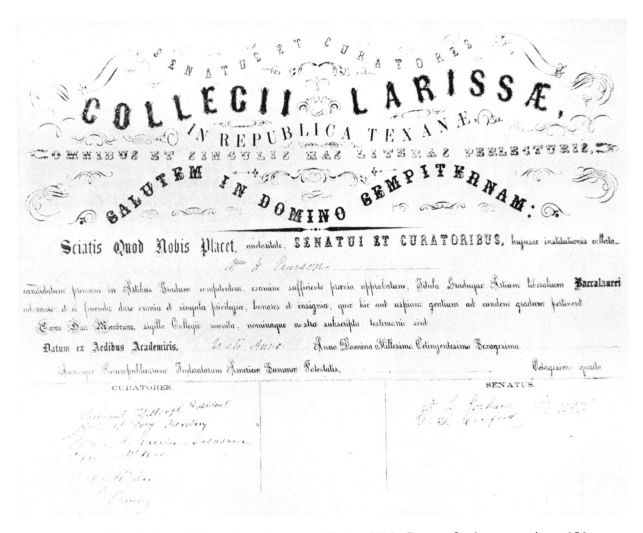

Diploma from Larissa College. From Hugo Fred Ford and J. L. Brown, *Larissa*, opposite p. 156.

Long quiet lodge hall at Larissa. Photograph by the author, 1981.

other new railway, this time the Kansas and Gulf Short Line, built southward to connect Jacksonville with Lufkin, missing Larissa by about three miles and spawning the nearby railroad town of Mount Selman. Soon Larissa withered away, black tenants moving into the abandoned homes belonging to some of the former white residents. Today scattered shanties, abandoned houses, and a quiet lodge hall are all that remain from what once was one of the cultural centers of Texas.

LOCATION: *To reach the site of Larissa, drive southward about 0.8 mile on a paved county road leading from Farm to Market Road 855 about 2.6 miles west of Mount Selman in northern Cherokee County. Beyond the site of the town one finds the memorial erected in 1934 for the victims of the 1838 Killough massacre.*

Linnville

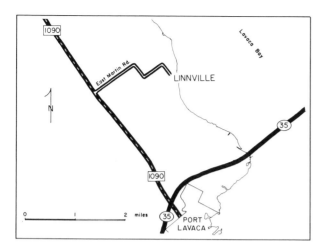

Linnville, a ghost town on Lavaca Bay near Port Lavaca, was established as a seaport by John J. Linn and William G. Ewing in 1831. First known as New Port, later as Linnville, within less than a decade the community grew to become a prosperous port of entry, complete with a Republic of Texas customhouse, several large warehouses, and a number of residences and places of business. In 1840 it was described as "the point to which most goods and merchandise are shipped for Victoria and other 'settlements' on the Guadalupe and Lavacca [*sic*]."

Today Linnville is known not for its importance as a Republic of Texas seaport, but rather for its death. The site possesses the distinction of having been one of the few communities in Texas to have been destroyed by Indians and never rebuilt. The story of its demise begins in San Antonio.

Throughout much of its early history, Texas witnessed successive bloody encounters between white settlers and the Comanche Indians. One of the best known of these clashes came in the Alamo City on 19 March 1840. After preliminary meetings, the Comanches agreed to enter San Antonio to meet with the Texans and to return white prisoners which they had captured. They arrived to confer with the Texans, but they brought only one captive, a horribly mutilated fifteen-year-old girl named Matilda Lockhart. A woman who saw the poor girl at the time described her as being covered with sores, bruises, and burns, her nose "actually burnt off to the bone—all the fleshy end gone, and a great scab formed on the end of the bone."

The Indians were led into a stone complex on the Main Plaza known as the Council House. A dozen chiefs entered a large meeting room, leaving their warriors and a number of women and children on the outside. Once they were in the meeting room, armed Texans informed the chiefs that they would be held hostage until the remaining white captives, thought to number over a dozen, had been returned from the Indians' camps. Soon a melee broke out between whites and Indians, resulting in all the outnumbered chiefs being killed outright. Almost all the warriors, women, and children outside the meeting room were either killed or captured.

Infuriated by the betrayal at the Council House fight, the Comanches determined to wreak their revenge on the Texans. Their efforts were in part encouraged by Mexican agents representing the centralist regime then ruling Mexico. Because Mexican federalists at the time were gathering supplies on the Texas coast in order to oppose the centralist Mexican government, centralist agents entered the Comanche camps and directed the Indians toward the main port of entry for these supplies—the town of Linnville.

Although the Indians met a handful of whites on their way into the interior of Texas, they encountered little opposition until their huge war party reached Victoria, on the gulf coastal plain, on 6 August 1840. There they harassed the residents, stole about fifteen hundred horses (a third of them from Mexican traders in the neighborhood), and killed a number of white men they found alone or in small parties. After spending two days unsuccessfully assaulting Victoria, they turned toward the coast and the bulging warehouses at Linnville.

Not knowing about the attacks on Victoria, most of the residents of the seaport were peacefully sleeping on the morning of Sunday, 8 August, when a horde of about six hundred Comanche warriors swept down on the town. Killing a few men on the outskirts, they rode into the very streets, whooping and shooting arrows in all directions. Most of the inhabitants ran for Lavaca Bay and waded through the shallow water to boats resting at anchor. The raiders overtook a few of them, among them H. O. Watts, the Republic of Texas customs collector for the port. In addition his attractive wife, a black slave woman, and a child were captured and taken away.

Granite monument erected by the State of Texas in 1936 to mark the site of Linnville. Photograph by the author, 1982.

Lavaca Bay seen from the site of Linnville. Photograph by the author, 1982.

"Safe" aboard the small boats in the bay, the townspeople had the heartrending experience of watching the red warriors loot and burn their town. The raiders spent the entire day plundering the seaport. They destroyed or took virtually everything of value, even driving the cattle into pens to burn them or cut them to pieces. In a warehouse owned by John J. Linn, one of the town's founders, the Indians found several cases of umbrellas and hats that had been sold to James Robinson, a San Antonio merchant. As Linn himself recalled: "These Indians made free with, and went dashing about the blazing village, amid their screeching squaws and 'little Injuns,' like demons on a drunken saturnalia, with Robinson's hats on their heads and Robinson's umbrellas bobbing about on every side." By afternoon the Indians retired from the devastated village, their booty tied on the backs of stolen horses and mules.

Fighting men from much of Texas combined to follow the huge war party, catching up with it on Plum Creek near present-day Lockhart on 12 August. In the ensuing fight the Texans overwhelmingly bested the Comanches, recovering many of the horses and other property stolen only days earlier at Victoria and Linnville. It was during this fight that the Texans rescued Mrs. Watts of Linnville, but not before one of the warriors had shot her in the breast with an arrow. A piece of steel in Mrs. Watts's corset saved her life by pre-venting the arrow from penetrating more deeply, and the lady recovered to live almost forty years longer as the keeper of the San Antonio House in Port Lavaca. Not being satisfied with the punishment exacted on the Comanches at Plum Creek, the Republic of Texas sent another strong body of men into their homeland on the Colorado River and on 24 October 1840 decisively defeated them a second time.

After the raid on Linnville, the town was never rebuilt. Its mercantile role was assumed by Port Lavaca, which was first settled in the year of the great raid and platted as a town in 1842. For almost 150 years the site of Linnville lay unoccupied, though in the last decade a handful of modern residences have been erected at its site.

LOCATION: *Linnville today is marked by a granite monument erected by the state of Texas during the 1936 centennial observances. The marker and townsite may be reached by taking a circuitous route that begins at Port Lavaca in Calhoun County. Drive 2.6 miles northward from Texas Highway 35 on Farm to Market Road 1090 to its intersection with East Martin Road, a paved county road, and then turn east for one mile, passing by two small bridges on the left over a drainage ditch. Take a gravel road that continues one mile south, then east, then south to a dead end amid a new residential subdivision. From the end of the road, the gray granite marker may be seen clearly about seventy-five yards to the southeast across a grassy area on the bluffs overlooking the bay.*

Lobo

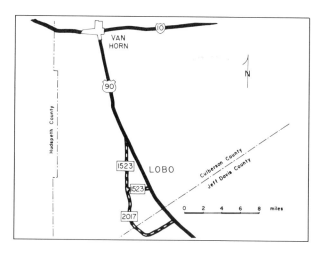

One of the many disused irrigation pumps that dot the former fields around Lobo. Photograph by the author, 1981.

Named for the lobo wolves which once commonly prowled the vicinity, Lobo for its entire history depended on its water resources for survival in an arid environment.

The Van Horn Wells, near what became the town of Lobo, served as a stop on the San Antonio–San Diego mail route in the 1850s and 1860s. These seep springs provided the only dependable source of water for miles in the surrounding desert. Then in the 1880s the Southern Pacific Railroad drilled a well and located a steam locomotive water stop, depot, and livestock loading pens in the same general area.

Early in this century settlers brought to the Lobo vicinity by land promoters began drilling wells so that they might pump groundwater to the surface to irrigate agricultural crops. For a while around World War I a minor agricultural boom centered on Lobo, which received its first post office in 1907. When Culberson County was organized in April 1911, Lobo actively competed with Van Horn for the distinction of becoming its seat of government. A newspaper at the time noted that "a good hotel, good water, a beautiful valley and a prosperous town are some of the claims that Lobo folks are urging." Despite the claims, however, Van Horn won the contest and secured the county seat.

The Lobo area experienced a second agricultural boom in the years following World War II until about 1950 when large-scale irrigation employing more efficient power pumps was introduced. For a few years cotton farming was king. Hundreds of acres were placed under cultivation and scores of large irrigation wells were drilled,

Tumbleweed-filled fountain and motel swimming pool in Lobo. Photograph by the author, 1981.

but the prosperity was only temporary. Because of the expense of pumping, virtually all of the wells eventually had to be abandoned by the late 1960s. Today, with the exception of a few small areas, Lobo has returned to the desert, with more of its houses abandoned than occupied. The 1950s town even includes an attractive but vacant motel complete with a tumbleweed filled swimming pool and empty rooms.

LOCATION: *The Lobo community lies scattered along U.S. Highway 90 about 12 to 16 miles south of Van Horn in southern Culberson County.*

Pumphouse which once provided boiler water to Southern Pacific steam locomotives stopping at the siding in Longfellow. Photograph by the author, 1981.

Longfellow

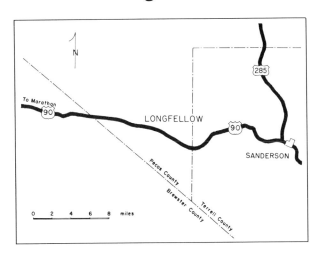

The area around Longfellow, a ranching community in extreme southern Pecos County, was first settled before the Civil War when Mexican ranchers entered the region and began grazing livestock on both sides of the Rio Grande. Its history as a village, however, began in 1881 with the construction of the Southern Pacific Railroad through the territory.

Longfellow, named by the railroad for poet Henry Wadsworth Longfellow, became a livestock shipping point which served a wide area. Many of its old trackside pens and chutes survive even to this day. It became a station on the Southern Pacific and had not only a depot and telegraph office but also extensive facilities for supplying water to steam locomotives on the transcontinental route. According to company water service records, the drillers sank their wells two thousand feet at Longfellow and in the process passed through an unexpected vein of silver ore. The railroad installed large steam pumps to elevate the water from the wells into overhead tanks from which it flowed into the locomotive tenders. Even today heaps of coal ash may be seen near the pumphouses, where the waste was dumped after removal from the boilers which generated the steam to power the pumps. The company for a while also operated a small ballast quarry near the station.

With the passage of time a considerable community grew up around the Longfellow station. It received a post office in 1890 and became the headquarters of the Longfellow Ranch. By the middle of this century, improved transportation removed the economic base for Longfellow. The freight and telegraph office for the railroad closed in 1944, and when diesel power took over for locomotives, the water column and well facilities were retired in 1954. Most local residents now shop in Sanderson, only fifteen minutes away by automobile over paved roads. Today one finds only the ranch headquarters and abandoned but interesting railway structures.

LOCATION: *Longfellow is located on U.S. Highway 90 in the southern tip of Pecos County. It is about 35 miles east of Marathon and 16 miles west of Sanderson.*

Los Ojuelos

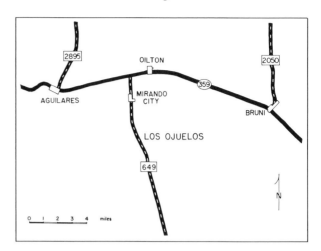

Los Ojuelos has experienced as varied a history as any ghost town in Texas. It has been an Indian camping ground, the site of Hispanic haciendas, a Texas Ranger camp, a rural community, and a ranch headquarters.

Los Ojuelos, today the headquarters for a privately owned ranch. Photograph by the author, 1981.

Water always has been the key to human existence in semiarid Webb County. Most habitation has been along the Rio Grande, where water always can be found, but historically most of the interior areas of the county were used only for grazing livestock. One of the exceptions to the local geography was Los Ojuelos, which in Spanish means "the springs," for it had small but dependable seep springs which came to the surface to supply water. The Indians knew of these springs and used them as a camping ground for centuries before the entry of the first Spaniards into the area.

In 1810, Eugenio Gutiérrez received a grant of land from the king of Spain which encompassed the springs. He attempted to settle the area but was driven away by hostile Indians who wanted to use the springs exclusively. Then twenty-five years later his son, Isidro Gutiérrez, returned, but he was no more successful than his father had been and he too was unable to withstand the Indians. Finally in 1857 a Gutiérrez descendant, José María Guerra, built a blockhouse around the springs and established a permanent settlement. Guerra constructed an irrigation system and a chapel, and he encouraged Mexicans from the Rio Grande valley to move to Los Ojuelos. By 1860 an estimated four hundred people had occupied the vicinity, creating a substantial ranch community.

Even before Guerra had founded the town at Los Ojuelos, it had served as a camp for John S. "Rip" Ford and his Texas Rangers. They moved there in 1850 from another camp thirty-four miles away so that they might better protect the trade route leading via Los Ojuelos from Laredo across South Texas to Corpus Christi.

Though it prospered for a number of years, by the early twentieth century Los Ojuelos had declined to fewer than two hundred inhabitants. Having had at least intermittent mail service since the mid–nineteenth century, its post office closed in 1917. The community briefly flourished again because of an oil boom in nearby Mirando City during the early 1920s, but the influx of transients ended almost as quickly as it had started. Today Los Ojuelos is virtually abandoned, serving as a privately owned ranch headquarters.

LOCATION: *Los Ojuelos stands on Farm to Market Road 649 about 2.5 miles south of Mirando City. Although it lies on private property, most of the old town may be viewed from the highway right-of-way.*

Loyal Valley

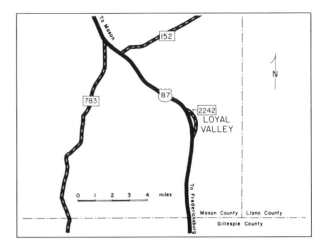

Loyal Valley originally was called Cold Spring from the springs that feed Cold Creek, a stream that passes through the community. Occupied by German immigrant farmers about 1858, it is one of the oldest towns in present-day Mason County.

By the late 1860s the area around Loyal Valley became thickly settled, and in 1869 John O. Meusebach came there. Meusebach had come to Texas from Europe in 1845 as the second commissioner-general of the Society for the Protection of German Settlers in Texas, the association of nobles which organized the mass migration of Germans to Texas in the mid-1840s. As an older man Meusebach moved to Loyal Valley with dreams of building it into a prosperous city. He platted the townsite, operated a general store and a nursery, served as justice of the peace and as notary public, and even ran the post office. He erected for himself a comfortable home and constructed beside it a still-standing open-air "Roman bath." The prominent German lived in the community until his death in 1897. He was buried at Cherry Spring, five miles south.

Loyal Valley was a stage stop on the road from San Antonio westward through Fredericksburg to San Angelo and El Paso. The old two-story stone stagecoach inn, now a residence, still stands at the center of the former town. In its heyday in the 1870s Loyal Valley had a church, school, hotel, general store, and a combined dry goods and millinery store. The school began in 1870, when Indian raids had forced farmers from outlying areas to move into the town for safety. The subsequent increased number of children prompted Phillip Burchmeier to erect a stone schoolhouse.

John O. Meusebach's store built in Loyal Valley in the late 1860s. Courtesy Sophienburg Museum, New Braunfels, Texas.

The two-story stone building in which Herman Lehmann's mother operated a stagecoach inn during the 1880s. Photograph by the author, 1981.

Graves in the Loyal Valley cemetery, where Herman Lehmann lies buried. Photograph by the author, 1981.

For entertainment the residents of Loyal Valley enjoyed horse racing on the flat prairie adjoining the town. There they frequently had matched races on Sunday afternoons. About the turn of the century, a community baseball team, the "Loyal Lads," was organized, and it competed with similar teams from surrounding communities for a number of years.

A second well-known resident of Loyal Valley was Herman Lehmann. He was born near the town in 1859, living there with his family until his eleventh year. In 1870 he was captured by a raiding party of Apache Indians, who initiated the German-speaking boy into the tribe. Lehmann lived with the Apaches for four years. Then after killing an Apache medicine man, the young German spent a year alone living on the plains, subsequently joining a Comanche band for an additional four years. While with the Indians he became a warrior and participated in numerous raids ranging from Mexico to his own home country in Central Texas. A member of one of the last Comanche bands to surrender to the U.S. Army at Fort Sill in 1879, he was identified as a white captive and forced against his will to return to his family at Loyal Valley. His mother had married

Phillip Burchmeier, builder of the first school at Loyal Valley, and when Herman returned home she was operating the stagecoach inn at the village. The former captive never fully adjusted to life in rural German Texas, though he relearned his native language as well as English. At first Herman refused to eat pork or to sleep in a bed, often entertaining hotel guests with exhibitions of riding, roping, and shooting with bow and arrow. Several times he embarrassed his family by appearing before visitors clad only in breech clout, leggings, feathers, and body paint. He later married and had a family at Loyal Valley, though he often visited his Indian friends in Oklahoma. He died in the town in 1932 and is buried in its graveyard.

Paved roads and the rerouting of the main highway around Loyal Valley brought about the decline of the community as commercial business went to larger towns in the vicinity. Today it is a sleepy rural community with only about half a dozen occupied residences, several abandoned houses, and a cemetery.

LOCATION: *Loyal Valley is just off U.S. Highway 87 on Loop 2242 about 18 miles southeast of Mason and 21 miles north of Fredericksburg.*

Luckenbach

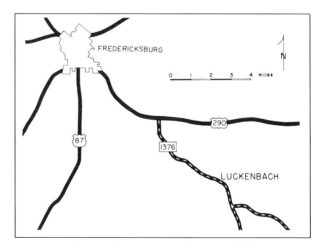

Luckenbach, an out-of-the-way ghost town about ten miles southeast of Fredericksburg, became an "in" community for country-and-western enthusiasts when Waylon Jennings and Willie Nelson recorded the popular song, "Luckenbach, Texas," in 1977. Its history, however, goes back well over a century.

German immigrant farmers began settling the area along Grape Creek in what became Luckenbach during the 1850s, not long after the founding of nearby Fredericksburg in 1846. The Reverend and Mrs. August Engel are credited with founding the town. Engel was a circuit-riding Methodist minister who spent much of his time traveling from place to place, leaving his wife with time on her hands. With her husband's assistance about 1860 she established a small country store near their home in order to supply the needs of local residents. In the early years even Indians came to the store, trading pelts for goods that they desired. About twenty years later, in 1880, they erected the present-day wood frame store building, which has served the community for over a century. In 1886, August Engel applied for a post office for the neighborhood, his sister, Miss Minna Engel, agreeing to work as its clerk.

When they received application forms from the postal authorities, they had to choose a name for the town. Since Minna was engaged to marry Albert Luckenbach, a local bachelor, she suggested his name, and the officials in Washington accepted it.

In 1881, August Engel erected a large cotton gin on the banks of Grape Creek about a hundred yards north of the store. After the first gin burned, it was rebuilt at the same location. In the days when cotton was an important crop, the Luckenbach gin turned out over a thousand bales annually. The steam powered plant still stands, its old equipment mostly intact, but it has not operated for many years.

In 1890 the Engel family made two more commercial additions to the town, a saloon and a dance hall. The latter became the social center of the town, where dances, reunions, wedding feasts, and other festive occasions were celebrated. The old saloon stood until 1954, when it was torn down and the sale of beer transferred to the back room in the store which formerly had

The Luckenbach store, still little changed by the years. Photograph by the author, 1981.

Steam-powered cotton gin remarkably well preserved in Luckenbach. Photograph by the author, 1981.

The steam engine which once powered the Luckenbach cotton gin. Photograph by the author, 1981.

been used for bulk storage of flour and animal feed. The dance hall stood until 1932, when it was rebuilt with a fine maple floor, making it one of the most popular entertainment centers in the area. For many years a blacksmith shop operated adjacent to the store.

Luckenbach purportedly witnessed activities in the 1860s which today seem almost unbelievable and indeed may never have occurred. The teacher at the town was one Jacob Brodbeck, a native of Württemburg, Germany. Later serving as county surveyor and as county school superintendent, Brodbeck spent many years attempting to invent a heavier-than-air flying machine. According to the stories still circulated in Gillespie County, he built an aircraft having a ship-shaped fuselage and wings somewhat like those of a bird. According to the stories, in 1863 Brodbeck is supposed to have flown the craft successfully. The purported machine had a large coiled spring to provide motive force to a propeller which drew it through the air. Though aviation historians discredit the tales about a German schoolmaster flying through Texas skies, many local residents are convinced that Brodbeck flew forty years before the Wright brothers' first successful flight at Kitty Hawk.

With the improvement of rural roads in Gillespie County, most of the farmers around Luckenbach began shopping in Fredericksburg, leaving the little town to wither away. In the early 1970s Hondo Crouch and others purchased ten acres encompassing most of the town. Hondo with white hair, white beard, and a never ending supply of stories became the center of attention in the little store. His interest in the Austin country music scene brought local musicians to play in the dance hall, and soon Luckenbach became a popular place for local people to enjoy new talent. Then in 1977 the song, "Luckenbach, Texas," rose to the top of music charts, and the little German settlement for a few weeks became a household word throughout America. Since then Luckenbach has been a Mecca for music fans, many of them visiting only to have their pictures taken in front of the old Engel store, sometimes tarrying long enough to drink a cold beer and to buy a bumper sticker. The handful of old residents still in the town view the notoriety of their community with mixed emotions. One of them recently complained: "Such a racket they make. All that singing and yelling and motorcycles. They used to have nice Saturday night dances with polkas and waltzes and the best dance floor in the country." Another remarked, "Once I used to go down there and sit under the trees and have a beer, but no more, not with all those folks coming in from here and there and wondering if this is all there is to Luckenbach."

LOCATION: *Luckenbach may be found on Farm to Market Road 1376 about 4.5 miles southeast of its intersection with U.S. Highway 290 about 5.6 miles east of Fredericksburg.*

Manning

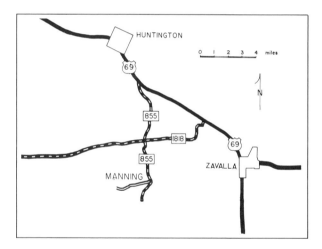

Manning, once a thriving lumber company town with as many as 1,500 inhabitants, today is a ghost with just one of its original buildings intact at the site, though the area is littered with the remains from the former town.

Lumber activity at Manning began in 1863, when Dr. W. W. Manning established a sawmill there. Major efforts, however, did not start for another forty years. About 1903, W. T. Carter of Houston and G. A. Kelley of Lufkin organized the Carter-Kelley Lumber Company and began buying timber lands in southern Angelina County. They built a small-scale mill in Polk County, but in 1905 they began constructing a major complex at the site of Dr. Manning's earlier mill. They named it in honor of the pioneer lumberman who had preceded them.

Concrete footing for long removed machinery at the Manning sawmill. Photograph by the author, 1981.

Mansionlike home of sawmill manager W. M. Gibbs at Manning. Photograph by the author, 1981.

The Shreveport, Houston and Gulf Railroad in 1907 built nine miles southward from the Cotton Belt line to serve the new facility, which in time became a self-sufficient city of 1,500 residents. In addition to its massive sawmill, at one time touted as the second largest in the South, Manning had an elementary school, an eight-teacher high school, a hotel, theaters, lodge halls, a warehouselike company commissary store, and scores of residences ranging from the mansionlike home of mill superintendent W. M. Gibbs to tiny frame dwellings for common laborers. At its peak the huge mill produced 34,000,000 board feet of lumber annually and employed 300 men.

Disaster struck Manning in 1934 and it never recovered. Fire broke out in the sawmill complex, burning it to the ground. The Carter-Kelley company decided not to rebuild the mill because the timber reserves in the area had already become depleted. The general economic problems

during the Great Depression only aggravated the financial difficulties. Gradually the hundreds of residents moved away, leaving a handful who turned to farming for their livelihood. Grass grew in the deserted streets and stray cattle roamed the empty yards and gardens. In 1938 the lumber firm decided to sell its empty buildings for their materials. M. B. Tyre of Lufkin made the best offer, so in 1939 he purchased more than 250 buildings in the nearly abandoned town. The press reported that Tyre in his bargain had acquired approximately 2,000,000 board feet of used lumber, enough to fill 100 railway cars, and that most of it went for reuse in Dallas, Lufkin, and Houston. Former plant superintendent Gibbs bought the land at the townsite and purchased twenty of the houses, which he then rented to the few remaining inhabitants.

Since the destruction of Manning for its building materials, the site has been virtually abandoned. Thirty residents and one store remained in 1940, but today only one original building is seen, the beautiful home built about 1905 for superintendent Gibbs. The former millponds have become popular fishing places for local anglers, who seldom think about the activity that once took place in the adjacent mill complex marked now only by massive concrete foundations.

LOCATION: *To reach Manning, drive southeast 2.1 miles from Huntington on U.S. Highway 69 to its intersection with Farm to Market Road 844. Proceed south on the farm to market road 7.4 miles to the townsite, Gibbs residence, and ruins of the mill complex beside the old ponds.*

1950 Studebaker sedan and lonesome shell of a former filling station, both slowly deteriorating in the elements at Mentone. Photograph by the author, 1981.

Mentone

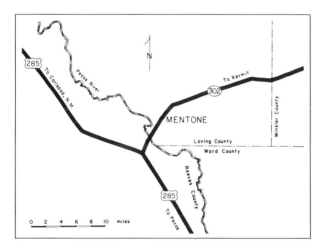

Mentone, though still the seat of Loving County, is a ghost of its former self. Once boasting five to six hundred inhabitants, today it has only about thirty. Its single largest employer is the county government.

Mentone first was laid out in 1922 by J. J. Wheat and B. Ramsey, but the site remained vacant for almost a decade. Then in February 1930 lots began to sell in the townsite after oil was discovered nearby in the Wheat Oil Field. Within a matter of months Mentone grew from a barren desert into a bustling oil field town. By July 1931 it had two hotels, two drugstores, five cafes, two recreation halls, five filling stations, a machine shop, a dry cleaning establishment, two bar-

Detail of a barn erected from railway crossties at Mentone. Photograph by the author, 1981.

bershops, a chamber of commerce, and an oil refinery.

Public education at Mentone began in spring 1931, when a frame schoolhouse/community church building was moved there from the older community of Porterville on the Pecos River. It had been erected there in 1910, but it was transported to Mentone when most of the residents of Porterville moved to the newer town with the opening of the oil field. Beginning in 1932 the first phase of a modern new brick school complex was built, which by the end of the decade consisted of a gymnasium and six classrooms. The old wooden school reverted to use as a community center and nondenominational church.

Loving County, for which Mentone in 1931 became the seat of government, has never been heavily populated. In 1890 it had but three inhabitants and in 1900 only thirty-three. The peak year for population in the county came in 1933, when it had an estimated six hundred residents, most of them in Mentone. Today it is the least populated county in all of Texas, with just over a hundred people in its 647 square miles.

Mentone, a thriving town during the oil boom, faded with declining petroleum production. By 1940 it had only 150 residents, and in the subsequent four decades the number decreased to about

thirty. Today visitors can find the Loving County Courthouse, one cafe, one filling station, a post office, and about a dozen occupied residences. The townsite is littered with the debris of historic petroleum production, has its preserved 1910 school/church building from Porterville, an abandoned 1930s brick school, and numerous empty former dwellings and commercial buildings.

LOCATION: *Mentone stands on Texas Highway 302 about 25 miles southwest of Kermit and about 25 miles north of Pecos.*

Early 1930s style worm-gear, single-crank "Lufkin" oil well pumping unit still in service on the outskirts of Mentone. Photograph by the author, 1981.

Mobeetie

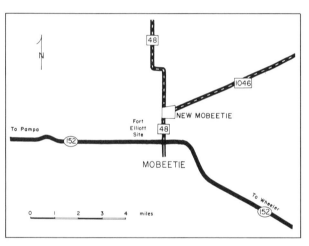

Mobeetie, the first permanent town in the Texas Panhandle, began as a supply base for buffalo hunters on Sweetwater Creek in 1874. At the southern terminus of the Jones and Plummer Trail that led northward to Dodge City and the nearest railroad, it was the logical place for Kansas merchants to build stores and to purchase hides from the professional hunters. Because the residents covered their picket and dugout shelters with green buffalo hides for protection from cold winter weather, their settlement came to be known as Hide Town.

In May 1875 the U.S. Army located its only substantial military post in the Panhandle at Fort Elliott, about two miles away from Hide Town. The army chose the site for the same reasons that had drawn the hunters: convenient access to water from the creek and abundant wood from the trees

U.S. Cavalry mounted troops with Indian scouts in the foreground photographed at Fort Elliott. Courtesy Panhandle-Plains Historical Museum, Canyon, Texas.

J. J. Long's general store in Mobeetie. Courtesy Panhandle-Plains Historical Museum, Canyon, Texas.

growing along it. By the time the troops occupied the post, Hide Town had approximately 150 inhabitants. George A. Montgomery, who later became the first postmaster, arrived in the early days and remembered the place this way:

There were three saloons, a dance hall, a Chinese laundry, and a restaurant. . . . The restaurant was run by Tom O'Laughlin and wife, Helen, who was the only virtuous woman in town. There were about fifteen dance hall girls there at that time. There was a barber shop and a big store owned by Bob Wright and Charles Rath. Also in the town lived bullwhackers, mule skinners, buffalo hunters, and gamblers galore.

In 1878 the town moved a short distance to be closer to the military post, for its officers and men represented a substantial proportion of the customers for its saloons, gambling dens, and "cribs of soiled doves." By no means all the residents of the town were of the "low life" variety, however, for the community contained numerous business and professional men including physicians, lawyers, and merchants.

In 1879, Wheeler County was organized with Hide Town chosen as its county seat, but before it

Street scene in Mobeetie around the turn of the century. Courtesy Panhandle-Plains Historical Museum, Canyon, Texas.

The 1889 jail at Mobeetie soon after its construction. Courtesy Panhandle-Plains Historical Museum, Canyon, Texas.

could legally receive the seat of government the community had to provide a post office. One was requested under the name of Sweetwater after the nearby creek, but unfortunately Texas already had one Sweetwater post office and the application was rejected. A local citizen suggested that they send to the fort for an Indian scout to tell them the Indian word for Sweetwater. Accordingly two Indians accompanied by civilian scout Billy Dixon as an interpreter came down to the town, and through Dixon the Indians were asked the word in their tongue for Sweetwater. One replied *mobeetie*, and that name was written down on the new application form. Accordingly on 4 September 1879 a post office with the Indian name was established. It was on a mail route that stretched from Vinita, Indian Territory, across the Panhandle to Las Vegas, New Mexico, a total distance of 725 miles for the round trip which was made once a week.

Through the decade of the 1880s Mobeetie remained one of the most prominent towns in the region, though soon other communities came into existence. In 1882 it had 300 inhabitants, in 1890, 400, and in 1910, 250. By the end of the 1880s, it began to suffer a decline when various railroads began building across the Panhandle and all of them missed it. Then in 1890 the War Department closed Fort Elliott as no longer needed to restrain the tribesmen in Oklahoma. Another shock came in 1898 when a tornado smashed through the town, killing six residents and destroying buildings, many of which were never rebuilt. Mobeetie was located in the northwest part of Wheeler County, and as the central and southern portions were settled in the 1890s and 1900s, the residents of these areas began requesting that the seat of justice be moved to a more central location. In a county-wide election in 1907, Wheeler won the county seat from Mobeetie, and many of the remaining residents followed the courthouse to the newer town. Finally in 1929 the Santa Fe Railway built a line from Clinton, Oklahoma, to Pampa, Texas, bypassing Mobeetie by two miles. Most of the last inhabitants moved the short distance to the steel rails to establish New Mobeetie, leaving the pioneer town virtually abandoned and marked only by its stone jail and a few old houses.

LOCATION: *The site of Old Mobeetie lies 0.5 mile south of Texas Highway 152 on a paved and gravel road that begins at the state highway opposite its juncture with Farm to Market Road 48 on the south side of New Mobeetie. At the former townsite the 1889 jail houses a local museum. The site of Fort Elliott lies northwest of a roadside park and historical marker on the state highway about 1.0 mile west of the intersection.*

Morales

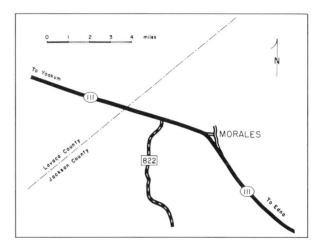

One of the oldest settlements in Jackson County, Morales (pronounced More-rails) today is just a memory. The town had its beginning in the late 1840s with a blacksmith shop established by Frank Morales (some sources say Seco Morales) on the Jonathan Vess land grant. Originally known as Morales de Lavaca from its location northeast of the Lavaca River, it had a post office as early as 1849. The town grew slowly over the next two decades, and by 1870 it had a post office, general store, drugstore, blacksmith shop, two or three saloons, and the first telegraph office in Jackson County. The office was on a telegraph line erected in 1870 to connect Victoria with Columbus. Later Morales had a Masonic lodge, gristmill, sawmill, cotton gin, and Methodist and Baptist congregations. The first school was a private pay school in which Miss Gustie Lymos was the initial teacher, but in time a public school opened.

Its location in lightly settled ranch country caused Morales to become a haven for the lawless element from other parts of Texas during the Reconstruction period following the Civil War.

Travelers along the Gulf coastal plain often chose routes which avoided the town because of its violent reputation. Numerous killings took place there during those years, and few residents felt safe unless they were armed. The more stable members of the community eventually formed an extralegal vigilance committee, but it operated primarily against horse thieves and rustlers rather than against the murderers.

The decline of Morales came in the 1880s when it was missed by railroads building through the area. Oral traditions state that the New York, Texas and Mexican Railway graded a roadbed to Morales, but track was never laid on it. Folklore explains that the belligerent attitude of the town toughs prompted the company to reroute the line southward through Edna. Without the steel rails, Morales lost its commercial life to competing towns. By 1940 it had only one country store and a population of fifty. Today even that evidence of life is gone, leaving Morales a scattered rural community marked by its cemetery and a few ruined building foundations.

LOCATION: *Morales is 12.8 miles northwest of Edna on Texas Highway 111.*

Mormon Mill

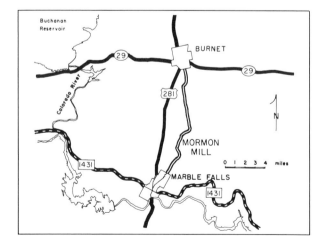

Mormon Mill was the site of a Mormon colony founded by Lyman Wight and his followers in 1851. Wight had come to Texas in 1845 after the death of Joseph Smith, the founder of the Church of Jesus Christ of Latter-day Saints. Upon Smith's death Brigham Young had assumed the role of leader, but Wight refused to acknowledge his direction. Dissident Wight had himself been a member of the Quorum of Twelve, a church governing body, and was a prominent leader.

Disassociating himself from the church under Brigham Young, Lyman Wight led 150 Mormons from Illinois to Texas, entering the state at Preston on the Red River and wintering in Grayson County. The group trekked southward to the Colorado River just above Austin, where they erected a gristmill. They remained there but a few months until their mill was damaged by high water. The party then moved westward to a site they called Zodiac on the Pedernales River a short distance below Fredericksburg. There they again erected their mill and formed a community that lasted until 1851.

At least in part to escape debts that they had incurred, the Wight colony in summer 1851 moved again, this time to a beautiful site on Hamilton Creek about ten miles downstream from Burnet, then called Hamilton. At this location in Burnet County the waters of spring-fed Hamilton Creek flow between rock banks and over a prominent stone bluff into a natural pool, the ideal setting for a mill. The Mormon colonists constructed a wooden dam that diverted water into a flume that carried it to the mill proper, a three-story wooden structure. There the flowing water dropped onto a twenty-six-foot overshot waterwheel that powered not only the gristmill but also a sawmill for cutting timber into lumber. Not all the colonists worked at the mill, for a number of them farmed and at least some produced locally noted furniture including bedsteads, chairs, and tables. The women gained a high reputation for their well-made willow baskets. The settlers built numerous small homes in the area near the mill, which as an adjunct also had a blacksmith shop.

The Mormons remained on Hamilton Creek until December 1853. At this time, again hounded by debt, the members, who now numbered about 250, moved again, this time to Bandera County, where they built another mill and engaged in shingle making. They stayed there until about 1858, when Lyman Wight died and the community disbanded.

Noah Smithwick purchased the old mill on Hamilton Creek from Wight and operated it for

The Mormon mill as it appeared in operation. Courtesy Mrs. Ernest A. Guenther.

The falls on Hamilton Creek which to this day mark the site of the Mormon mill. Photograph by the author, 1984.

a number of years. He erected the first school there, in part for the benefit of the children of the handful of Mormons who remained to operate the mill for its new owner. Soon Smithwick opened a store, which for several decades served the community. A post office was granted to John R. Hubbard, Smithwick's nephew and partner, in 1856, and the community had intermittent postal delivery until the post office was discontinued in 1875. Finally in 1901, because of increasing competition from newer mills in surrounding towns, the old Mormon mill closed. The next year the wooden flume to the mill accidentally burned. The mill was then torn down, its salvageable materials being removed for use in erecting a nearby barn. Then in 1915 the last of the homes to have housed members of the Mormon colony burned. Today one finds only foundations, the old Mormon cemetery, and an almost hidden historical marker at the site of the colony.

LOCATION: *To reach Mormon Mill, drive south from Burnet 9.6 miles on the paved county road extension of Boundary Street. Alternately the site may be reached by taking Mormon Mills Road, a paved county road, 5.4 miles northward from Marble Falls starting at an intersection on U.S. Highway 281 about 0.1 mile north of its juncture with Farm to Market Road 1431. The site is on private property, but the falls and natural pool may be seen from the public right-of-way.*

Morris Ranch

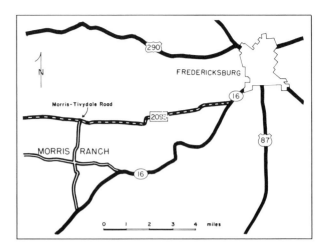

Morris Ranch is unique in Texas history, for it was an entire community devoted exclusively to the breeding and training of thoroughbred race horses. Its story begins in 1856 when Francis Morris, a noted breeder and racer of fine horses, purchased 23,000 acres about twelve miles southwest of Fredericksburg in Gillespie County. Three decades passed before Morris employed his nephew in 1884 to convert the rangeland in Texas into a center for horse raising and training. The property came into the hands of John A. Morris in 1886 upon the death of his father, and

Morris Ranch as drawn by nineteenth-century Texas German artist Herman Lungkwitz. Courtesy Helene Klappenbach Richter Estate.

Headquarters building at Morris Ranch. Photograph by the author, 1984.

1893 Morris Ranch schoolhouse, where classes met until 1962. Photograph by the author, 1984.

the son proceeded with the work already initiated.

By the end of the decade, Morris Ranch had become a nearly self-sufficient community dedicated to horses. Not only was there a large headquarters with home and offices for the manager, but also an entire complex devoted to animal husbandry. Across from the headquarters a huge barn was built to house the stallions, while on another side a two-story hotel was erected for single employees and visitors to the ranch. East of these buildings was a two-story stone store building which had a recreation room on its upper floor for dances and social gatherings. Beside it stood a small drugstore. Also on this part of the ranch were a cotton gin, where cotton raised on the ranch and on adjoining properties was processed, and a steam-powered roller mill that not only chopped oats for the horses but also produced three different grades of commercial flour.

Northeast of the headquarters was the actual training center. There the Morris family erected a one-mile racetrack, now a cultivated field, and constructed barns for mares, colts, and young horses in training. Also here stood a two-story jockey house, where young men resided while receiving training. It had their quarters on its upper floor, while the ground floor served as kitchen, dining room, recreation room, and cook's quarters. Nearby stood a luxurious home erected for the owners, who occasionally came from the East to visit and observe progress. One more building completed the major structures at Morris Ranch, a beautiful stone schoolhouse, complete with steeple and bell, which for many years served the ranch and its surrounding area. It was also the site of church services led by Episcopal, Presbyterian, Methodist, and Baptist ministers. A graveyard was begun behind the school.

Morris Ranch reached its peak in population and activity in the late 1880s, but outside events caused its demise. In the 1890s numerous states enacted laws curtailing horse racing, and this dramatically affected the market for the stock raised and trained on the Texas ranch. In 1902 the Morris family decided to end their operation in Texas and held a dispersal sale of their remaining horses. They gradually sold off most of the land as well. The post office was discontinued in 1954 and the store closed its doors soon thereafter. Today the former town is marked by a number of its handsome century-old buildings.

LOCATION: *To reach Morris Ranch, drive westward on Farm to Market Road 2093 about 7.2 miles from its intersection with Texas Highway 16 about 2.2 miles west of Fredericksburg. Then turn south on the paved Morris-Tivydale Road and drive 1.9 miles to a four-way intersection at the center of the former Morris Ranch community.*

New Birmingham

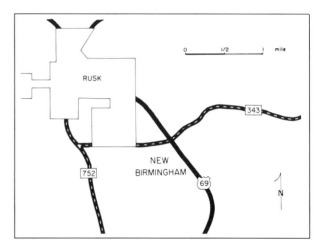

Once the "Iron Queen of East Texas," New Birmingham had four hundred buildings, electrically lighted streets, a brick business district, and even a streetcar system. Today it is an absolute ghost on the southern outskirts of Rusk.

Since the 1840s iron had been smelted in East Texas, but never on a truly large scale. Alexander B. Blevins, a sewing machine salesman from Alabama, traveled the area, heard the stories, and observed the limited iron production at the furnace in the Rusk State Penitentiary in the mid-1880s and decided that the area could become "a second Birmingham." Enthusiastic about the prospects, with the backing of a wealthy brother-in-law he acquired options to buy thousands of acres of East Texas forest land which he felt could provide not only iron ore but also charcoal with which to smelt it.

Blevins then traveled to the East, secured the backing of capitalists there, and with them in 1888 formed the Cherokee Land and Iron Com-

Dallas Street in downtown New Birmingham about 1890. From *Texas, New Birmingham as It Is, October, 1891*, p. 30.

The Southern Hotel, in its day one of the showplaces of Texas. From *Texas, New Birmingham as It Is, October, 1891*, p. 3.

Pouring molten iron at the Tassie Belle furnace. From *Texas, New Birmingham as It Is, October, 1891*, p. 17.

Furnace remains preserved at the Tassie Belle Historical Park. Photograph by the author, 1981.

pany. This firm made plans not only to exploit the natural resources but also to develop a complete town to become the center of the new industrial complex. The company sold its first town lots for New Birmingham on 12 October 1888, and within a matter of months a small city sprang up where only trees had stood before. By 1891 New Birmingham had an estimated 1,500 inhabitants, two iron furnaces (the Tassie Belle named for Alexander Blevins's wife and the Star and Crescent), not to mention an iron pipe foundry, a large brick kiln, and other industrial enterprises.

The pride of New Birmingham was the Southern Hotel, which was acclaimed as the largest hotel in Texas outside of Dallas, Houston, San Antonio, and Galveston. It featured hot and cold running water, electric lights and call bells, restaurants, reception rooms, a smoking room, and a billiard parlor. Among its better known guests were President Grover Cleveland, railway magnate Jay Gould, and Texas Governor James Stephen Hogg.

New Birmingham died only a few short years after its birth. Its promoters lacked the capital necessary to weather the economic hard times that began with the Panic of 1893. Contributing to the problems was the recently passed Texas Alien Land Law, which made it difficult for the promoters to secure willing investors in England, a major potential source of capital. Then in 1893 an explosion destroyed the charcoal beds and power plant at the Tassie Belle furnace, and the company lacked the funds to rebuild them. In a matter of months New Birmingham died and its residents moved away. By the beginning of this century most evidence of the town had already disappeared, the buildings having been demolished for construction materials to be used in nearby Rusk. The last intact building, the hotel, burned in 1926, and its shell was demolished in 1932 to make way for a new highway. New Birmingham was forgotten by all but a few.

LOCATION: *The site of New Birmingham is crossed by the business route of U.S. Highway 69 on the extreme south side of present-day Rusk in Cherokee County. A historical marker for the town stands near the highway intersection with Farm to Market Road 343. Ruins of the Tassie Belle furnace may be seen by visitors at the Tassie Belle Historical Park on the west side of the business route south of the farm to market road juncture and historical marker.*

Old Gomez

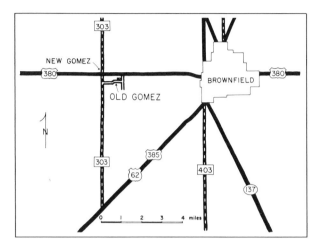

Gomez, the first town in Terry County, had its beginning in 1902. In that year three local speculators purchased a section of ranch land which they believed to be at the center of then-unorganized Terry County. Their plan was to establish a town which would become the seat of government when the area would become formally organized as a county. They named it Gomez in honor of Máximo Gómez y Báez, a prominent leader in the Cuban fight for freedom from Spain only a few years earlier.

The promoters had their land surveyed and then platted the town around a large public square which they hoped one day would be the location for a courthouse. Merchants and professional men

Northwest across the overgrown Old Gomez cemetery. Photograph by the author, 1984.

Empty house at "New Gomez," a short distance from Old Gomez. Photograph by the author, 1984.

began moving to the new settlement, which within a couple of years contained several mercantile stores, a blacksmith shop, livery stable, post office, public school, saloon, dance hall, hotel, drugstore, the *Terry County Voice* newspaper, real estate offices, a barbershop, lunchroom, and even a state bank. A cemetery, the first in the county, was begun in 1902 with the donation of land by local citizens.

The year after the founding of Gomez, other entrepreneurs established a competing townsite called Brownfield five miles east. Their community, though it had a school, did not prosper as well as its predecessor, but its boosters remained confident that it might someday eclipse Gomez. Their first opportunity came in 1904, when Terry County was organized. In an election Brownfield won the county seat by a margin of three votes, primarily because cowboys from the Rose Ranch in the eastern portion of the county were induced to support the site nearer their range. The Brownfield Townsite Company reputedly had offered to give every voter in the county a free lot in their town.

Despite losing the county seat to "upstart" Brownfield, Gomez prospered for a decade longer. Since it was the largest town in the county, its residents expected that when a railway was built into the area, it would automatically pass through their community. As the years passed, more and more people located in Gomez, building homes and opening business establishments. Then in

1916 the Panhandle and Santa Fe Railway projected a line from Lubbock southwestward to Seagraves, traversing Terry County. The Brownfield promoters promised the company a free right-of-way across the county if it routed the line through their town, and the offer was too much for the railroad to resist. The rails reached Brownfield in 1917, spelling doom for landlocked Gomez. The owners of businesses and homes in the older town had their buildings moved either to Brownfield or to Plains in Yoakum County. When J. T. Gainer moved his residence to the latter town, it took forty-two mules to draw it over the sandy roads.

Gomez died over the next decade, losing its post office in 1916. A few of the residents moved their homes and businesses about half a mile to the northwest to a crossroads on a new highway later built from Brownfield westward to Roswell, New Mexico, calling the place "New Gomez." In the intervening years even this community has withered away, leaving only a cotton gin, a Baptist church, and mostly abandoned buildings.

LOCATION: *To reach Old Gomez, drive 4.4 miles west from Brownfield on U.S. Highway 380 to a historical marker at the south side of the road. The townsite lies about half a mile south in a cultivated field, while 0.6 mile farther west are the remains of New Gomez. To find the overgrown Old Gomez cemetery, turn south on a sandy county road 0.4 mile east of the historical marker, passing by the Southwest Seed and Delinting Company plant, and drive 0.3 mile to the graveyard.*

Peach Tree Village

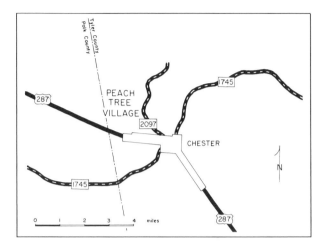

Built on the site of an Alabama Indian village, the name of which translates to English as Peach Tree Village, this community was one of the pioneer Anglo-American settlements in southeast Texas. The first known white settler in the vicinity was Peter Cauble, a native of Guilford County, North Carolina, who came to Texas from Alabama in 1829. He settled in Tyler County by 1831 and fought in the Texas War for Independence, receiving a headright grant of land from the Republic of Texas in 1839. During the 1840s Cauble became a prosperous planter, by the outbreak of the Civil War having over five thousand acres of woodlands and agricultural fields. He is noted locally for having erected one of the first cotton gins in the area.

In 1843, Cauble's daughter, Helen Elmira, married Valentine Ignatius Burch, who had come to Texas from Kentucky in 1826 and who had participated in the 1836 Battle of San Jacinto. After the marriage Burch came to Peach Tree Village and managed his father-in-law's plantation as well as his own properties in East Texas. Burch and others built and maintained a private academy which for a number of years operated in the community. In 1853 the town had already gathered sufficient population that it was granted a post office under the name Peach Tree Village.

The best known offspring of the village was John Henry Kirby, who was born there in 1860. Having earned a law degree, Kirby entered the lumber business as a young man representing timber companies in court litigation. By the 1880s he had been employed as general manager for both the Texas and Louisiana Land and Lumber Company and the Texas Pine Land Association. Through the economically depressed years of the mid-1890s, Kirby invested in East Texas timberland. He also built the Gulf, Beaumont and Kansas City Railroad through these areas between the Neches and Sabine rivers, beginning lumbering on his and his associates' lands. In 1901 he secured a charter for the Kirby Lumber Company, which he directed. At its peak in the second decade of this century, the firm owned thousands of acres of timber, operated twelve sawmills, had ten logging camps, and employed over 16,000 men. Remembered mainly as a lumberman, Kirby also was a Texas legislator, an able corporate lawyer, an oilman, and a federal government administrator.

Though an industrial magnate in the truest sense of the word, Kirby found his solace not at Newport or Saratoga but rather in the simple village where he had grown up. John Henry Kirby built a rural home for his parents at Peach Tree Village, and it was there that he retreated for the peace he sought, far from the noise and bustle of the city. A local schoolteacher once recalled that

The red brick chapel erected by industrialist John Henry Kirby at Peach Tree Village in 1912. Photograph by the author, 1981.

the industrialist "worshiped his father and mother and loved the village greatly." In 1912, three years after his father passed away, lumberman Kirby erected a beautiful red brick chapel in the town in honor of his parents. He even hired a Russian artist to paint wall-sized pictures for the church depicting his father's baptism. The faces in the painting were so lifelike that local people visited the chapel just to pick out familiar faces in the crowd the artist portrayed. Peach Tree Village residents used the chapel both as a church and as a school until after Kirby's death in 1940, but then it fell into disuse. Twenty years later Tyler County citizens restored the beautiful building as a memorial to Peach Tree Village's most famous son.

LOCATION: *Peach Tree Village, now only a scattered rural community, and its beautiful chapel stand on Farm to Market Road 2097 about 1.6 miles northwest of Chester in Tyler County.*

Perico

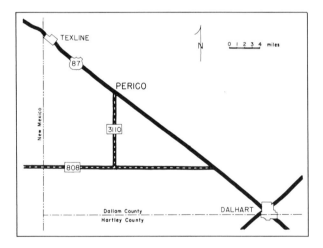

Perico, once a bustling farm community beside the Fort Worth and Denver Railway tracks in the northern Panhandle, today is a virtual ghost with only two residents. It had its beginnings about 1888 as a siding on the railroad. Three years earlier the surrounding area had become part of the XIT Ranch after title to three million acres of Texas Panhandle rangeland was given to a Chicago-based syndicate in exchange for the construction of the present state capitol building.

Initially the siding was known as Farwell, taking its name from the nearby Farwell Park line camp on the Buffalo Springs division of the XIT Ranch. In 1905 George Findlay of the Capitol Syndicate requested that the railroad change the name to Perico, and the shift was made. About this time much of the ranch land in Dallam County was being broken up for sale to farmers from other parts of the country. In 1900 there were only four farms in all of Dallam County, but by 1910 there were over two hundred farms, which represented 35 percent of its area. As agriculture boomed, towns sprang up to serve the farmers, and one of these was Perico.

The initial population of Perico before the land boom was very limited, consisting of the railroad station agent and his family, a track maintenance crew chief and his family, and eight track section laborers. When the farmers began entering the territory early in this century, Perico prospered and became the center of rural education in the vicinity. By 1931 it had not only the T. W. Timmerman store, which also served as a John Deere implement dealership, a gasoline station, and post office, but also the Blotz-Henneman Grain Company elevator, and the large Foxworth-Galbraith Lumber Company lumberyard. The original depot, which had operated in a converted boxcar, was removed and the railroad built a commodious wooden passenger and freight station.

The great pride of Perico was its educational system. The first school building was a two-room concrete structure which in 1924 was replaced by a two-story building with six classrooms and an auditorium seating two hundred. The complex also contained a teacherage and a large gymnasium. In the late 1930s it averaged fifty pupils in daily attendance and employed four teachers.

As happened to many communities throughout rural Texas, the improvement of highway transportation drew trade away from Perico. Though it had an estimated thirty residents in 1947 and even forty in the 1960s, Perico in the subsequent two decades died. Almost all its buildings stand vacant or in ruins and its sole operating business is a grain elevator.

LOCATION: *Perico lies alongside the Fort Worth and Denver tracks on U.S. Highway 87 about 24.3 miles northwest of Dalhart and 11.1 miles southeast of Texline.*

Cowboys from the XIT Ranch posed on horseback for a picture in front of a wooden "Eclipse" windmill near Perico. Courtesy Southwest Collection, Texas Tech University, Lubbock, Texas.

Outside the Perico post office early in the twentieth century. Courtesy Panhandle-Plains Historical Museum, Canyon, Texas.

Shell of a once bustling commercial building in Perico. Photograph by the author, 1984.

Peyton Colony

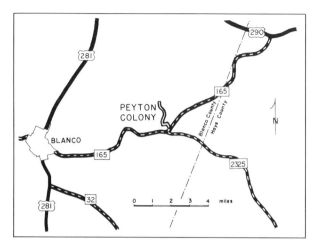

Interior of the now quiet Peyton Colony school. Photograph by the author, 1984.

Peyton Colony is one of the most interesting communities in the Texas Hill Country, for it was founded exclusively by black freedmen after the Civil War. The former slaves decided that the best way to demonstrate their newfound freedom was to leave their old homes and build for themselves a separate community.

Peyton Colony barbecue pit, with the abandoned wooden school in the background. Photograph by the author, 1984.

The blacks formed a settlement near a natural divide between the drainages of the Blanco and Pedernales rivers in eastern Blanco County. There in a beautiful setting they built not only a considerable number of homes, but also a church and about 1870 the first black school in Blanco County. In honor of its founder, Peyton Roberts, the residents named their community Peyton Colony, although most of the whites who lived around them called it Freedmen's Colony or simply Colony.

When the town was placed on regular mail service from Blanco in 1918, its post office was named Board House after an old wooden frame structure which had been erected over a spring that had furnished water to the earliest settlers in the area, thus giving the place a confusing third name. The post office operated well into this century.

Through the years Peyton Colony has declined in population, but much of the land in the vicinity is still owned by the descendants of its initial black settlers. The school, integrated in the 1960s, was abandoned several years ago, though it still stands, and the community still supports the active Mt. Horeb Baptist Church. Ruins and foundations from former structures may still be seen around the church and school.

LOCATION: *Peyton Colony is located 0.5 mile north on a graded county road over two cattle guards from Farm to Market Road 165 about 0.3 mile northeast of its intersection with Farm to Market Road 2325 about 8 miles east of Blanco. The turnoff is marked by a pink granite sign for the church.*

Pine Spring

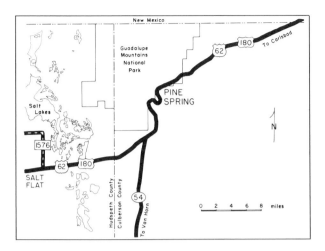

Pine Spring twice in its history has served as a way station for travelers at the remote Guadalupe Pass in far West Texas. It first was a stop on the Butterfield Overland Mail in the late 1850s and then starting in the late 1920s became a stop for auto travelers when a highway opened from El Paso to Carlsbad, New Mexico.

The Butterfield Overland Mail provided mail and passenger service from St. Louis and Memphis by way of Fort Smith across the entire American Southwest to San Francisco, California—a total distance of 2,795 miles. It began operation on 15 September 1858 and ran until 1 March 1861, on the eve of the Civil War. Its principal function was to carry the U.S. mail, for which users paid ten cents per half ounce for letters, the post office department requiring that the trip be made in a maximum of twenty-five days. Two coaches went each direction weekly, with the passengers paying an average fare of about two hundred dollars one way.

The Pine Spring station, popularly called the Pinery, was one of the original stops on the transcontinental route. Its site was chosen with several considerations in mind, but probably the most important was that it was located near the crest of the Guadalupe Pass, making it the optimum point for changing the teams of animals drawing the coaches. It received water via an open ditch from the constantly flowing Pine Spring and thus had a dependable supply of water. Because of its proximity to the mountains and the higher elevation of this location, it received greater rainfall than surrounding lower areas and provided good grazing for the draft animals.

The station supported a small community of

Stone ruins of the 1850s Pinery stagecoach station, with the Guadalupe Mountains and Pine Canyon in the background. Photograph by the author, 1982.

The Pine Spring Camp Cafe, little changed since the 1920s. Photograph by the author, 1982.

company employees. Heading the crew was Henry Ramstein as station keeper. Assisting him were six to eight helpers who worked as cook, blacksmith, and herders. For part of its history the site also was occupied by a detachment of U.S. Army troops, there to protect the station from marauding bands of Indians, and they made their own quarters in dugouts near the station. The Pinery remained in use until August 1859, when the route for the mail was changed to a more southerly one through Fort Stockton and Fort Davis so that it might better serve the army posts along the old military road to El Paso. After the route was changed, the Pinery station fell vacant, but it provided shelter for the next thirty years to freighters, drovers, emigrants, and soldiers as they crossed the pass. Finally with no maintenance it fell into ruins.

The stage station was striking in appearance. The main structure was a fortresslike building with three-foot-thick stone walls eleven feet tall forming a roofless rectangular enclosure measuring just over forty-one by fifty-seven feet. Within this area were four lean-to type rooms for station keeper, employees, and work areas. At the front was a wooden stockade protecting the entrance to the main enclosure, while at the opposite end was a five-foot-tall rock-walled corral about thirty-five by sixty-seven feet.

For a number of years no one permanently occupied the area of the former stage station, but in 1928 Walter and Bertha Glover constructed a filling station, cafe, and tourist court only a few hundred yards away from the old Pinery. A new road was being built to connect El Paso with Carlsbad, and the top of the pass again became the logical place for travelers to stop. Only now overheated automobiles had replaced frothing mules. Since that time the Pine Spring Camp Cafe has operated as a way station for auto travelers much in the way that the Pinery functioned for Butterfield passengers. Within a mile of the cafe are recently constructed quarters for personnel working for the state highway department and the Guadalupe Mountains National Park, but the site of the stage station is utterly abandoned.

LOCATION: *Pine Spring is just on the north side of the crest of the Guadalupe Pass over 5,600 feet in elevation in the Guadalupe Mountains National Park on U.S. Highway 62/180 about 96 miles east of El Paso and 56 miles south of Carlsbad, New Mexico. Interpretive brochures ordinarily are available at the Pinery ruins, and the Pine Spring Camp Cafe, little changed since the 1920s, is still open for business.*

Port Sullivan

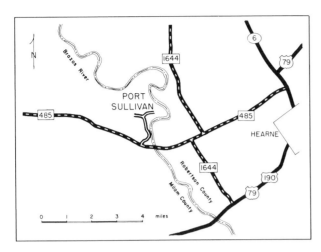

In the water just above the present-day Farm to Market Road 485 bridge over the Brazos River west of Hearne lie abandoned concrete locks constructed by the U.S. Army Corps of Engineers early in this century. These locks stand immediately downstream from the site of Port Sullivan, the effective head of steam navigation on the Brazos, and they represent an unsuccessful effort to make the river navigable to Waco.

The town of Port Sullivan, one of the best-known Texas steamboat ports, had its origins in the activities of Augustus W. Sillaven. In 1835, Sillaven secured title to a tract of land on a high bluff on the west side of the Brazos beside a substantial shoal. The site in time came to be known as Sullivan's [*sic*] Bluff. In 1851 the landowner at the urging of Reuben Anderson laid out a portion of his property into a townsite. Anderson was a wealthy cotton planter who lived across the river, but he wanted to reside on the bluff where his home would be safe from flooding. Accordingly Sillaven started a town, selling the first lots to two of Anderson's sons. In time the new town became the home for many local planters from both Robertson and Milam counties.

Sillaven and Anderson expected the town to become primarily a river port, but even in good years it was accessible by steamers only during high water. Through most of the following decade a handful of steamboats actually did call on the port, but it never became a regular port of call.

The Galveston *Weekly Journal* on 5 November 1852 published a description of Port Sullivan written by one of its correspondents. The writer

Concrete locks in the Brazos River at Port Sullivan. Photograph by the author, 1981.

noted that the town was a new village just a year old which had about two hundred inhabitants, four stores, two blacksmith shops, three carpenters' shops, a circular sawmill, and two or three warehouses for goods brought in by the steamboats. He added that the community had weekly mail delivery from Independence, one lawyer, and several doctors. In time Methodist, Baptist, and Episcopal churches came to serve Port Sullivan, not to mention the educational facilities provided by the Port Sullivan Male and Female College founded in 1860 and operated into the 1870s. Another institution at Port Sullivan was its Masonic lodge established in 1856.

With the passage of time, Port Sullivan grew increasingly independent of the river. Its location on the shoals gave it importance as a ford for teams and wagons. More significant in the development of the town, however, was its freedom from flooding, since much of the surrounding agricultural land was considerably lower in elevation and subject to occasional inundations.

Port Sullivan survived the Civil War only to die during Reconstruction. A number of men from the town served in the Confederate Army, several of them in Hood's Texas Brigade, and many of them gave their lives during the conflict. By the time that the grey-clad men had returned from the war, the winds of change were blowing for Port Sullivan. Through the late 1860s and 1870s, more and more railway lines were being constructed in the direction of the town, but all of them missed it. The railroads changed the lives of all with whom they came in contact. Nearby communities which gained rail connections boomed while Port Sullivan stagnated. The former steamboat port lost nearly all its trade to such railway towns in the vicinity as Calvert, Cameron, and Hearne. By 1880 the Port Sullivan population had dropped to 123, less than a tenth of the 1,423 a decade earlier. The village, no longer a town, had one doctor, one schoolteacher, and one druggist-merchant.

By the 1890s the town had disappeared completely, leaving only scattered building foundations and the cemetery. Later, around the turn of the century, a cotton gin and store were built near the site of the former community, but the newer settlement had no ties with the old steamboat port other than its location. It was near here that the U.S. Army Corps of Engineers between 1910 and 1920 constructed the still standing but never used locks on the Brazos as an aid to the navigation which never revived.

LOCATION: *The site of Port Sullivan is approximately 8.2 miles west of Hearne on the Milam County side of the Brazos. To reach the townsite drive 0.9 mile northeast from Farm to Market Road 485 on a graded county road which leads from the pavement 0.5 mile west of the Brazos River highway bridge. The abandoned town is marked by a 1936 Texas Centennial granite historical marker (with an inaccurate inscription), while the preserved but overgrown cemetery may be found just beyond a sharp right fork in the road.*

Praha

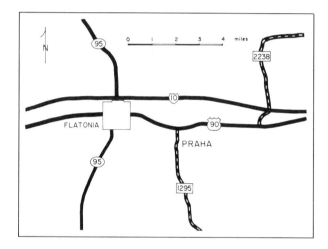

Praha, which means "Prague" in Bohemian, is the mother colony of the many Czech settlements scattered across Texas. Known originally as Mulberry from Mulberry Creek, which flows through it, the town began when Mathias Novak settled there in 1854. A penniless immigrant, Novak worked for Americans around him until he had saved enough money to buy his own farm and erect a log home. Over the succeeding years numerous other Czechs coming from Europe joined him.

The first church services at Praha were held in Novak's home, but by 1866 there were enough Bohemian Catholics in the community to erect their first church. It was followed by other structures until 1890, when the present magnificent Gothic Revival stone sanctuary was begun. Work progressed on the massive undertaking for five

Praha as it appeared in the 1890s. Courtesy Institute of Texan Cultures, San Antonio, Texas.

Turn-of-the-century advertisement for a Praha blacksmith. From F. Lotto, *Fayette County: Her History and Her People*, p. 403.

Crucifix with Czech language inscription in front of the church in Praha. Photograph by the author, 1981.

of seven hundred. By the turn of the century its business district consisted of two mercantile stores, two saloons, a combined blacksmith and wheelwright shop, a meat market, and an open-air dance platform. The platform was replaced by an enclosed dance pavilion in 1927.

Praha's economic development was stunted by the construction of the Southern Pacific Railroad, which in 1873 passed just one mile north of the town. Three miles away Flatonia was founded beside the tracks, and in time it drew away most of the commercial business from Praha. Then in the middle years of the twentieth century the improvement of rural roads took away more trade to surrounding towns, leaving Praha today with a filling station and a cafe as its only places of business.

The Czech colony remains very quiet and seemingly almost abandoned except for Sundays, when its parking lot fills with automobiles belonging to worshipers who come into Praha from miles around for regularly scheduled Masses in the big stone church. Even today the community is known throughout the state for its Veterans Day observances on the Sunday preceding the holiday and for its 15 August homecoming for the Feast of the Assumption. During the latter event the little town bulges with over ten thousand visitors, who come to attend one or more of the three Masses offered in the church, to enjoy home-cooked

Entry to the Praha cemetery. Photograph by the author, 1981.

years until its dedication in 1895. With a spire towering over the surrounding green countryside, visible from miles away, it is one of the most beautiful of all churches in Texas. After the basic structure was completed, the parishioners hired an artist from Europe to paint the interior. Not only did he paint vines, ferns, and flowers on the blue ceilings, but also angels, a jeweled cross, and other religious symbols. Above the altar are pictured a cathedral and a convent in Prague of the old country.

For many years Praha had two schools, a public school established in 1868 and a parochial school opened in 1896 and taught by Catholic sisters. Both were well attended, the church school often enrolling over a hundred pupils. Both operated until 1973.

Praha for most of its history was the bustling center of a rich agricultural section. In the 1880s it had a post office, saloon, restaurant, general store, liquor store, and an estimated population

Czech food, and to dance to the strains of "The Blacksmith Waltz," "Annie the Foreman March," and "The Long Road to Praha."

LOCATION: *Praha lies on Farm to Market Road 1295 about 0.8 mile south of its intersection with U.S. Highway 90 approximately 2.7 miles east of Flatonia in southern Fayette County.*

Preston

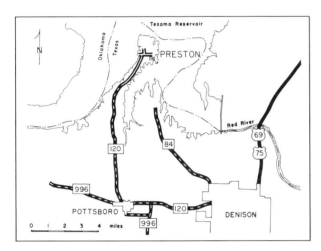

Preston, site of one of the most important crossings on the Red River, is opposite the point where the Washita River flows into the Red from the north. Before entry of white men to the region it had served as a crossing for Indians in the region, making it the ideal site for a trading post.

Silas Cheek Colville and Holland Coffee established a trading post about 1837 on the south side of the river. Coffee during the decade built a number of posts along the Red River, but the one opposite from the mouth of the Washita, known at the time as Coffee's Station, was the most famous and probably the most important. In 1839, Coffee wed Sophia Suttonfield Aughinbaugh, a native of Indiana then in her early twenties but already once before married. Coffee took her to his log stockade on the Red River, later building for her a plantation house named Glen Eden, which became renowned for its luxury.

In 1840–41 Colonel William G. Cooke for the Republic of Texas blazed a military road leading from Austin northward to the Red River at Cof-

fee's Station and established a temporary military supply depot near the post. From this time onward the community that grew up around Coffee's Station came to be known as Preston or Preston Bend, but the origin of the name is lost to history. By 1845 a considerable population had gathered at Preston, with an estimated one thousand wagons of immigrants to Texas crossing the river there in a single year. By 1851 a municipal government was set up with Tom Jackson as the first mayor. A Masonic lodge followed in 1852, and a post office was granted in 1856. The U.S. Army operated a small supply depot at Preston from 1851 to 1853.

After the death of Holland Coffee at Preston in 1846, his widow, Sophia, married Major George Butts, but the marriage lasted only a short time. In 1856 she was married for the fourth time, on this occasion to Judge James Porter. Sophia through the Civil War years was perhaps the most prominent resident of Preston. She is best known today as having been a spy for the Confederacy, giving to Southern officers intelligence that she gleaned from groups of Union soldiers passing through Preston. Once she unexpectedly became the hostess for a party of Northern scouts who were searching the area for Confederate James Bourland, who headed Southern forces along the river. Knowing that Bourland was on his way to Fort Washita, north of Preston, and realizing that he and his men were in peril, she opened her wine cellar and entertained the Yankee officers

Glen Eden, the plantation house built by Holland Coffee for his bride, Sophie. Courtesy Texas State Library, Austin, Texas.

until late at night. While they were still frolicking in her home, Sophia quietly left the party, went to the stable, saddled a mule, and swam the river to carry a warning to Bourland, who with his men escaped danger. Sophia, confident that she had saved the Southerners, returned the same evening unnoticed by the Union troops.

During the late nineteenth and early twentieth centuries, Preston remained alive as the center of a rural community. In this century it had general stores, a public school system, two churches, a cotton gin, and a cemetery on the hill overlooking the settlement. In the late 1930s, when the community still had about twenty residents, the U.S. Army Corps of Engineers purchased all the land in its immediate area, because Preston would be flooded upon the completion of the Texoma Dam a few miles downstream. When the gates of the dam were closed in 1944, the site of Preston was inundated, leaving only its cemetery intact.

LOCATION: *The area of the Preston community in Grayson County is now covered by the waters of Lake Texoma, but its fascinating cemetery, with burials dating back to the 1850s as well as the 1897 grave of Sophia Porter, may be viewed. To reach the graveyard drive north from Pottsboro on Farm to Market Road 120 about 7.0 miles to the end of state maintenance, where a paved county road begins. Proceed northward an additional 2.2 miles on the county road through a beautifully wooded countryside to a "T" intersection. At the intersection turn east onto another paved county road that leads 0.8 mile to the end of the pavement at the Preston cemetery.*

Proffitt

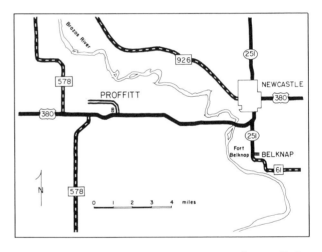

Although Proffitt as a town did not exist until the late nineteenth century, it was a ranching community as early as the 1860s. In 1852 the Reverend Robert S. Proffitt, a part-time Methodist minister and storekeeper from Tennessee, had come to Texas, settling at Center Mills, in present-day Hood County. A decade later he acquired title to ranch property eighty miles northwest on Elm Creek, near Fort Belknap. Soon two of his sons and two herders drove cattle to the unfenced area and set up a ranch. Other settlers had occupied much of the area for several miles up the Brazos from Fort Belknap, many of them locating along Elm Creek in the general area occupied by the Proffitts.

In one of the most famous of all Indian raids into Texas, known to this day as the Elm Creek

Detail from the grave marker for Sophia Suttonfield Aughinbaugh Coffee Butts Porter, who is remembered today as the Texas Confederate spy. Photograph by the author, 1984.

The common grave of the three young men killed by raiding Indians at Proffitt in 1867. Photograph by the author, 1984.

Detail of a long silent Proffitt home. Photograph by the author, 1984.

Raid, Plains Indians swooped down on the settlers in the valley of Elm Creek on 13 October 1864. They killed ten persons, ransacked over a dozen homes, and carried off two women and five children into captivity. Among those captured were the wife and two children of Brit Johnson, a black slave belonging to James Allen Johnson, a local rancher. The next year Brit Johnson made a trip into the Indian Territory in search of his family, but without success. In 1865 his wife and children were released with the aid of Indian agents. Johnson remained in the area until he himself was killed by Indians in 1871.

The 1864 raid was by no means the only depredation suffered by settlers on Elm Creek; another major raid followed in July 1867. Three young men, one of them a son of Robert S. Proffitt, were rounding up cattle when they were surprised by a war party. Since their guns were on the saddles of their horses some distance away, the boys had no defense. The warriors killed and

scalped them on the spot, their bodies later being placed in a common grave.

Despite the attacks by Indians, settlers remained in the Elm Creek valley. With the end of Indian danger in the mid-1870s, more and more people entered the area. Another of Robert S. Proffitt's sons, John William, in 1894 established a store on the north bank of the creek, even though there already had been a Proffitt post office nearby as early as 1880. John donated land for the construction of a church, which also served as a schoolhouse for the growing town. An upper room, which was added later, became the meeting place for the Proffitt Masonic lodge. In addition to ranching and operating his store, John Proffitt also engaged in the telephone business, providing the first telephone service to Graham and building lines to the Cornelius Reynolds ranch and to the town of Throckmorton. The first telephone exchange at the town of Proffitt was in John Proffitt's home.

A farmer with his son posed for a picture in his wagon at Proffitt early in the 1900s. Courtesy Southwest Collection, Texas Tech University, Lubbock, Texas.

Proffitt thrived for a number of years as a rural community with general store, public school, and both Methodist and Baptist churches, retaining its post office until 1925. The consolidation of farms coupled with the improvement of rural roads in the middle of this century, however, eventually killed Proffitt as a town. Today it consists only of its former school (now a residence), a handful of scattered rural homes, the Proffitt Baptist Church, an abandoned Methodist church, and an interesting cemetery.

LOCATION: *To visit Proffitt, drive west from Newcastle 7.3 miles on U.S. Highway 380 to a paved county road leading north. Take this paved road 1.0 mile north and then west to the end of the pavement in the center of the former town. The Proffitt cemetery, which was begun with the burial of the three boys killed by Indians in 1867, is located on the north side of the federal highway 0.2 mile beyond the turnoff to the town. The common grave of the 1867 Indian victims is designated by a historical marker.*

Pumpville

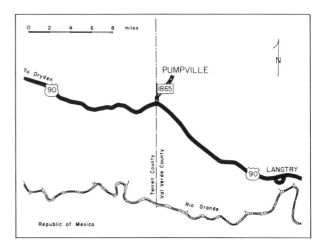

Pumpville was a Southern Pacific Railroad town between Langtry and Dryden in Val Verde County. As its name suggests, it existed primarily to provide water to the steam locomotives which pulled trains through the isolated semiarid ranch country. In the early 1880s the company drilled a well for fresh water, installed steam pumping equipment to elevate it to the surface, and erected steel water tanks in which to store it until needed by the locomotives. Then crews swung the gooseneck arm on a water column over the locomotive tender and opened the valve to let the water flow into the reservoir in the car.

In addition to its company water service personnel, a station agent and his family, and track maintenance workers, Pumpville gained population in the form of local businessmen as well as ranchers and former ranch employees who preferred to live in town rather than in the isolation of their ranges. As early as 1899, James N. Morgan received a post office at Pumpville, and the town grew to have a general store, livestock holding pens and loading chutes, the Pumpville Baptist Church, and a number of dwellings along a main street parallel with the tracks.

The decline of Pumpville came after World War II when the Southern Pacific gradually withdrew its personnel from the town. In 1952 the depot closed, while the railway water service was abandoned in 1955 when diesel locomotives had completely supplanted steam engines on the transcontinental route. Today Pumpville has one remaining abandoned Southern Pacific water tank, the foundations of the pumphouse which gave the town its name, a steel derrick over the old well, a Baptist church, several abandoned residences, an abandoned combined store, post office, and filling station, and foundations or ruins of several other structures.

LOCATION: *Pumpville stands at the northern end of Farm to Market Road 1865 about 2.2 miles north of U.S. Highway 90, approximately 13.6 miles northwest of Langtry, and 26.6 miles east of Dryden.*

123
P

A Southern Pacific freight train passing through Pumpville, where the steam locomotives once stopped for water. Photograph by the author, 1981.

The old Stonewall County courthouse, the last intact structure from the town of Rayner, now a privately owned ranch headquarters. Photograph by the author, 1984.

Rayner

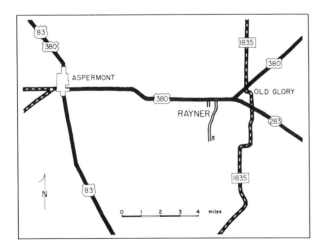

Rayner represents an attempt by a speculator to profit from the organization of a county. In 1888, W. E. Rayner, the manager of the St. Louis Land and Cattle Company holdings in King County, became interested in creating a town in adjacent Stonewall County so that it might become the seat of justice when that county was formally organized. He first approached A. S. Rhomberg, another local rancher, about the possibility of placing the townsite on his property, but Rhomberg at the time was opposed to the organization of the county because of increased taxes that it might impose.

Accordingly Rayner acquired a section of land about eight miles east of Rhomberg's property and in late spring or early summer 1889 laid out the site on the ground. As platted by its founder, the town of Rayner consisted of sixty-three city blocks with streets running north-south and east-west. Within a year the entrepreneur successfully induced a number of businessmen to locate in the new town, among them operators of three general merchandise stores, a photography studio, a barbershop, and a printing shop. Written sources record that the town even had water hydrants at the corners of all the business blocks, with water supplied from a reservoir on a hill west of the site. Within a short time both a cotton gin and a

Typical burial sites in the overgrown Rayner cemetery. Photograph by the author, 1984.

grain mill were added. Education was provided in a schoolhouse built at an expense of eight hundred dollars.

Even before the town was formally laid out, Stonewall County in 1888 became organized, with W. E. Rayner's new community as its seat. Subsequently the county commissioners issued bonds for the construction of an imposing three-story stone courthouse, reportedly costing forty thousand dollars to build.

The impressive edifice housed county offices, records, and courtrooms for less than a decade. Within two years after the founding of Rayner, other areas of the county began to settle up sufficiently that local residents were able to have a special election called to consider moving the seat of government to a more central location. A new town named Aspermont nearer to the center of the county vied with the older settlement in the contest, and when the ballots were counted the newer town won. The victory, however, began eight years of dispute and litigation over the re-sults of the election that finally ended on 4 June 1888 with the actual transfer of county records to Aspermont.

After Rayner lost the county seat, its population dwindled, many of its citizens moving to Aspermont. In time Rayner became a ghost, its post office being discontinued in 1906. Today the former town has only one family, that of a rancher residing in the old courthouse.

LOCATION: *To reach Rayner, drive east from Aspermont on U.S. Highway 380 about 8.4 miles to a graded private road leading 0.3 mile south to the townsite around the three-story former courthouse. The site is on private property but may be viewed from the highway. To visit the Rayner cemetery, filled with graves almost exclusively from the 1890s, drive east on the U.S. highway an additional 0.3 mile and then turn south onto a graded county road that leads 2.2 miles through open range to the graveyard. Avoid all turns and stay on the main road. The cemetery, mostly grown up in mesquite and brush, lies behind a barbed wire fence about seventy-five yards east of the county road.*

Salt Flat

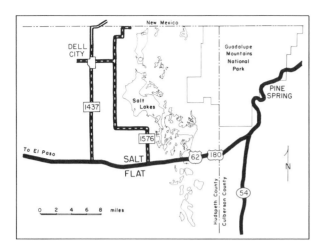

Salt Flat sprang up in the desert beside a new highway linking El Paso with Carlsbad, New Mexico, in the late 1920s, though the area had seen human activity for many years previously.

The story of Salt Flat as a community begins with the arrival of J. W. Hammack in 1905. He moved to the area from Arlington, Texas, and worked for a number of years on surrounding ranches while also raising irrigated garden produce that he sold in Van Horn. The largest ranch in the vicinity was the five-hundred-section Figure 2, which the year after Hammack's arrival branded a remarkable twenty thousand calves. There was no formal education for children at Salt Flat, so parents had to board teachers in their homes for short periods of time to give their children a measure of "schooling." The nearest schoolhouse was at Orange, New Mexico, and the young people from Salt Flat generally went there not for education but for dances that were held every two or three months.

In 1928, Ed Hammack, son of J. W. Hammack, learned that a new highway was to be built over the Guadalupe Pass to connect El Paso with Carlsbad, New Mexico. Up to that time the only roads between the flats and El Paso had been rude affairs that paralleled buried petroleum pipelines. Learning the exact route of the road from the

Abandoned tourist courts constructed by the Hammack family at Salt Flat in the 1930s. Photograph by the author, 1984.

Commercial salt extraction from the natural salt flats on the southwest side of the Guadalupe Mountains early in the twentieth century. Courtesy Texas State Library, Austin, Texas.

Idle but still furnished kitchen in the cafe established by Arthur Grable at Salt Flat about 1930. Photograph by the author, 1984.

highway department surveyors, Hammack constructed a store and gasoline station beside the proposed highway, opening it when traffic began in 1929. A few hundred yards to the west Arthur Grable built another store and station. Both businessmen also opened cafes and eventually added tourist courts. From the outset the Hammack store doubled as a bus station serving a broad area of ranches.

Another source of income for inhabitants at Salt Flat was salt production. The town takes its name from natural salt flats that lie on the southwest side of the Guadalupe Mountains. These flats, which after rains become shallow salt lakes, had provided salt to residents of the Rio Grande Valley around El Paso for centuries and were the subject of violent confrontations in the 1860s and 1870s. The complex dispute ethnically pitted Mexicans against Anglo-Americans and politically placed Republicans opposing Democrats, and before the arguments were settled a number of men on both sides were killed. By the 1920s the salt flats had been relegated to use as a source of salt for cattle and other livestock. Salt operators hired men with picks and shovels to load the natural mineral into wagons or trucks which hauled it to customers as far north as the Sacramento Mountains and as far south as Van Horn and Marfa. The mining continued until the late 1930s, when pumping of irrigation wells at Dell City a few miles to the north lowered the water table so much that natural salt ceased to be deposited in its previous amounts, and mining became unprofitable.

An unexpected event augmented the population at Salt Flat. About 1932 an American Airlines passenger plane crashed in the nearby Guadalupe Mountains with the loss of several lives. Consequently the federal government constructed an emergency aircraft landing strip at Salt Flat so that planes could safely land there if the peaks were shrouded in fog. The government employees worked around the clock in eight-hour shifts, were housed in seven special residences, and operated the airport until the early 1960s, when it closed because the installation of new automated radio equipment permitted planes to fly over the mountains in all weather.

At its maximum population Salt Flat had fifty-four inhabitants, but today it is virtually deserted, with only a post office, a cafe, and one filling sta-

tion, though it contains several other abandoned and deteriorating buildings and vast amounts of surface debris.

LOCATION: *Salt Flat is located in northeastern Hudspeth County on U.S. Highway 62/180 about 0.2 mile west of its intersection with Farm to Market Road 1576 approximately 69 miles east of El Paso.*

Salt Gap

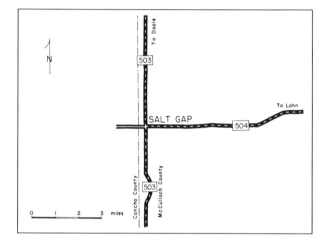

Salt Gap half a century ago was a prosperous agricultural community, but today it is virtually dead, almost all of its homes and businesses standing empty and deteriorating.

The area around the town was first occupied by ranchers in the 1870s, with farmers following just after the turn of the century. Before settlement the vicinity witnessed at least one Indian depredation. Cibern Ghoens, a member of a three-man party trailing wild horses in 1861, was surprised in his camp and slain by warriors who took his scalp. His partners escaped and later returned to bury him in a shallow grave on a nearby hill.

James N. Craig secured a post office for Salt Gap in 1905, about the same time that the community received its first school. The school met in an eighteen- by twenty-foot frame structure that served the surrounding area until 1938, when a much larger brick building in the same general location took its place. Classes met there until the early 1940s, when the Salt Gap school merged with that at Melvin. A local rancher bought the

Pupils and teacher posed for a picture at the Salt Gap school about 1914. Courtesy Wayne Spiller.

former school in order to salvage some of its building materials, leaving the roofless and windowless walls a gaping ruin.

By the 1930s, Salt Gap had become a tidy little community with about sixty residents. It consisted of a school, post office, cotton gin, two grocery stores with filling stations, a blacksmith shop, automobile garage, and a gristmill. The consolidation of agriculture in the forties and fifties, however, reduced the importance of the town as more and more small family farms disappeared and their owners moved to larger towns and cities. During the same years improved roads drew trade away from Salt Gap to Eden and Brady. Over the past thirty years the community has withered away to the point that it has no commercial business whatever and only one occupied home, though the site is strewn with abandoned

The Salt Gap post office, now abandoned, at the side of the road. Photograph by the author, 1984.

structures, foundations, and debris from former buildings.

LOCATION: *Salt Gap is located at the intersection of Farm to Market Road 503 with Farm to Market Road 504 in western McCulloch County.*

Samfordyce

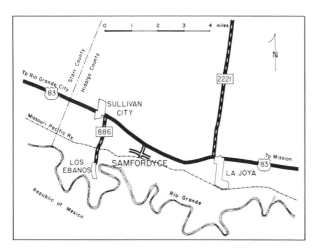

Samfordyce, three times a boomtown, is now a ghost for the third time in its history. It began as the western terminus of an extension of the St. Louis, Brownsville and Mexico Railway in 1905, a town planned to become a center for irrigated agriculture. Benjamin Franklin Yoakum, a builder of railroads in several parts of the United States, projected the railway line from near Brownsville up the Lower Rio Grande Valley. At the same time he promoted agriculture along the new route. Railroad construction began in 1903 and it reached Samfordyce, about seventy miles up the valley, in 1905. Yoakum named the station Sam Fordyce after one of his financial supporters, but postal officials refused to grant a post office name consisting of the two words. They combined them into one as Samfordyce and granted the post office on 3 November 1905.

When John Lawrence, who became a major landowner in the area, first came to Samfordyce in 1904, before the arrival of the railroad, he found that it had "all the earmarks of a boomtown." Its streets had been laid out on the ground,

blocks and lots numbered, and a new two-story frame hotel had opened for business, with a larger one under construction since the first hostelry could not handle all the trade. Already a number of four- and five-room cottages had been erected, and more pretentious residences were under construction.

The reason for the prosperity was that Yoakum had organized another company with local backing to construct a major irrigation system taking its water from the Rio Grande above Samfordyce, elevating it with three pumping stations, and then carrying it by gravity flow all the way to Harlingen. This system would have become the largest irrigation project in the Lower Rio Grande Valley and would have watered much of the land served by Yoakum's railroad. About the time that the tracks reached Samfordyce, however, questions were raised concerning the validity of the land titles at the upper end of the proposed development. Consequently the irrigation company had to abandon its plans for the long gravity canal and was forced to draw its water from the river downstream near Mercedes. Although Yoakum had constructed extensive brick warehouses and large freight and passenger depots at Samfordyce, by 1910 it had withered away to nothing more than two vacant hotels, a post office, the quiet railway facilities, and three or four families.

In the latter part of 1910, life returned to Samfordyce with the beginning of revolutionary activity across the Rio Grande in Mexico and the subsequent introduction of U.S. Army troops to protect the border communities on the American side of the river. Samfordyce was the nearest railway point for Fort Ringgold and much of Starr County, and the War Department shipped thousands of cars of freight to the Samfordyce depot. On some individual days the freight receipts totalled seventy-five to one hundred thousand dollars. At Samfordyce the army constructed a three-troop permanent post complete with hospital, waterworks, and sewage plant. With all the military activity the Samfordyce post office handled as many as one hundred thousand pieces of mail daily. The town boomed until the War Department, without ever fully occupying the military post, declared the Samfordyce encampment abandoned and moved the soldiers away. By 1920, Samfordyce again was declining, and within a few years it had dwindled to one hotel unfit for habi-

U.S. Army troops stationed at Samfordyce during the border troubles with Mexico early in this century. Courtesy Hidalgo County Historical Museum, Edinburg, Texas.

The last railway station to serve Samfordyce, a small wooden structure, a sad successor to the large freight and passenger depots once in the town, as it appeared in 1963 before its destruction by fire. Courtesy Hidalgo County Historical Museum, Edinburg, Texas.

tation, the railroad facilities, vacant warehouses, and a post office that closed in 1926.

Yet a third boom came to Samfordyce in the mid-1930s. In September 1934 local oilman Otto Woods discovered oil in Hidalgo County with the No. 1 John Lawrence oil well at Samfordyce. This opened the Samfordyce Oil Field, which was located just north of the town and which produced considerable amounts of petroleum through the World War II years. Much of the production was carried to Port Isabel and Brownsville through a ninety-mile five-inch pipeline laid shortly after the discovery.

With the decline in petroleum production, Samfordyce for the third time became a ghost. Today it is marked by a few ruins, the ashes of its last railroad station, and scattered detritus from former buildings.

LOCATION: *The Samfordyce townsite lies on the present-day Missouri Pacific Railroad tracks at the end of a graded county road that leads south 0.4 mile from U.S. Highway 83 about 1.8 miles east from its intersection with Farm to Market Road 886. The turn-off, marked by a highway department sign, is 18.0 miles east of Rio Grande City and 13.6 miles west of Mission.*

Sanco

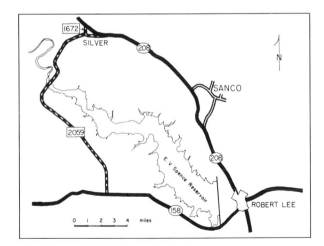

Sanco, a picturesque ghost town in scenic northern Coke County, moved to its present site in 1907, but it originally stood about a mile east where settlement began in the 1880s. The first

post office for the town was opened by John L. Durham in 1888, and about this same time the members of the surrounding rural community erected a meetinghouse which five days a week served as a school and on Sundays housed worship services when a minister was available. During the same time a general store opened, and Sanco became a typical country town. Most of its residents were stock raisers and later cotton farmers, for cotton cultivation spread into Coke County from the east during the late nineteenth century.

Because the residents became convinced that the site of their town was not conducive to further growth, they moved it one mile west in 1907 to a location on the south bank of Yellow Wolf Creek. Already a Methodist church had been built at the site, which offered the advantages of more level ground and dependable water from springs along the creek. Ulmer Bird donated land for the con-

Gravity gasoline pump and hand oil pumps in front of the last store and post office to serve Sanco. Photograph by the author, 1984.

Inside the abandoned Sanco Baptist Church, complete with furniture and a forty-eight-star American flag. Photograph by the author, 1984.

struction of a new school, which took the place of two former rural schools in the area. Within a decade Sanco contained a general store, school, Methodist and Baptist churches, cotton gin, and blacksmith shop which later became an automobile garage. In the mid-1920s an open-air tabernacle was built adjacent to the Methodist church.

At its peak of population Sanco had probably thirty families, but drought, boll weevils, and changes in agriculture spelled its demise. Drought struck the community a severe blow during World War I, forcing many of the small farmers to sell out to those with larger holdings. Then in the 1920s low commodity prices combined with increased boll weevil infestation to force many farmers out of agriculture altogether. The people who were able to hold onto their land frequently purchased the holdings of those who were leaving. With the opening of new cotton land on the South Plains and in the Panhandle, the small

farmers in Coke County found themselves unable to compete with more efficient growers on the level plains. Gradually almost all the former cotton fields returned to grassland and range use. The last cotton gin at Sanco closed in the mid-1920s, signalling the effective end of most cultivated agriculture in the immediate vicinity. Improvement of roads in the 1940s and 1950s sealed the doom for Sanco, its last store closing in the early 1970s.

LOCATION: *Sanco is located about midway on a five-mile paved county road loop known locally as the "Sanco Loop" northeast of Texas Highway 208. The ends of the loop meet the state highway 6.7 and 9.7 miles northwest of Robert Lee. Care should be exercised while driving on the loop because much of its length is open range, and livestock may be encountered on the roadway. The ghost town of Silver may be seen 8 miles farther to the northwest.*

Shafter

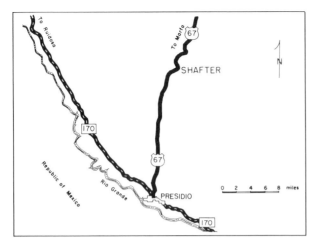

Established in the 1880s, Shafter was the site of the most intensive development of underground mining in Trans Pecos Texas. From its discovery in 1880 until 1942, the Shafter Mine dominated Texas silver production.

The silver deposits were discovered in September 1880 by a teamster named John W. Spencer. A civilian employee of the U.S. Army, he went to several military officers soliciting their aid in developing the silver deposits that he discovered in the Chinati Mountains north of Presidio. With samples of ore from his strike, Spencer convinced William R. Shafter, Louis Wilhelmi, and John L. Bullis to join him in purchasing several sections of land around the discovery site.

The four men agreed to split the ownership of their new lands as well as dividing equally any profits that they might derive. Since they did not have the money to begin mining, in 1882 the four men contracted with Daniel Cook, a San Francisco mining entrepreneur, to develop the property. Cook's field parties found what they believed to be considerable amounts of high-grade silver ore in the area owned by the four men. Accordingly the Californian incorporated the Presidio Mining Company of San Francisco to begin mining operations.

The Presidio Mining Company offered to buy the mining property for 5,000 shares of company stock plus $1,600 in cash to each of the four partners. Three of the men agreed to the offer, but John Bullis declined. Most of the ore had been located on the land he had purchased, and he wanted to secure full payment for the minerals coming from "his" property. After the passage of time he did agree to the offer, but only after he had lost a major court case against the mining company.

Activity in the area began in earnest during the spring of 1884 with large-scale excavations of shafts and tunnels and the installation of an ore reduction mill near Cibolo Creek about a mile away. Year after year the Presidio Mining Company prospered as more ore bodies were located in the Shafter Mine. The ore was found principally in pockets within the surrounding limestone. Some of these pockets were remarkably large. It was not considered unusual for the miners to excavate pockets of ore as large as fifty to seventy-five feet high and five hundred to a thousand feet long. The most impressive measured 2,500 feet long, 250 feet high, and 10 to 40 feet wide—all underground. Since the ore bodies frequently were connected with each other, the underground workings took a highly irregular form.

After the ore was brought up to the surface, it was hauled to the reduction mill in mule-drawn wagons. This method of transportation continued in use until 1913, when an aerial tramway was erected to reduce the expense of moving ore. The milling operation began as a small stamp mill, but it grew as the years passed. Initially pan amalgamation was used to aid in the breakdown of the ore, though in later years cyanide treatment took its place. The concentrated ore then was hauled to Marfa for shipment by rail elsewhere for smelting.

As early as 1884 a community began to grow around the ore reduction mill beside Cibolo Creek. It took the same name as the mining district, Shafter. As the mining operations grew in scale, the town grew as well, for increasing numbers of men were needed to work in the mines. At one time the town boasted four thousand inhabitants. The majority of the workers were Mexicans who labored under the supervision of Anglo-Americans. The Anglo employees lived in comfortable stone and adobe houses, while the Mexicans lived in generally smaller and often less comfortable quarters. Many of the prominent edifices in the town lined its winding main street, among them the Catholic church and adjoining parochial school, stores, post office, saloons, and jail. Stories are told of topsoil being hauled in for the yards at the homes of the supervisory staff to enable their wives to enjoy flowers, fruit trees,

The adobe U.S. post office still open at Shafter. Photograph by the author, 1982.

and green lawns. Single Anglo male employees at the mine were housed in a men's clubhouse managed by an Englishman named Bryant. This building also provided rooms for visiting company officials from California.

Soon the hills and valleys around Shafter were denuded of trees in order to fuel the boilers producing steam to operate equipment in the mines. A writer in 1910 noted that within hauling distance "nearly all of the original wood has been cut and used, so that for years the fuel has been crude oil hauled 45 miles, in tank wagons, from the railroad." The same observer described the water supply at Shafter in this way: "Cibolo Creek affords abundant water from Shafter toward the upper springs, but ceases to flow above ground below the town. The water is good enough for all ordinary purposes and is also used for drinking, although most of the white people use distilled water from the condensers at the boilers. The

Mexicans are not so particular. Now and then there is a little typhoid fever in the settlement, but, on the whole, health conditions are good."

Life in Shafter seems to have been good for most of its inhabitants. An early twentieth-century visitor noted that "plenty of shade, good water," and other amenities rendered life in Shafter unusually pleasant when one considered its arid location. One resident recollected from the mining days that "we were so far away from everything that we had to make our own good times." She remembered especially the serenades played in the evenings by Mexican miners in the shade of trees still standing along Cibolo Creek, their musical strains floating through the air to the area where the Anglos lived. The element of social discrimination did exist, however, with the Mexican workers living in their own distinct sector of the town. Discrimination also entered in the determination of pay for services rendered. An ob-

A mine headframe looming above the ruins of former Shafter buildings. Photograph by the author, 1982.

Pinup picture of the type enjoyed by miners at Shafter. Courtesy Southwest Collection, Texas Tech University, Lubbock, Texas.

server early in this century noted that "wages vary from $1.25 per day for Mexicans to $3 per day for white miners, but the Mexican at $1.25 does as much and as good work as his American rival."

The Shafter Mine remained in production for six decades, finally closing in September 1942. Its record was more than impressive. During its history it produced two million tons of silver ore which also carried minor values of gold and lead. This ore when smelted produced 30,293,606 ounces of silver, 90 percent of the entire silver output of the state of Texas.

With the closure of the Shafter Mine, the town of Shafter began withering away. As residents moved elsewhere, those who remained began removing anything of value from the vacant homes, even tearing off the roofs for firewood. This left only open shells where formerly the miners and their families had lived, and without coverings the bare adobe walls began eroding back into the soil. Today only about twenty-five residences in Shafter are occupied. Among the surviving remains are the still operating Catholic church, abandoned public and parochial schools, a functioning post office in an adobe house, two disused stores, dozens of abandoned houses in varying states of disrepair, and the ruins of the former three-story ore reduction mill of the Presidio Mining Company.

Shafter Lake

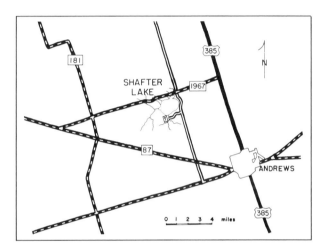

Standing near a large natural salt lake named in honor of Colonel William R. Shafter, who first discovered it in 1875, the town of Shafter Lake came into existence as the result of promotion by speculators. The "father" of the town was J. F. Bustin, who lived nearby and who saw the rolling countryside as the ideal site for a town. It was located in Andrews County, which had not yet been formally organized and which did not have a single town, and Bustin hoped that the place would become the seat of government when that occurred. Touting the dry climate, scenic lake, and natural drainage, the entrepreneur interested the firm of Pierce and Powers in establishing a townsite on the north side of the lake. The firm had just finished promoting the town of Hamlin in Jones County.

In 1906, Pierce and Powers printed up thousands of handsome brochures extolling Shafter Lake as the most promising community in a wide trade area of big ranches. Soon immigrants from all parts of the United States began traveling by rail to Midland, the nearest railway station, and thence by buggy and automobile the fifty-one miles to Shafter Lake, "the city of a thousand wonders." Many of them were so impressed with the site and its skillful promotion that they bought town lots and set up businesses. One of the first commercial concerns was the *Shafter Lake Herald*, owned and edited by James T. Cumley. He filled its pages with praises for the new town, and sent thousands of copies throughout the country, especially to the Midwest.

Considerable numbers of people located in Shafter Lake, giving it a peak population of approximately five hundred in 1910. In addition to over fifty homes, it had two hotels, the Cowboy State Bank, a drugstore, large general merchandise store, post office, lodge hall, doctor's office, telephone exchange, three churches, a six-room concrete schoolhouse, newspaper and printing shop, blacksmith shop, and livestock commission merchants, but never a single saloon, for the town was "dry." In 1908 a cemetery for the community was begun on the opposite side of the lake. Virtually all of the businesses in the town served the ranches in the surrounding territory, as the climate was too arid to support most forms of cultivated agriculture.

In 1910, the same year that Andrews County was legally organized, a competing town named Andrews was established about eleven miles southeast of Shafter Lake. The towns contended with each other very actively in the voting to select the seat of government in an election that year, Andrews winning by a very slim margin. After losing its bid to become the county seat, Shafter Lake began losing its population to the newer town. A severe drought in 1917–18 and accompanying hard times hastened the decline, though the community retained its post office until 1929.

Today only one original building from Shafter Lake survives intact. This is a concrete block residence built in 1908, the sand and gravel in its blocks coming from the banks of the salt lake. In addition visitors to the former town see several modern dwellings belonging to the descendants of Bert M. Irwin, the first postmaster, who today have a ranching operation at the site. Near the highway east of the ranch headquarters are numerous foundations of long forgotten Shafter Lake buildings.

LOCATION: *To visit Shafter Lake, drive west from U.S.*

The natural salt lake named for Colonel William R. Shafter which gave the nearby town of Shafter Lake its name. Photograph by the author, 1984.

The 1908 Irwin ranch house, built of concrete blocks made with sand from the banks of Shafter Lake, the last surviving intact structure from the former town of the same name. Photograph by the author, 1984.

Highway 385 about 3.7 miles on Farm to Market Road 1967 to a four-way intersection. The turn-off from the U.S. highway is 8 miles north of Andrews and 20 miles south of Seminole. From the four-way intersection proceed west an additional 2.1 miles to the townsite. To reach the cemetery turn south at the four-way intersection and drive 1.5 miles on pavement past the lake to a historical marker and sign for the graveyard. Cross a cattle guard to the west and drive 1.3 miles over a very rough occasionally graded road (disregarding minor roads to the sides serving oil wells) to the fenced cemetery. This road is not recommended after any wet weather.

Sher-Han

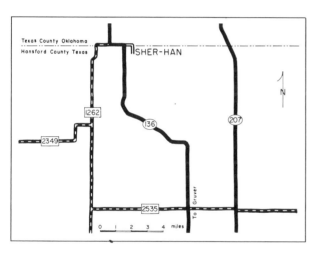

Sher-Han is the name most often given to a natural gas/petroleum company camp established in 1944 by the Phillips Petroleum Company just south of the Oklahoma state line in northern Hansford County. It takes its name from Sherman and Hansford counties. Soon after Phillips built its facilities, two other companies constructed adjoining pipeline compressor stations with housing for employees, creating a community which had an estimated three to four hundred inhabitants.

The story of Sher-Han begins in 1944, when the Phillips Petroleum Company built a natural gas liquids extraction plant at Sher-Han. The purpose of the facility was to remove liquid petroleum from natural gas coming from the huge Hugoton gas field in southwestern Kansas. Beginning operation in late 1944, it remains in service today, sending natural gas liquids by pipeline

to Borger, Texas, for processing. Not long after Phillips built its facilities, it was joined at Sher-Han by the Michigan-Wisconsin Pipe Line Company and by the Panhandle Eastern Pipe Line Company, both of which purchased gas from Phillips after the liquid petroleum had been removed. These two firms built compressor stations to force the gas through their pipelines to customers in other parts of the country. Much of the natural gas eventually reached consumers in the upper Midwest.

Guymon, Oklahoma, is the nearest town to Sher-Han, and according to oral traditions Phillips originally planned to locate its gas extraction plant closer to the town. Lower property taxes in nearby Texas, however, encouraged Phillips to place its facilities just across the state line outside Oklahoma.

The reason the camps had to be built lay in the remote location chosen for the plants. Although the camps stood only a few miles south of Guymon, in the 1940s no paved roads reached the site. It was not feasible for the workers to commute to their jobs from the surrounding communities because wet weather and snow often made the dirt roads impassable. The petroleum and gas companies were forced to build housing for their employees near the plants, which they rented to the workers and their families at reasonable rates as an incentive for them to live and work in the isolated locale.

The first company housing at Sher-Han was built by the Phillips Petroleum Company, which between 1944 and 1949 erected eighty-one dwellings for its employees and supervisory personnel. In addition the Phillips camp included a community building, a grocery and general store, a small cafe, and a Baptist church.

After Phillips established its plant and company housing at Sher-Han, it was joined in similar efforts by its two natural gas customers. In 1949 the Michigan-Wisconsin Pipe Line Company constructed the large E. G. Hill pipeline compressor station at Sher-Han, and just north of it in 1949–50 erected twenty-one residences for its employees. The camp, like that built by Phillips, included paved streets, fire protection system, concrete curbs and sidewalks, and attractively planted elm trees. This community was known popularly as the "Mish-Wish" camp. About the same time the Panhandle Eastern Pipe

Aerial view of the Michigan-Wisconsin Pipe Line Company camp at Sher-Han, with the E. G. Hill compressor station in the background. Courtesy American Natural Resources Company, Detroit, Michigan.

Children standing in front of Phillips Petroleum Company employee housing in 1952, when Sher-Han was a bustling community. Courtesy Phillips Petroleum Company, Bartlesville, Oklahoma.

Line Company constructed its own compressor station just south of the Phillips plant and erected three residences as housing for its personnel.

For almost twenty years Sher-Han lived as a thriving community. It had not only its homes, community building, businesses, and church, but also such amenities as a baseball park, tennis and basketball courts, playgrounds, and even a nine-hole golf course. In the early 1960s, however, improved transportation in the form of paved roads made it possible for the men employed at Sher-Han to live in Guymon or other surrounding towns and commute by automobile to work. The companies began selling their housing units to their employees and others, either requiring or encouraging them to remove them from company land, and by the late 1960s, Sher-Han's camps had become virtual ghosts. Today no intact homes re-

Entrance to the former Phillips Petroleum Company camp at Sher-Han as it appears today. Photograph by the author, 1984.

main from either the Michigan-Wisconsin or the Panhandle Eastern camps, while only eight remain from the eighty-one formerly in the Phillips camp. Even so, the sites of dozens of former residences and other buildings are clearly marked to this day by paved streets, concrete sidewalks, planted trees, shrubs, and flowers, and the disturbed earth marking the locations where houses once stood.

LOCATION: *Sher-Han is located directly east of Texas Highway 136 at the Oklahoma state line 18 miles north of Gruver in Hansford County. The site of the Michigan-Wisconsin camp is clearly visible but enclosed by a chain-link fence. The former Phillips camp, with its handful of remaining structures, is just north of the Phillips industrial complex. The site of the Panhandle Eastern residences is south of the Phillips plant and is not accessible to the public.*

Long quiet playground equipment standing idle at Sher-Han. Photograph by the author, 1984.

Sherwood

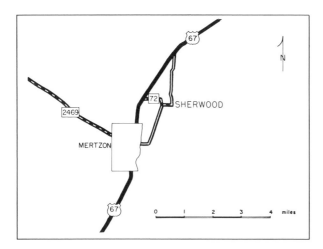

Sherwood, the seat of Irion County for almost half a century, fell victim to the railroad and today is a ghost of its former self, its magnificent stone courthouse towering over the few remaining buildings in the town.

The area around Sherwood received its first permanent residents, mostly ranchers, in the 1870s. In time settlers began to congregate on the banks of Spring Creek, with a post office named Sherwood, after a former owner of the land, granted in 1881. By the mid-1880s the town around the post office had two grocery stores, a blacksmith shop, livery stable, two saloons, and a horse racetrack. A one-room school was added in 1886. In that year the townsite was platted and in the next half dozen years the community began more active growth.

In 1889, Irion County was organized and Sherwood was chosen by its citizens to become its seat. The county commissioners issued bonds in the amount of $6,500 for the construction of a courthouse and jail, which were completed and accepted later in the year. More and more businesses located in the town, which by the 1890s had three hotels, a newspaper and printing office, livery stables, blacksmith shops, several mercantile stores, three churches, Masonic and Odd Fellows lodges, drugstore, telephone exchange, cafes, barbershop, meat market, optician's shop, undertaking parlor, saddlemaker's shop, freight yards, a two-story school, and the Bank of Sherwood. In 1890 the census takers counted 264 people in the town, and more kept coming.

On 24 May 1900 the voters of Irion County approved a bond issue for the construction of a

The 1900–1901 Irion County courthouse standing at the center of Sherwood. Photograph by the author, 1982.

new and larger courthouse in Sherwood. Work on the structure, erected by the firm of Martin and Moody, progressed into 1901, and was accepted by the commissioners' court in March of that year. The new stone structure had two stories of offices and courtrooms surmounted by a tower bearing a false clock with its hands set at the supposed time of Abraham Lincoln's death. It was (and still is) a handsome work of architecture with long, slender windows and decorative details in its stonework.

Sherwood grew at its site because Spring Creek afforded its inhabitants a dependable supply of water. The beautiful tree-lined setting, however, eventually caused the demise of the town. In 1907 the Kansas City, Mexico and Orient Railroad announced plans to build across Irion County, and its surveyors selected a route which stayed north and west of Spring Creek on a comparatively level path. In order for it to pass through Sherwood, the company would have been required to construct two costly bridges across the creek. Instead of undertaking the added expense, the railroad bypassed the town in 1911, establishing nearby a railroad town named Mertzon after M. L. Mertz, a company backer. The new town boomed, drawing away much of the mercantile activity which formerly had centered on the county seat. Within a matter of years Sherwood was left with only the county administration, Mertzon having the commerce, the railroad, and later the highway. This situation persisted until 1936, when the citizens of Irion County overwhelmingly voted to move the seat of justice to Mertzon. This shift sealed the fate of Sherwood, and during the subsequent fifty years it withered away into little more than a rural community. Today it has the vacant courthouse, about forty to fifty occupied residences and mobile homes, a number of abandoned buildings, and a cemetery, making it one of the most picturesque ghost towns in Texas.

LOCATION: *Sherwood is located about two miles northeast of Mertzon. The most convenient access is found by taking Farm to Market Road 72 about 1.2 miles eastward to Sherwood from its intersection with U.S. Highway 67 about 1.3 miles north of Mertzon.*

Silver

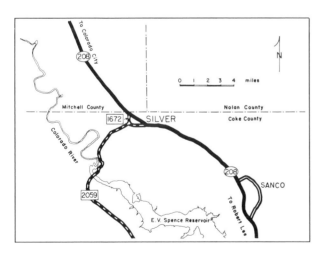

Silver began its existence as a ranching community in northern Coke County with the entry of stock raisers into the area in the 1870s, although the first settlement at Silver itself probably did not come until the late 1880s. Willie I. Tubb owned the land surrounding what became the town. In 1890 a post office was granted with the name of Silver, and about the same time the neighborhood

received a one-room school. The town was never more than a rural community until the 1940s, the censuses from 1900 to 1940 enumerating an average of only about ten inhabitants.

The history of Silver dramatically changed in 1946, when oil was discovered on the Allen Jameson property about half a mile east and one mile south of the schoolhouse. By July 1949 the Sun Oil Company had brought in fifty-nine producing wells in what came to be known as the Jameson Oil Field. The petroleum company investments were so extensive that by 1950 they had doubled the tax valuations in Coke County.

In a few short years Silver became one of the larger towns in the county with an estimated one thousand residents, almost all of them living in homes built and owned by the oil company. One camp alone, the Tubb Camp, in 1961 had a total population of 527, the residents living in standard housing units with 908 square feet of floor space and consisting of two bedrooms, a bath, living room, kitchen, and breezeway that most people used as a den. The company built four other camps in the immediate area.

The school and churches became the focus of social life for the Silver population. From a one-room shack the Silver school grew to become a one-million-dollar complex housed in a modern brick physical plant. The teachers reportedly were paid the highest rate in all of Texas, $700 above the basic state pay schedule, and they also received free rent in school-owned housing as a further inducement to teach at Silver. The petroleum companies paid approximately 80 percent of the taxes in the school district. The churches represented the Methodist, Baptist, and Church of Christ denominations. Events were planned so that nothing at the churches or school conflicted with activities elsewhere. In addition to the school and churches, Silver had a company recreation hall, grocery store, two cafes, post office, and service station.

Residents of Silver exhibited a remarkable community spirit. Perhaps one reason for this situation was that virtually every inhabitant earned approximately equal income, each salary coming to within a few hundred dollars of the same level. In the 1950s the great national charity was the March of Dimes, and in some years Silver contributed more than the remainder of Coke County combined. Silver citizens gained a reputation for

The "Sun Oilers" amateur baseball team from Silver posed for a picture in 1952. Courtesy Bob Edwards.

A "womanless wedding" staged as a fund-raising event for the March of Dimes at Silver in the early 1950s. Courtesy Bob Edwards.

A vendor selling fruit from a hovel at Smeltertown early in the 1900s. Courtesy Southwest Collection, El Paso Public Library, El Paso, Texas.

The story of Smeltertown begins with the smelter. In 1887 the Kansas City Consolidated Smelting and Refining Company constructed a smelter beside the Rio Grande above El Paso to process ore originating from Mexico. In time it grew more important as a smelting center for both lead and copper ores coming from the American Southwest, especially from the famed Santa Rita Mine in New Mexico. In 1899 the Kansas City firm joined several other companies that merged to form the American Smelting and Refining Company, which since that time has operated the facility. For almost a century it has been a landmark in the upper El Paso valley.

At the west side of the smelter lay a narrow strip of level ground between the industrial plant and the Rio Grande. In the 1880s Mexican employees of the smelter had begun erecting houses there, and in 1891 the Catholic diocese purchased a site where it erected what initially was called San Rosalía Church, named for the town in Chihuahua from which most of the first parishioners came. The church later came to be known as San José del Rio Grande. The community grew through the years and became the site of the E. B. Jones School. In 1946 the old church burned, but it was replaced by the new San José de Cristo Rey Church.

Smeltertown was a very closely knit Hispanic community. Though many of its inhabitants lived at or below the poverty level, the neighborhood had comparatively little crime. A resident de-

Scene on Veterans of Foreign Wars Street looking past the church and school after the expulsion of Smeltertown residents in 1972 and the subsequent demolition of their homes. Photograph by the author, 1981.

clared: "When I leave I can keep the house unlocked, because nobody steals from anyone." The community had not only its school and church but also grocery stores, a billiard parlor, and taverns. At one time during the 1930s it even boasted of having a live theater, social clubs, and a forty-piece band. Smeltertown's east-west streets were marked and named for its boys killed serving in World War II, while its long north-south thoroughfare was called Veterans of Foreign Wars Street. The neighborhood had water, electric, and telephone service in later years comparable with other parts of the city, which in time had grown out around it. The population of the parish served by the church in Smeltertown averaged between two and five thousand people for most of its history. During the middle of this century families in the community paid fifteen to twenty dollars a month to rent the ground on which their homes were built.

In 1972 medical tests indicated that a quarter of the children in Smeltertown were suffering poisoning from lead originating in the adjacent smelter. A controversy erupted over what actions should be taken, resulting in the expulsion of all residents by the private landowners in late 1972. Many of the former inhabitants were forced to accept shelter in public housing projects and the community was torn apart. All the former homes were razed, leaving only rows of elm trees, sidewalks, underground utilities, the disused school, and the shell of the church.

LOCATION: *The site of Smeltertown, marked by the still-standing Jones school and ruins of the church adjacent to the International Boundary and Water Commission headquarters may be seen on the west side of U.S. Highway 85 immediately west of the ASARCO smelter on the northwest side of El Paso.*

Soash

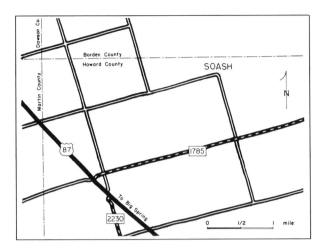

Soash, named for its founder, William Pulver Soash, existed for about three years northwest of Big Spring on the Slaughter Long S Ranch. It was the central point of a tract of several thousand acres which Soash promoted for sale to farmers.

W. P. Soash, a native of Iowa, already had successfully disposed of several thousand acres in the Texas Panhandle in 1905–1908, selling it primarily to midwestern farmers seeking cheap land in an area with a mild climate. He became acquainted with Christopher Columbus Slaughter during this time and made arrangements to sell about two hundred thousand acres on his Long S Ranch. Having signed a contract with the rancher in January 1909, Soash organized the Soash Development Company and began advertising the lands.

As part of the promotional scheme, Soash laid out and founded a town which he gave his own name. Employees graded the streets, numbered the blocks and lots, and planted so many trees that two men reputedly worked full time just watering them. Soon construction began on the two-story Lorna Hotel, named for Soash's daughter, and on a garage to house the thirty automobiles that were needed to transport prospective customers the twenty-five miles over the plains from Big Spring, the nearest railroad town. Other components of the town built by Soash included a two-story school building and an electricity generating plant and waterworks. The most imposing structure in the town, however, was Soash's own office building, which also housed the Bank of Soash. Knowing that potential customers judged a land company by the amount of money that it invested in the area being promoted, he contracted with a St. Louis firm to erect a forty-four-by eighty-eight-foot reinforced concrete structure at a cost of ten thousand dollars.

The first of several special trains carrying potential buyers from the Midwest arrived in Big Spring on 5 March 1909, with others following during the months to come. Even before this time

Crowd enjoying the Independence Day festivities at Soash in 1909. Courtesy Panhandle-Plains Historical Museum, Canyon, Texas.

The impressive shell of W. P. Soash's concrete bank and office building that remains to mark the site of Soash. Photograph by the author, 1984.

steam tractors had been at work breaking the sod on some of the farm tracts so that customers might begin immediate cultivation if they desired. W. P. Soash was so convinced that the town and farms would prosper that he himself moved there in 1909. He participated in the planning of the Gulf, Soash and Pacific Railroad, which was projected to pass through his lands as it connected Big Spring with an extension of the Santa Fe Railway from Lubbock, but only a few miles were ever graded for the line.

Independence Day in 1909 was the most festive event in the history of Soash. An estimated two thousand five hundred people came to the new town to participate in a traditional West Texas barbecue lunch and to watch as cowboys rode bronc horses and the Soash and Lamesa teams played baseball. In the evening the visitors enjoyed vaudeville entertainment after which they danced to live music under electric lights on a platform in the middle of the main street.

Although W. P. Soash had been eminently successful in selling former ranch land for farms in

the Panhandle, his efforts on the South Plains failed. The fault was not his, for beyond his control a drought began in 1909 that continued through 1910 and 1911. Land prospectors ceased coming to the parched plains, and those who already had purchased lands began leaving. Even though the town had attracted two general merchandise stores, a hardware store, a machine shop, a post office, and a barbershop, most of the businessmen left by the end of 1911. Soash managed to hold his financial affairs under control until the summer of 1912, but then he went bankrupt. The unsold lands reverted to C. C. Slaughter's ownership and the town of Soash completely died. Today only the impressive shell of W. P. Soash's concrete bank and office building remains to mark the site.

LOCATION: *At a point 21 miles northwest of Big Spring on U.S. Highway 87, turn east onto Farm to Market Road 1785 and drive 2.1 miles to an intersection with a paved county road leading north. Turn north and proceed 1.0 mile to a sharp bend in the road at the Soash townsite.*

Spanish Fort

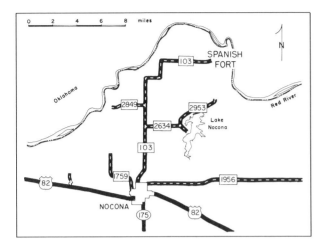

Three centuries ago a major Indian village and trading center, today Spanish Fort is a sleepy little village overlooking the Red River at the end of a farm to market road that goes nowhere else.

As an Anglo-American settlement, Spanish Fort was occupied in the 1850s. Its heyday came two decades later in the 1870s, when the town offered many drovers the last stop on their way up the Chisholm Trail before they crossed at the Red River Station into the Indian Territory on their way to Kansas markets. Many of the cattlemen bedded down their stock at the river and rode into Spanish Fort to buy supplies and quench their thirst. The most popular destination in the town was the once-famous Cowboy Saloon, which for many years thereafter in its walls bore bullet holes marking the drovers' revelry and merriment.

Although most of the town's residents attempted to stay aloof from the activities of the transient population, Spanish Fort for several years maintained a reputation as a tough town. Its boot hill cemetery included forty-three burials. Three of these occupants had committed suicide, but the other forty were the victims of killings. A resident who came to the town during its heyday recollected years later that on one Christmas morning, as the cowboys celebrated the holiday, a shooting took place in which three men were killed before breakfast.

It is interesting to note that the Nocona Boot Company had its origin at Spanish Fort during the days of the trail drives. H. J. Justin started the business in a building on the town square, taking custom orders from the cowboys on their way north on the Chisholm Trail. While they were gone he made the boots, which they picked up on their way back, giving rise to a firm which later moved to Nocona that today sells western style boots throughout the nation.

At its peak Spanish Fort contained four hotels, five physicians, and numerous commercial businesses and saloons. It received its post office as early as 1877 and in 1897 was incorporated as a city. The first school was established in a log building in 1884, followed by two frame schools and finally by a still standing but now abandoned red brick school erected in 1924. The Baptists and Methodists established churches in the town, and the Baptist church, founded in 1875, occasionally still holds meetings.

Spanish Fort began declining about the turn of the century, and today it is merely a shadow of its former self. There is only one place of business, a general store and billiard parlor on the town square, to which are added several disused filling stations and stores, the now vacant school, and several dwellings, many of them abandoned. As one of the remaining inhabitants told the author, "All Spanish Fort is now is the end of the road."

Spanish Fort draws its name from a historical misunderstanding, and it is known to most historians not from the American town but rather from a much older Indian village which formerly stood nearby. In reality there was *never* a Hispanic fort at the site, but instead a fortified Indian village. From artifacts and remains found by the early Anglo-American settlers, an incorrect assumption was made that the Spaniards had occupied the area.

The first known European to visit the village of the Taovaya Indians near the present-day town was a French trader, Bénard de la Harpe, in 1719. There he found a large village of sedentary Indians living in beehive-shaped thatch lodges, and he established trade between them and French settlers in Louisiana which persisted for decades. The Taovaya Indians were enemies of the Lipan Apaches, and this eventually placed them in conflict with the Spaniards far to the south in Texas.

In 1757 the Spaniards established a mission and fort on the San Saba River in present Menard County. Their purpose was to convert the Apaches to Christianity and at the same time to use the tribe as a buffer between the Spanish settlements and the hostile Comanches farther to the north and west on the plains. The effort had the addi-

The Spanish Fort business district about 1910. Courtesy Louise Addington.

An abandoned Spanish Fort residence. Photograph by the author, 1981.

tional role of helping to prevent any intrusions by Frenchmen from Louisiana, who were trading along the Red River, principally in and around the Taovaya village. Infuriated by the Spanish entry into what they considered to be their territory, the Comanches on 16 March 1758 attacked and destroyed the mission, leaving only three surviving witnesses to the massacre, while the soldiers in the fort some distance away were unable to render any effective aid.

Diego Ortiz Parrilla, the commander of the fort, in August 1759 led a punitive expedition against the Tribes of the North, choosing the Taovaya village as the point for attack. The expedition was to consist of five hundred Spanish troops and mission Indians supported by five hundred Apache auxiliaries, but not all the group actually arrived. They were equipped with such supplies and munitions as six cannons, seven hundred pounds of powder, scores of muskets, and food for both men and horses. Parrilla's men successfully attacked a Tonkawa village on their route, where they found spoils from the San Saba mission, and they used some of their captives to lead them to the Taovaya village, reaching it on 7 October 1859.

What the Spaniards found surprised them greatly. They discovered a large, fortified village composed of numerous thatch lodges surrounded by a wooden palisade and moat, a French flag flying in the breeze above everything. A reputed six thousand warriors were either inside the village or encamped behind it. Not only were the Taovaya Indians there, but also their Comanche allies. The volleys of gunfire from within the stockade combined with attacks by the warriors on the outside were so overwhelming that the Spaniards were forced to retreat, even leaving behind two of their cannons. The four-hour battle represented one of the greatest Spanish military defeats on the entire frontier of New Spain.

The Spaniards later claimed that the Taovaya villagers had received training from French agents, but the reason for the Indian success more likely came from their superior numbers and abilities as fighting men. The French flag noted in the Spanish annals was probably one received in a treaty ceremony, for it was a popular custom at the time to present the tribes with flags on such occasions. The supplies of guns, lances, and sabers used by the warriors undoubtedly came from the regular process of trade rather than from any organized effort by French authorities to arm the tribes.

The Taovaya Indian village remained inhabited throughout the eighteenth century and into the early years of the nineteenth century. Through the combined effects of smallpox and the entry of white men into the region, however, the village declined in population. From the 1820s the Taovaya villagers increasingly associated with their linguistic and cultural relations, the Wichita Indians, and finally in the late 1830s they merged with that tribe in present-day Oklahoma. Today the site of the Taovaya village is a plowed field just northwest of the town of Spanish Fort, where over the decades thousands of Indian artifacts have been picked up by visitors and collectors.

LOCATION: *Spanish Fort is located at the extreme northern end of Farm to Market Road 103 in northern Montague County.*

Stewards Mill

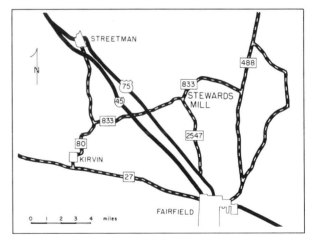

The vicinity of present-day Stewards Mill was first settled in the 1850s, and it was named for a water-powered gristmill constructed by Washington Steward, a native of South Carolina. The mill was one of only a handful serving the area between Dallas and Houston, and often farmers had to wait until the miller could grind their wheat and corn into flour and meal. In later years the mill was converted to steam power.

The back porch of the old Stewards Mill Store. Photograph by the author, 1984.

The nineteenth-century Harmony Chapel at Stewards Mill. Photograph by the author, 1984.

The gristmill was the first structure built in the community, but soon more settlers came into the area and gave it a more substantial population. In 1867, Dr. James I. Bonner opened the first store, known as the Stewards Mill Store, and it served the area in the same building for over a century before it finally closed. Its lumber had been transported up the Trinity River to a landing at Troy and then hauled by teamsters to the construction site. After all the work was completed, Dr. Bonner's records noted that the building had cost him a total of $528.20 to erect. Goods for the store came either overland from the coast or up the Trinity by steamboat to Troy and thence by wagon. After railroads entered the region, the shipping points became Kirvin and Streetman. A post office came in 1872. The first school began at Stewards Mill in the 1880s, and the town maintained public education until its school consolidated with the one in Fairfield in 1929.

Although the dominant economic activity in the surrounding area was agriculture, the neighborhood became known for its well-bred mules. Some of the raisers even purchased jacks from as far away as Tennessee. They prided themselves on the stamina of their draft animals, which were able to work from sunrise to sunset day after day.

Stewards Mill received its first church building in 1876, when the Harmony Chapel was erected by the Reverend T. J. Bonner and the Reverend W. L. Patterson. The wooden structure, which still stands, was shared by members of three denominations, the Presbyterians using it two Sundays a month and the Baptists and Methodists using it the other two. For a while the Baptist congregation worshiped in its own sanctuary about a quarter mile west of the store. Two cemeteries served the community, one directly behind the Harmony Chapel and the other, the Bonner cemetery, about three miles north of the church. Both have burials dating back to the 1860s.

The community maintained its population until after World War II. With a reported seventy inhabitants in 1880, it had fifty-five residents in both 1930 and 1947, but today it has declined considerably. Part of this condition may be attributed to its being bypassed by the modern federal highway and part to the general consolidation of agriculture and reversion of cultivated fields to stock raising. Today Stewards Mill has no places of business; its immediate area has about half a dozen scattered occupied residences and about the same number of abandoned houses. The sites of several former structures are evident from foundation stones, uneven ground, and still living daffodils, irises, and lilies in the yards of long-demolished homes.

LOCATION: *Stewards Mill is found at the intersection of Farm to Market Road 833 with Farm to Market Road 2547 on the old route between Fairfield and Streetman in Freestone County. The most convenient access is east 3.8 miles on Farm to Market Road 833 from an exit on Interstate Highway 45 about 7.4 miles north of Fairfield and 6.3 miles south of Streetman.*

Stiles

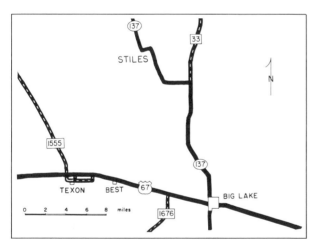

Stiles, the first seat of Reagan County, stands virtually abandoned in range country near the center of the county. Its area became occupied by sheep and goat ranchers in the 1890s, Gordon Stiles locating on Centralia Draw in the neighborhood about 1890. Because there was no post office serving the vicinity, William G. Stiles applied for one in the name of Stiles, receiving it on 17 April 1894. A store apparently operated nearby or in conjunction with the post office, for when G. W. Shield purchased the land from the Stiles family in 1900, it included a store. The immediate area was traversed by the Butterfield Overland Mail in 1859–61, but the later activities had no historical associations with the famous stage route.

In 1903, Reagan County was organized for-

mally, and the voters of the new county selected Stiles as its seat of justice. The county first erected a temporary frame courthouse at a cost of five hundred dollars, replacing it in 1904 with another wooden one costing five thousand dollars. Then in November 1910 the county commissioners called an election to approve bonds for the construction of a permanent building. The voters approved the issuance of twenty thousand dollars in bonds for the erection of a two-story structure built of stone from a nearby hillside. Constructed by William Martin of Comanche, Texas, the structure was completed on 25 October 1911.

Together with its courthouse, Stiles had several places of business including a mercantile store, blacksmith shop, livery stable, and the like. Its population in 1904 was seventy-five. J. Marvin Hunter, who later published the monthly *Frontier Times* magazine, in 1907 began the Stiles *Journal* as a weekly newspaper serving the county.

The demise of Stiles began in 1910, when the Kansas City, Mexico and Orient Railroad surveyed a route from San Angelo to Fort Stockton. The owner of a large ranch on the initial route planned through Stiles refused to grant a right-of-way for the line, so company engineers selected an alternate route twenty miles to the south. In 1911 the railway company began and promoted a

The 1910 Reagan County courthouse, still standing at the center of what once was Stiles. Photograph by the author, 1982.

new town beside its recently laid tracks and named it Big Lake from a natural depression found nearby. Within a decade the new community had nearly caught up with Stiles in population, and then in 1923 oil was discovered in southern Reagan County. Big Lake boomed as a major railway shipping point for the petroleum development, while Stiles, isolated in ranch country with no rail connections, stagnated. In a county-wide election in 1925, Big Lake won the county seat away from Stiles in a 292 to 94 vote.

In the subsequent sixty years Stiles deteriorated into a minor ranch community noted in the region for its big, empty courthouse. Today it has only a handful of residents, numerous abandoned structures, and its vacant courthouse that today is reportedly unsafe to enter.

LOCATION: *Stiles lies on State Highway 137 approximately 19 miles north of Big Lake.*

Swartwout

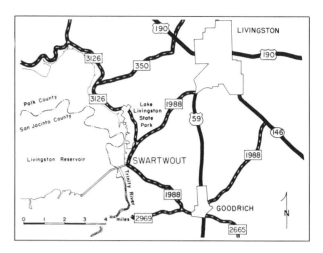

A landing on the Trinity River, Swartwout was founded in the 1830s, prospered through the 1840s and 1850s, but soon thereafter declined, as steamboat traffic decreased and it failed to receive the

The Methodist church in Swartwout. Photograph by the author, 1983.

seat of justice when Polk County was organized in 1854.

The initial settlers came to the Swartwout area in the 1830s, among the first being Arthur Garner and Thomas Bradley. These two men formed a partnership with James Morgan of Houston to develop the site into a town because it offered the combination of a natural steamboat landing with a townsite having sufficient elevation to be safe from most floods. At the suggestion of Sam Houston, the three entrepreneurs approached Samuel Swartwout of New York City for financial support in their venture, naming the town in his honor. Each of the three partners purchased fifty acres at a chosen site and then in 1838 platted the area into a town consisting of eighty-six city blocks. They carefully reserved two blocks as public squares, undoubtedly hoping that a courthouse in the future might grace one of them. They also reserved two lots for churches and one for an academy. At the first sale seventeen people purchased lots in the new town.

Swartwout became a prosperous trading center. When the Trinity was running high from rains upstream, steamboats were able to come there to unload goods and carry back raw products like cotton, hides, and peltries. As early as 1840 the town received a Republic of Texas post office, and after annexation a United States post office on 22 May 1846. The community thrived, by the 1850s having two hotels, stagecoach service, a large warehouse, Masonic lodge, ferry across the Trinity, and such skilled and educated residents as a tailor, wagon maker, carpenter, blacksmith, physician, and several ministers.

For several years Swartwout served as a "sub-county" seat for the Northern District of Liberty County, assuming this role as early as 1838. When Polk County was formed from the northern portion of Liberty County in 1854, everyone expected Swartwout to become the seat of government. To the surprise of many, however, a town nine miles away called Springfield won the election. A promoter of the other town offered the county one hundred acres of land if the name of the community could be changed to Livingston after his hometown in Alabama, and the bargain was struck. Since that time Livingston has been the first and only seat of the county. With decreased river traffic and the loss of the expected county seat, Swartwout began a gradual decline.

Crumbling remains of a Swartwout home. Photograph by the author, 1983.

Though its ferry operated into this century, it was disappearing as a town by the 1870s. Its post office survived until 1875, but by this time the town was virtually gone. With the departure of most of the old settlers and their families, their places were taken mainly by blacks, who maintained a rural community in the area for a century.

LOCATION: *The site of Swartwout is located near the east end of the Lake Livingston dam on Farm to Market Road 1988 about 9.8 miles southwest of Livingston and 5.4 miles northwest of Goodrich. Less than a mile to the southeast is the fascinating Whites cemetery with grave markers dating back to the 1850s. Just north of the ghost town is the beautiful Lake Livingston State Recreation Area.*

The well-maintained Tarrant cemetery. Photograph by the author, 1984.

Tarrant

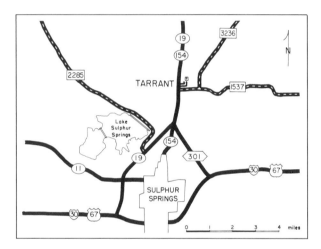

Tarrant, the first seat of Hopkins County, came into existence in the winter of 1842–43 when David Hopkins and his family moved there from Clarksville. When the county was organized in 1846, the voters had a choice of a site offered by David Hopkins or one offered by his brother, Eldridge Hopkins, only a few miles away. The voters chose the one proposed by David, and in time the place was named Tarrant in honor of General Edward H. Tarrant, a noted Texas Ranger, Indian fighter, and politician popular among the settlers.

Having discovered that a man named Pleasance had driven a herd of cattle into the area to graze but was not a resident of Texas, thus breaking a statute enforced at the time, the county court confiscated the three hundred animals and sold them to raise money for the construction of a jail. The two-story structure erected in 1852 was unusual even in its day, being built from ten-inch hewed timbers laid crosswise and doubled, the interior walls and floor being covered with ten- and twenty-penny nails driven in every four inches. During the early years the county officials maintained their offices and records in their own homes or places of business, but in 1854 the commissioners constructed a log courthouse.

By the 1850s Tarrant had become a thriving community. Among its institutions and businesses were a tannery, steam gristmill, blacksmith shop, brick kiln, post office, school, hotel, Masonic lodge, mercantile store, the *Texas Star* newspaper, and a small Methodist college. Its location with creeks comparatively close on two sides, however, prompted its decline. At times of high water the town became nearly inaccessible to people from other parts of the county. During the Union army occupation of Texas after the Civil War, the commander at nearby Sulphur Springs in 1868 removed the county records to that town so that they might be more easily available. After the return of civilian rule to Texas the records came back to the legal county seat, but by an election in 1870 Tarrant lost the seat of justice to Sulphur Springs. The loss of the county seat coupled with a location prone to isolation during floods caused Tarrant to dwindle away until today it is little more than a scattered rural community marked by its attractive cemetery.

LOCATION: *To reach the Tarrant cemetery, the last readily visible vestige of the town, turn east down a paved lane to the graveyard from Texas Highway 19/154 about 0.2 mile north of its intersection with Farm to Market Road 1537 approximately 4.2 miles north of Sulphur Springs.*

Tascosa

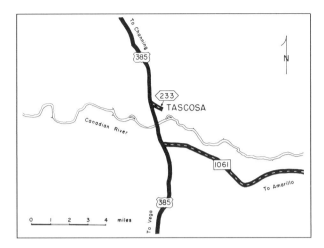

Tascosa, known during its heyday as the "Cowboy Capital of the Plains," was the first true town in the western Texas Panhandle. During its early years it served as the shipping point for numerous large ranches and grew into a booming community with several hundred residents. With its adobe houses, many saloons, and notorious red-light district, Tascosa came as close as any town in Texas to fulfilling the popular image of Western towns as portrayed in films.

The first non-Indian residents of the Tascosa area were New Mexicans who came there first to trade with the Plains tribesmen and later to herd sheep after the warriors had been forced to reservations. They were followed by Anglo-American cattle raisers, who began entering the region after the middle of the 1870s to establish huge ranches. The area around what became Tascosa had been a center of human activity for centuries, for it was an easy crossing point on the Canadian River, with several creeks flowing into it from the north and a broad meadow four miles wide on the south. One of the creeks on the north was named Atascosa, the Spanish word for "boggy," and later the name was shortened to Tascosa by the Anglos.

Although New Mexican sheep herders had already moved into the Atascosa valley, the first place of business at what became Tascosa was a blacksmith shop opened by Henry Kimball in 1876. Soon others, both Mexican and Anglo, moved into the little valley, some with livestock and others with merchandise or tools to open stores or other enterprises.

In 1880 the western Panhandle gained sufficient population that it was legally able to organize as a separate county. An election among local citizens approved the plan, and in a subsequent vote on 8 December 1880 Tascosa, the only town in Oldham County, was chosen as its seat of government. It held that distinction for thirty-five years. Eventually a fine two-story stone courthouse was constructed at the taxpayers' expense to house the courtrooms, offices, and records of the county.

Tascosa thrived through the late 1870s and early 1880s. At one time boasting well over three hundred residents, it had such businesses as the *Tascosa Pioneer* newspaper, numerous saloons, a barbershop, livery stables, several hotels, a public school, Catholic church, post office, millinery shop, jewelry store, drugstore, blacksmith shop, several large general merchandise stores, and a surveyor's office.

The town had its share of violence during the days of the big ranches. One of its three cemeteries was known as "boot hill" because its twenty-two occupants had all lost their lives violently. Among the badmen known to have frequented the community were William Bonney, known to most as Billy the Kid, Dave Rudabaugh, and Sostones L'Archeveque.

The decline of Tascosa began when the Fort Worth and Denver Railroad built past the town on the opposite side of the Canadian River in 1887. Within a matter of years other railways crisscrossed the Texas Panhandle, all of them bypassing the old community. Within a decade Tascosa became a ghost of its former self, with only the county seat seemingly keeping it alive. Resident after resident left for more promising locations like Amarillo, Dalhart, and Channing, all places with rail connections. Even the newspaper left in 1891. The deathblow came in 1908 when the Rock Island Railroad constructed a line westward from Amarillo through southern Oldham County, establishing along its route a series of towns in what became agricultural territory. As early as 1911 one of these new communities, Vega, challenged the right of Tascosa to remain the seat of the county. Vega lost the balloting but tried again in 1915 and won. Oral traditions state that Tascosa had only fifteen inhabitants at the time of the second vote. A handful of old-timers and hangers-on remained at Tascosa for the next few years, but in 1939 the last resident departed.

In the same year Tascosa was reborn in a com-

Cowboys enjoying drinks and each other's company in a Tascosa saloon. Courtesy Panhandle-Plains Historical Museum, Canyon, Texas.

Tascosa at the beginning of the twentieth century, showing the adobe schoolhouse in the foreground and the two-story stone courthouse behind it, both of them still standing at the site in 1985. Courtesy Panhandle-Plains Historical Museum, Canyon, Texas.

pletely different form. In March of that year Julian L. Bivins, the owner of the land around and encompassing the abandoned town, donated 120 acres and the old rock courthouse to become the site of a home for boys founded by Cal Farley. Beginning with half a dozen boys, it has grown over the years into a major facility consisting of residence halls for approximately four hundred boys, a school, dining hall, chapel, athletic fields, operating farm and ranch, and homes for staff. Cal Farley's Boys Ranch, on the very site of Tascosa, now has more people than the old town probably ever had. Surviving from the former days are the stone courthouse, now open to the public as a historical museum, and the 1889 schoolhouse, which in recent years has served as a polling place.

LOCATION: *Tascosa, now the site of Cal Farley's Boys Ranch, is located at the east end of Texas Highway Spur 233 about 0.6 mile off U.S. Highway 385 approximately 12 miles south of Channing and 24 miles north of Vega.*

Terlingua

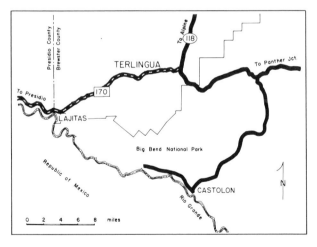

Whenever the topic of abandoned towns in Texas comes up in conversation, someone always mentions Terlingua—the most famous ghost town in the state.

"Terlingua" actually refers to a mining district. The name is taken from the two Spanish words, *tres* and *lenguas*, meaning "three tongues."

Whether this refers to the three languages of the area, Indian, Spanish, and English, or to the three forks of Terlingua Creek is debated among Texas etymologists, but long before the discovery of quicksilver in the area in the 1880s Terlingua meant a small Mexican village on a creek near the Rio Grande which bore that name. After the discovery of minerals upstream on the creek, the old community came to be known as Terlingua Abaja, or lower Terlingua.

The earliest commercial production of quicksilver, or mercury, in the Terlingua area came in the 1880s, with primitive mining and refining being conducted through the decade of the 1890s. The laborers were all Mexicans who crossed the Rio Grande to work under Anglo-American supervision at the mines. Using burro-drawn carts they hauled the cinnabar ore from surface outcrops and slight excavations to collecting points where it was hand sorted. Then men placed the ore in retorts, especially designed furnaces, where it was heated to high temperatures. As the ore heated, the mercury vaporized, rising to the top of the retort, where it condensed into its liquid form. The initial ores at Terlingua were so rich that only a simple furnace was needed to produce quicksilver in commercially salable amounts.

By the turn of the century the richest surface deposits had been exploited, so the workers were forced to begin excavating to find ore in the needed quantities. Using only such hand tools as shovels, picks, hand drills, and sledge hammers, they dug shafts into the ground as they followed slender "stringers" of bright red cinnabar toward hoped-for concentrations of ore. By 1902 these excavations had reached about eighty feet deep, but in the decades to come the shafts reached ten times that depth. During the early years the Mexican laborers often were required to bring the ore to the surface in rawhide buckets strapped to their backs as they climbed notched wooden poles that served as their "ladders."

The major development of the Terlingua mining district began in 1903, when Howard E. Perry incorporated the Chisos Mining Company. Several years before he had acquired some large acreages in the Big Bend country which happened to include some of the most valuable mineral-bearing areas of the quicksilver district. His Chisos Mine became the largest enterprise in the Terlingua district, at one time becoming the largest quicksilver

Collapsed headframe at the shaft leading to one of the Terlingua quicksilver mines. Photograph by the author, 1975.

Mine owner Howard E. Perry's now vacant home on a prominence overlooking Terlingua. Photograph by the author, 1975.

Hulk of a mid-1930s automobile where it was abandoned years ago at Terlingua. Photograph by the author, 1982.

producer in the entire United States. The name "Chisos" became virtually synonymous with "Terlingua." Of the several mining camps that came into being in the district, the one around the Chisos Mine became the largest. For a number of years it boasted having over a thousand inhabitants, most of them Mexican.

The Chisos Mining Company did more than excavate cinnabar and refine it into quicksilver. It owned and operated the entire town of Terlingua. The company ran a large general store, the Chisos Store, as well as operating a post office, a simple water system, and the Chisos Hotel, not to mention in later years a gasoline filling station, a motion picture theater, and even a confectionary shop. Though the miners received minimal wages, they were permitted to live in simple adobe and stone "company housing" at no cost.

Terlingua was divided into two parts, the "Mexican side" east of the Chisos Store and the "Anglo side" north and west of the store complex. Overlooking all the camp was the mansion built by mine owner Howard Perry in 1906. Hav-

ing returned from a trip to Spain to view the quicksilver mines at Almadén, he was intrigued by the Spanish and Moorish architecture that he had seen. Thus when he built his home on a prominence above the town, it represented his own version of these combined architectural styles. Originally only one story, after 1911 it was enlarged into a two-story nine-bedroom structure with a ninety-foot front porch. Although Perry only rarely visited his mine, the home stood waiting for his arrival at all times as a symbol of his power as the owner of the whole town.

Housing for the Anglo-American workers at Terlingua began on a fairly primitive level but improved with the passage of time. Shelter might be as simple as a tent erected on a level spot, but often it took the form of wooden plank walls and floors with a tent roof. Many employees added chicken wire suspended above the tent roofs into which they placed sotol leaves as a sun shade. In time adobe and stone houses replaced the "permanent tents."

The majority of the workers at Terlingua were

Mexican. They occupied adobe and rock huts east of the company store, many of which in the course of years were built into comfortable homes complete with flower beds and electric lights. Mine owner Perry sought to secure the greatest level of productivity at the least cost, so he paid his Mexican laborers the lowest possible wages, usually around a dollar a day. The men received their money in Mexican pesos, most of which were spent in the company store.

The most popular entertainment for the miners at Terlingua took the form of dances. Like almost everything else in the town, they were scheduled to fit the industrial needs of the company. The men worked in three eight-hour shifts which alternated every two weeks, leaving an evening without work every second Saturday. Usually sometime between sundown and dark on these evenings, one could see processions of señoritas with older women as chaperones as they filed toward a large corrugated metal dance hall. The older ladies kept the girls under their vigil throughout the evening, as the dances were conducted with extreme decorum and formality. The processions to the hall were events of rare beauty in the dusty village, as the lines of girls in their best dresses wound their way among the little adobe houses on the east side of town.

Beginning in various parts of Terlingua, the processions arrived at the hall about the same time. After the girls had seated themselves on benches around the dance floor, the boys came in to choose the one with whom they wanted to dance first. They stood in front of the girls until the latter either accepted or rejected them. The boys who were refused then moved on to other girls until all the dancers were paired. Then the affair was ready to start. The same couples danced through the first set of three or four selections, and then the boy by custom had to dance with a different girl for the next set, though he could return to his favorite for the third. Local Mexican bands provided the music for the Terlingua dances. They usually consisted of two or three guitars, several violins, and sometimes an added trumpet or saxophone. The music was almost all Mexican, with a few popular American pieces added for variety.

Terlingua remained alive even after the Chisos Mine closed in 1942, still having about 350 people as recently as 1947. In time, however, the popula-

tion dwindled to only a handful. After having fallen vacant, the Chisos Store today again has merchandise on its shelves, though certainly not comparable to its stock when it claimed to be "the biggest store between Del Rio and El Paso," and it houses the office of an excursion company that operates float trips on the nearby Rio Grande. A number of the old employees' houses have been repaired and reoccupied by individuals who have moved to the old camp for its peace and quiet.

LOCATION: *Terlingua is located just north of Farm to Market Road 170 approximately 3.8 miles west of its intersection with State Highway 118 in Brewster County. Extreme care should be taken by anyone looking around the remains of the former mining camp because of the presence of numerous unprotected open mine shafts, many of them hundreds of feet deep. Children and pets should never be left unattended.*

Texon

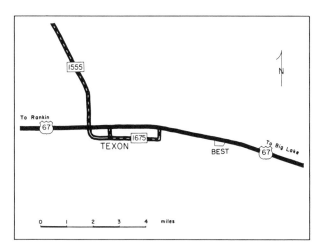

Texon sprang up as a company town to house workers employed by the Big Lake Oil Company soon after the discovery of petroleum on University of Texas lands at the Santa Rita No. 1 well in Reagan County. When the well blew in on 28 May 1923, the site had only two wooden shacks and the drilling rig, but within a year it had become a booming oil field community with hundreds of residents.

The Big Lake Oil Company owned Texon entirely. The company erected all the houses, stores, school buildings—everything. By 1930 it pro-

The Santa Rita No. 1 oil well, which still employs historic pumping equipment at Texon. Photograph by the author, 1982.

Streets, street signs, and concrete sidewalks still marking the town of Texon though most of its residences disappeared two decades ago. Photograph by the author, 1982.

vided housing and necessities for a thousand inhabitants, all of them either employees or dependents at Texon. It had scores of houses, paved streets, avenues of planted elm trees, waterworks, a hospital, union church with Sunday school, boy scout troop, ladies' study club, swimming pool, golf course, restaurant, grocery store, drugstore, and library, and all of this in its first decade and a half. Even when a boy scout meeting place was erected by volunteer labor in 1937, the company provided the "logs" from which it was built in the form of utility poles from its nearby tank farm.

Texon thrived from the 1920s through the 1940s, though its population had declined to about 750 by the end of World War II. As oil production from the field diminished, Texon residents either were moved by the company to other jobs or lost their employment. By the late 1950s the town was fading, and in 1962 the company sold its operations, and most of the structures in the former community were either moved or razed so that their building materials might be reused elsewhere.

Today Texon, formerly home for a thousand people, has only about a dozen occupied dwellings. The site is littered with the debris and foundations from former buildings, and its streets and yards are choked with weeds, but the now dead elm trees and painted metal street signs still stand above the desolation.

LOCATION: *Texon is located about 0.5 mile south of U.S. Highway 67 on Farm to Market Road 1675 approximately 13.5 miles west of Big Lake. Most of the town stood on the south side of the Santa Fe Railway tracks, but on the north side beneath a steel derrick one can view the Santa Rita No. 1 discovery well for the Big Lake Oil Field.*

View along the unpaved main street of The Grove. Photograph by the author, 1984.

The hand-dug public well in the center of the main street in The Grove. Photograph by the author, 1984.

The Grove

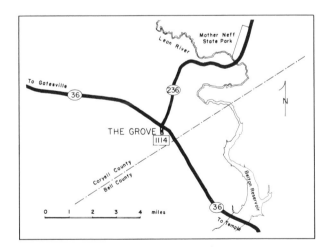

In an area settled by Anglo-Americans in the late 1850s, The Grove began as a town when its immediate area was occupied by Wends coming from Lee County in the early 1870s. Ethnically these people were representatives of the westernmost Slavs in Europe, coming originally from a region now part of East Germany. They settled first at Serbin in Lee County in 1854, and several groups later sought land elsewhere in the state. The Grove was one of these places.

The community takes its name from the trees which stood at the site when the first settlers arrived. It had sufficient population by 1874 to receive a post office, and by 1880 it had a reported three general stores, a drugstore, two barbershops, a physician, dentist, Lutheran church, school, undertaker, lumberyard, cafe, and confectionary shop. In 1890 it numbered 105 residents.

The Grove had an economy based primarily on farming and stock raising, and it maintained a fairly stable population until the 1940s, when it began to dwindle. The main reasons for the decline were its being bypassed by the new highway connecting Gatesville with Temple, improvement in rural roads in general, and the consolidation of agriculture. Today it consists of about fifteen occupied dwellings, eight or ten abandoned residences, a beautifully restored row of commercial buildings consisting of general store, post office, cafe, and blacksmith shop, the active St. Paul

Lutheran Church, and numerous sites of former buildings marked by ruins, foundations, and wells.

LOCATION: *The Grove stands on Farm to Market Road 1114 about 0.2 mile south of Texas Highway 36 near its intersection with Texas Highway 236 in Coryell County. Five miles north is the beautiful Mother Neff State Park, the oldest state park in Texas.*

Thurber

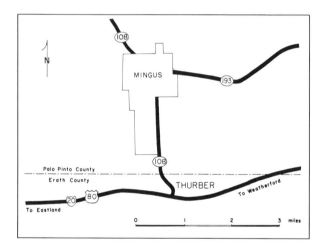

For half a century Thurber was an incongruous and unexpected industrial city surrounded by farm and ranch country seventy miles west of Fort Worth. At its peak of population it numbered ten thousand inhabitants, making it in its day the largest city between Fort Worth and El Paso.

Coal was the economic base for Thurber, as the town lay on top of the only known bituminous coal reserves in lignite-rich Texas. William Whipple Johnson, an engineer for the Texas and Pacific Railway, discovered the deposits in the mid-1880s. After purchasing several thousand acres encompassing most of the underground mineral, he resigned from the railroad and in 1886 initiated large-scale mining at the site. Encountering agitation by the Knights of Labor among his employees, he closed the mines in 1888 rather than concede to his workers' strike demands. In November of that year he sold the property to three Eastern investors who formed the Texas and Pacific Coal Company specifically to purchase and operate the Johnson mines.

With the miners still on strike, the new company fenced part of their property and began constructing a complete town and mining complex. The strikers outside the newly erected barbed wire fence watched as an entire town was built, though it had virtually no inhabitants. Thurber came to have over two hundred dwellings, mercantile stores, waterworks, churches, schools, offices, stables, and later an opera house seating over six hundred fifty people, a fifteen-teacher high school, dairy, meat market, two-hundred-room hotel, ice and electric plant, the only library in the county, and two saloons, the "Snake" and the "Lizard." In time the labor unrest was settled, and the miners and their families moved into the town.

All mining at Thurber was underground, with

Thurber as it appeared about 1910. Courtesy Texas and Pacific Oil Company, Dallas, Texas.

Two Thurber miners with mules that were used to draw the coal-filled cars inside the mines. Courtesy Southwest Collection, Texas Tech University, Lubbock, Texas.

Italian miners at Thurber relaxing on a holiday. Courtesy Joe Martin.

Underground in the Thurber coal mines. Courtesy Southwest Collection, Texas Tech University, Lubbock, Texas.

fifteen different shafts used at one time or another. By the mid-1890s between a thousand and fifteen hundred men worked for the company and they produced between fifteen hundred and two thousand tons of coal each day. In 1897 another industry came to the town with the construction of a large brick kiln which used clay also found on company property. Its principal product was paving brick, but the kiln also made construction brick and related goods.

The greatest economic boom at Thurber came after oil was discovered on company lands near Ranger in 1917. For a while the population rose to over ten thousand residents with the addition of oil field employees and their families for whom new housing was built. The oil discovery coupled with those elsewhere, however, indirectly caused the demise of Thurber. By 1917 most railroads were converting from coal to oil as fuel for their

steam locomotives. Since the railways constituted the most important market for Thurber's bituminous coal, this change struck at its industrial heart. When the miners went on strike for higher wages in 1920, the company was unable to meet their demands and the next year closed the mines. With the abandonment of mining, the company began systematically selling or scrapping many of the homes and buildings in the town. Another transportation change sealed the fate of Thurber, for the demand for paving brick diminished with increasing use of concrete and asphalt. Consequently the brick kilns ceased operating in 1933, leaving the town with neither of its industries. In 1933 the company closed the last mercantile store, removed most of the remaining housing, and in 1936–37 razed the brick kiln.

About 1939 an automobile with Arizona license tags drove up to the last place of business in

The once famous horseshoe-shaped bar serving Thurber. Courtesy Southwest Collection, Texas Tech University, Lubbock, Texas.

Thurber, a filling station, and the couple inside looked around in amazement. "What in the world has happened? . . . Where are all the houses?" the lady asked the attendant. "You been here before?" he replied. Holding her tears back with a handkerchief, she said, "We were married here in 1901. . . . This is our first trip back."

Today Thurber consists of acres of foundations from its former buildings, a handful of surviving company structures, one of which houses a restaurant, and the dominating smokestack from the 1908 ice and electric plant. The site is listed in the National Register of Historic Places.

LOCATION: *Thurber is bisected by Interstate Highway 20/U.S. Highway 80 in northwestern Erath County at its intersection with Texas Highway 108 about 14 miles east of Eastland and 35 miles west of Weatherford.*

Whon

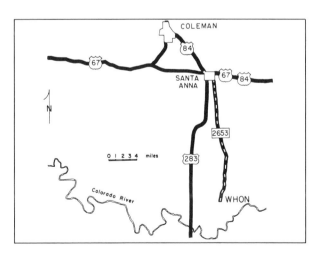

Whon, in extreme southern Coleman County, takes its name from a Mexican laborer who worked for Mr. and Mrs. Sam McCain at their

Ruins of the McCain family dugout home at Whon. Photograph by the author, 1984.

Abandoned commercial building at the center of Whon. Photograph by the author, 1984.

ranch in what became the town. The McCain family had moved to the area in 1903, purchasing a half section of land along Camp Creek from Mrs. Wagie Cooper. Mrs. McCain later recalled, "I wanted to make some money and so I decided to petition for a post office."

When Mrs. McCain as the potential postmistress sent the papers to Washington requesting a post office, a Mexican employee named Juan was working for her. She later recalled, "I thought that would be a good name for the post office. I didn't know how to spell Juan so I spelled Whon, which was the way it sounded to me." Ever since that time the town has been known by the name of the Mexican ranch hand.

As the big cattle ranches in the area were being broken up and parceled out to farmers in the 1910s and 1920s, the population of Whon grew considerably. By the twenties the town consisted of a cotton gin, a barbershop, two combined filling station/stores, a grocery store, a laundry, and a public school. The town had both Baptist and Nazarene churches, a teacherage providing accommodation for schoolteachers, and eight to ten other occupied dwellings. Coupled with those on outlying farms, the community had forty to fifty families. One hundred fifty to one hundred sixty children regularly attended classes in the Whon school, located a short distance south of the town. The schoolhouse was heated by wood-burning stoves and had water from a cistern for drinking purposes.

During the 1920s and national prohibition, the remote country along the Colorado River south of Whon became a favored retreat for local bootleggers. One of the last residents of the town related that "there used to be lots of whisky made here," and that once in a while the revenue agents "would come around, but not too often." Whon remained isolated for many years, the first paved road reaching the community in 1967.

The Whon cemetery was established by rancher Sam McCain in 1905 after the death of his one-year-old daughter, Lillian Ruth, who drowned in a stock tank. Since the community had no graveyard, McCain donated the land and started the cemetery with the burial of his own daughter. Her tombstone to this day states that the land was dedicated "to all that follow."

The community declined with the demise of small-scale intensive cotton farming in Coleman County. This regression started in the 1930s and today is virtually complete, leaving Whon a well-preserved ghost. Today only two residents remain from the scores of people who once inhabited Whon. Visitors to the townsite find the still operating Whon post office, located in a former filling station, where patrons mail letters simply by placing them through a slot cut in the wooden wall of the building. Surviving structures from the old town include three abandoned residences, the now quiet teacherage, one last empty commercial building, one occupied dwelling, and the remains of the McCain family's stone-front dugout.

LOCATION: *Whon is located in southern Coleman County 15 miles south of Santa Anna at the extreme end of pavement on Farm to Market Road 2653. To reach the Whon cemetery, drive 0.3 mile west from the post office and then 0.4 mile north on a gravel road. The gravel road is not recommended after wet weather.*

Williams Ranch

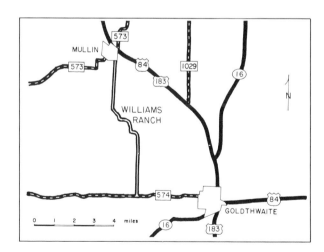

John Williams, a Tennessean who had lived in Missouri, founded a settlement at Williams Ranch when he located there about 1855. He was passing through the country and camped overnight beside a beautiful spring on Mullin Creek. He became so impressed with the qualities of the area that he stayed there to establish a ranch centered

Furniture and luggage deteriorating in the elements beside a demolished home at Williams Ranch. Photograph by the author, 1984.

on the springs. Within a decade a flourishing community had grown up around Williams's initial ranch. In the 1860s it consisted of numerous homes, several saloons, a general store, the Florida Hotel, livery stable, school, blacksmith shop, and a stop on the stagecoach road connecting Austin with Brownwood. In a few years Williams's son constructed a stone gristmill that served a wide area. Williams Ranch beginning in 1876 was on a telegraph line erected between Austin and Fort Concho (San Angelo), the telegraph office being in the Florida Hotel. The hotel owner's nine-year-

old daughter, Hallie Hutchinson, was the first telegrapher. By the early 1880s the community boasted a population of 250 residents.

Williams Ranch declined in importance and size in part because it was missed by the railroads building through the area, the Santa Fe Railway passing within five miles in 1885. Another reason for its demise, however, was a brutal feud which broke out in its population after the Civil War. The feud pitted the old settlers against the newer arrivals. The two groups called themselves the "Honest Man's Club" and the "Trigger Mountain

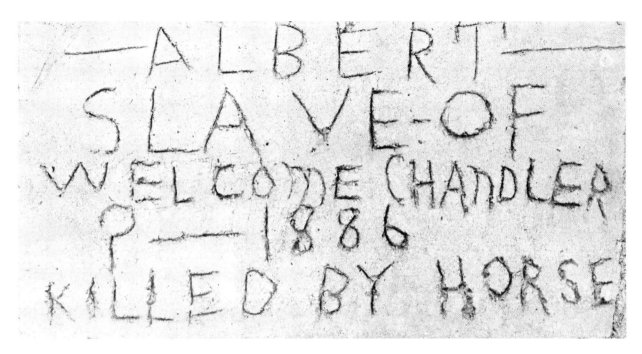

Grave marker for a former slave in the Williams Ranch cemetery. Photograph by the author, 1984.

Mob." The beginnings of the feud may have come in cattle rustling, but whatever the origins the violence ended in fence cutting and the loss of several lives. One resident later recalled, "Neither side gave the men they were after a chance to defend themselves." The violence came very near to destroying the community, which never again regained the vitality it had enjoyed prior to the vendetta.

Today Williams Ranch is composed of about half a dozen scattered rural residences, about the same number of abandoned dwellings, and ruins and foundations from several other buildings. The well-maintained cemetery contains numerous interesting grave markers over a century old.

LOCATION: *Williams Ranch is located in central Mills County and it may be reached either from Goldthwaite or Mullin. From Goldthwaite drive 4.5 miles west on Farm to Market Road 574 and thence 4.8 miles north on a graded county road to the site. From U.S. Highway 84/183 in Mullin, drive 3.8 miles south on a county road that begins opposite the intersection with Farm to Market Road 573. A historical marker for Williams Ranch stands beside the federal highway in Mullin.*

Zella

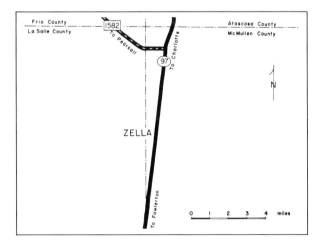

The center of a promotional scheme to sell thousands of acres of range land to farmers from Central Texas, Zella died shortly after it was born in 1913. Named for Zella Bland, a beautiful young relative of one of the town's founders, the site was developed by the Zella Townsite Company incorporated at Taylor in Williamson County. The members of the company planned to create an ag-

The 1913 Zella Hotel. Photograph by the author, 1981.

ricultural community beside the tracks of the San Antonio, Uvalde and Gulf Railroad in extreme northwestern McMullen County.

In 1912 they employed W. S. Goff to survey the perimeter of their proposed colony and in 1913 hired H. L. White to lay out the townsite. It covered several hundred acres, some of them in adjoining LaSalle County, and consisted of an ambitious 189 city blocks. As part of the land promotion the founders in 1913 built the imposing two-story Zella Hotel as well as schoolhouse, railway depot, and combined general store and post office. Their plans were to construct a large irrigation system to bring water to the agricultural fields.

A number of farms and town lots were sold to farmers mainly from Williamson and surrounding counties, but many of the buyers were disappointed when they came to view the lands. They found the country semiarid and their farms too small to grow sufficient crops to make a living.

The promoters lacked the capital and equipment necessary to build the promised irrigation project, so most of the farmers abandoned their lands. The death blow came with drought in 1917. Zella, which in 1915 probably had as many as seventy-five inhabitants, quickly withered away. It remained a ranch community with stock pens and loading chutes beside the railway tracks and perhaps twenty-five residents until about 1930. Since that time virtually everyone has moved away from the townsite, leaving about half a dozen inhabitants today. The owners of the property now use it as a ranch headquarters and utilize the old hotel and a few scattered mobile homes to provide accommodation to hunters, who use it as a base of operations during deer season.

LOCATION: *Zella stands at the west side of Texas Highway 97 about 8.0 miles north of Fowlerton. Although the townsite is on private property, it and the Zella Hotel may be viewed from the highway right-of-way.*

Bibliography

Aarts, Dorothy. *Ghost Towns of the Republic of Texas*. N.p.: Sons of the Republic of Texas, [ca. 1939].

"Acme Mill Our Largest Industry: Gypsum Plant Records Long Colorful Story in Hardeman." *Quanah Tribune-Chief* (Quanah, Tex.), 1 May 1958, sec. 6, p. 8.

Adams, Alice Mary. " 'Tis Life in Shafter: There, Betimes, Big Bend Border Folk Find Their Fun at the Little Theater across Cibolo Creek." *West Texas Today* 18 (August 1937): 5, 20.

Adams, Florene Chapman. *Hopkins County and Our Heritage*. N.p.: privately printed, [ca. 1976].

Allen, Henry Easton. "The Parrilla Expedition to the Red River in 1759." *Southwestern Historical Quarterly* 43 (1939): 53–71.

Andrews County History, 1876–1878. Andrews, Tex.: Andrews County Heritage Committee, 1978.

Arrow Investment Company, Houston, Tex. *Lajitas on the Rio Grande*. Houston, Tex.: Arrow Investment Co., [ca. 1982]. Folder.

"As Boom Nears: Town Upset by Claim to Oil under It." *Dallas Morning News* (Dallas, Tex.), 26 April 1950, sec. 1, p. 1.

Babcock-Hall, Ida. "Memories of Mormon Mill." *Frontier Times* 18 (1941): 463–67.

Bailey, Clyde, and Mabel Bailey. *Vignettes of Coryell County*. Gatesville, Tex.: Gatesville Printing Company, 1976.

Baird, G. H. *A Brief History of Upshur County*. Gilmer, Tex.: Gilmer Mirror, 1946.

Baker, T. Lindsay, and Billy R. Harrison. *Adobe Walls: The History and Archeology of the 1874 Trading Post*. College Station: Texas A&M University Press, 1986.

Banks, C. Stanley. "The Mormon Migration into Texas." *Southwestern Historical Quarterly* 49 (1945): 233–44.

Banta, John. "Ghost Town Remembered: Lake Whitney Killed Kimball, Founded in 1850s." *Waco Tribune-Herald* (Waco, Tex.), 20 April 1977, sec. B, p. 1.

Barfoot, Jessie Laurie. "A History of McCulloch County, Texas." Master's thesis, University of Texas, 1937.

Bartholomew, Ed. *800 Texas Ghost Towns*. Fort Davis, Tex.: Frontier Book Publishers, 1971.

———. *The Encyclopedia of Texas Ghost Towns*. Fort Davis, Tex.: privately printed, 1982.

"Belcherville Has Peace." *Austin Statesman* (Austin, Tex.), 29 April 1954, sec. B, p. 4.

Bennett, Bob. *Kerr County, Texas, 1856–1956*. San Antonio, Tex.: Naylor Company, 1956.

Berger, Catherine. "Praha: Once Visited, Never Forgotten." In *Fayette County: Past & Present*, edited by Marjorie L. Williams, pp. 154–60. N.p.: privately printed, n.d.

Betsill, Oscar B. Interview with T. Lindsay Baker at Doole, Texas, 24 May 1984. Typescript. Doole file, Texas ghost town research files of T. Lindsay Baker.

Beverly, Bob. "Two Texas County Seats That Disappeared." *Cattleman* 37 (April 1951): 29, 78, 80.

Bierschwale, Margaret. *Fort McKavett, Texas: Post on the San Saba*. Salado, Tex.: Anson Jones Press, 1966.

Biggers, Don H. "Fort Griffin in Her Glory Days." *Frontier Times* 28 (February 1951): 129–35.

———. "Old Fort Griffin." *Frontier Times*, 27 (February 1950): 122–27.

Bowman, Bob. *This Was East Texas*. Diboll, Tex.: Angelina Free Press, 1966.

———. *The Towns We Left Behind*. Diboll, Tex.: Angelina Free Press, 1972.

Boyer, Louise. "The Story of the Old French Colony." *Frontier Times* 13 (October 1935): 47–50.

Bradshaw, Mrs. John. "History of Calf Creek Community." *Brady Standard* (Brady, Tex.), 14 May 1976, sec. V, p. 8.

Bradshaw, Noma. "The History of Calf Creek." *Junior Historian*, 12 (November 1951): 23–25, 32.

Braly, Earl Burk. "Fort Belknap on the Texas Frontier." *West Texas Historical Association Year Book* 30 (1954): 83–114.

Branda, Eldon Stephen. *The Handbook of Texas: A Supplement*. Austin: Texas State Historical Association, 1976.

Brewer, Steve. "Frontier Spirit Grips Tourists in Border Town." *Dallas Morning News* (Dallas, Tex.), 26 September 1982, sec. AA, p. 5.

———. "Texas Town Finding New Life." *Sunday Express-News* (San Antonio, Tex.), 27 June 1982, sec. G, p. 14.

Brice, Donaly Edward. "The Great Comanche Raid of 1840: Its Causes and Results." Master's thesis, Sam Houston State College, 1968.

Brockman, John Martin. "Port Sullivan, Texas: Ghost Town." Master's thesis, Texas A&M University, 1968.

Brown, John Henry. *Indian Wars and Pioneers of Texas*. Austin, Tex.: L. E. Daniell, n.d.

Buckner, Oran Silas. "History of Terry County." Master's thesis, Texas Technological College, 1943.

The Bullard Area: Its History and People, 1800–1977. [Bullard, Tex.]: Bullard Community Library Committee, [ca. 1977].

Burgess, Roger Andrew. "The History of Crosby County, Texas." Master's thesis, University of Texas, 1927.

———. "Pioneer Quaker Farmers of the South Plains." *Panhandle-Plains Historical Review* 1 (1928): 116–23.

Burke, Jan. "The Rise and Decline of Port Sullivan." *Texas Historian* 37 (November 1976): 10–15.

Burns, Nancy. *The Collapse of Small Towns on the Great Plains: A Bibliography*. Emporia State Research Studies, no. 31. Emporia, Kans.: Emporia State University, 1982.

Burton, Gerry. "Thurber Now Just Ghost of Once Thriving Town." *Lubbock Avalanche-Journal* (Lubbock, Tex.), 21 May 1978, sec. G, p. 5.

Bush, W. A. "Washington County." *State Gazette* (Austin, Tex.), 26 March 1859, p. 3.

"Calliham Drowning Town: Dam Will Destroy Community." Unidentified newspaper clipping. McMullen County, Texas, vertical file, Barker Texas History Center, University of Texas at Austin.

Carlson, Paul H. "The Discovery of Silver in West Texas." *West Texas Historical Association Year Book* 54 (1978): 55–64.

Carlson, Paul H., and Michael Stark. "Shafter Lake Boom Town Bust." *Greater Llano Estacado Southwest Heritage* 4 (Winter 1974–75): 31–33, 48.

Carmack, George, and Bonnie Carmack. "Praha Inspiring in 2 Lands." *San Antonio Express-News* (San Antonio, Tex.), 3 September 1983, sec. D, p. 1, sec. K, pp. 16–17.

———. "'Praszha Pout': Homecoming to Praha." *San Antonio Express-News* (San Antonio, Tex.), 6 April 1974, sec. C, pp. 1, 8.

———. "Shafter: Mining Town Has Few Rivals as Most Interesting Ghost Town." *San Antonio Express-News* (San Antonio, Tex.), 4 November 1978, sec. B, pp. 1, 6.

Casey, Clifford B. *Mirages, Mysteries and Reality: Brewster County, Texas, the Big Bend of the Rio Grande*. Seagraves, Tex.: Pioneer Book Publishers, 1972.

Castolon. N.p.: Big Bend Natural History Association, [ca. 1975]. Folder.

Cervin, Paul. "A History of the Famed 'Morris Ranch.'" *Radio Post* (Fredericksburg, Tex.), 26 August 1976, sec. B, pp. 1, 2, 4, 5.

Chrisman, Brutus Clay. *Early Days in Callahan County*. Baird, Tex.: privately printed, 1966.

Clarke, Ollie E. *Fort Griffin: A Brief Sketch of the Old Fort and Its Relations to the Great Southwest*. Albany, Tex.: Albany Chamber of Commerce, 1935.

Clark, Pat B. *The History of Clarksville and Old Red River County*. Dallas, Tex.: Mathis, Van Nort & Co., 1937.

Coffee, Hattie Mae. Letter, Blanco, Texas, to T. Lindsay Baker, Canyon, Texas, 3 June 1985. Autographed letter signed. "Peyton Colony" file, Texas ghost town research files of T. Lindsay Baker.

"Comyn to Build and Equip a $30,000 School Building." *Comanche Chief* (Comanche, Tex.), 6 June 1924, sec. 3, p. 1.

Conkling, Roscoe P., and Margaret B. Conkling. *The Butterfield Overland Mail, 1857–1869*. 2 vols. Glendale, Calif.: Arthur H. Clark Company, 1947.

Cox, Mike. "It's Heyday Wasn't Long-Lived." *San Angelo Standard-Times* (San Angelo, Tex.), 24 September 1967, sec. A, p. 11.

Crane, R. C. "Ghost Towns of West Texas." *West Texas Historical Association Year Book* 17 (1941): 3–10.

Crawford, Leta. *A History of Irion County, Texas*. Waco, Tex.: Texian Press, 1966.

Crouch, Carrie J. *A History of Young County, Texas*. Austin: Texas State Historical Association, 1956.

Crumbaker, Marge. "Exploring a Ghost Town." *Houston Post* (Houston, Tex.), 4 February 1968, Tempo sec., pp. 6–7.

Curtis, Sara Kay. "A History of Gillespie County, Texas, 1846–1900." Master's thesis, University of Texas, 1943.

Daggett, Marsha Lea, ed. *Pecos County History*. 2 vols. Fort Stockton, Tex.: Pecos County Historical Commission, 1984.

Davy, Dava McGahee. *The Pinery Station, Guadalupe Mountains National Park, Texas*. Carlsbad, N.Mex.: Carlsbad Caverns Natural History Association, 1979.

Day, James M. "Brown County's Fry Oil Boom, 1926–1927." *West Texas Historical Association Year Book* 50 (1974): 31–46.

Dealey, Edward M. "The Story of Old Tascosa." *Frontier Times* 4 (October 1926): 33–41.

"Death Claims T. W. Timmerman, Prominent Dallam County Citizen and Merchant of Perico: Services in Dalhart Thursday." *Dalhart Texan* (Dalhart, Tex.), 17 February 1931, pp. 1, 6.

Debo, Darrell. *Burnet County History: A Pioneer History, 1847–1979*. 2 vols. Burnet, Tex.: Burnet County Historical Commission, 1979.

DeCordova, J. *Texas: Her Resources and Her Public Men*. Philadelphia, Pa.: E. Crozet, 1858.

De Shields, James T. *Border Wars of Texas*. Edited by Matt Bradley. Tioga, Tex.: Herald Company, 1912.

Dietrich, Wilfred O. *The Blazing Story of Washington County*. N.p.: privately printed, 1950.

Dinn, R. E. ANR Pipeline Company, Detroit, Michigan, to Joe Martucci, Public Relations, [American Natural Resources Company, Detroit, Michigan], 27 February 1985. Typescript. Research Center, Panhandle-Plains Historical Museum, Canyon, Texas.

Dixon, Bobby. "Ghost Towns of the South Texas Coast." *Junior Historian* 7 (September 1946): 27–28.

[Dixon, Olive K.] *Life and Adventures of "Billy" Dixon of Adobe Walls, Texas Panhandle*. Edited by Frederick S. Barde. Guthrie, Okla.: Co-Operative Publishing Co., 1914.

Doan, C. F. "Reminiscences of the Old Trails." In *The Trail Drivers of Texas*, edited by J. Marvin Hunter, pp. 772–79. 2d ed. Nashville, Tenn.: Cokesbury Press, 1925.

Dockery, Joe. Letter, Marble Falls, Texas, to William L. Cummiford, Lubbock, Texas, 30 September 1976. Typescript. "Mormon Mill" file, Texas Historic Engineering Site Inventory, Center for the History of Engineering, Texas Tech University.

Donnell, Guy Renfro. "The History of Montague County, Texas." Master's thesis, University of Texas, 1940.

Duddlesten, Loy W. "Will 'Forgotten City' of Texas 'Come Back'?" *Houston Post-Dispatch* (Houston, Tex.), 28 June 1925, magazine sec. [p. 5].

Dugas, Vera Lee. "Texas Industry, 1860–1880." *Southwestern Historical Quarterly* 59 (1955): 151–83.

Dunn, Robert W. "The History of Loving County, Texas." Master's thesis, University of Texas, 1948.

Early-Day History of Wilbarger County. Vernon, Tex.: Vernon Times, 1933.

Early Settlers of Terry: A History of Terry County, Texas. Hereford, Tex.: Pioneer Book Publishers, 1968.

"East Texan Purchases Angelina County Town." *Dallas Morning News* (Dallas, Tex.), 29 August 1937, sec. I, p. 12.

Edwards, Bob. Interview by telephone with T. Lindsay Baker, 17 November 1982. Typescript. Research Center, Panhandle-Plains Historical Museum, Canyon, Texas.

————. Letter, Dallas, Texas, to T. Lindsay Baker, Canyon, Texas, [January 1983]. ALS. "Silver" file, Texas ghost town research files of T. Lindsay Baker.

1855–1955 Centennial of Praha Celebrated on Parish Patron Feast, August 15, 1955. N.p.: privately printed, [1955].

1854–1954 Bosquerama Centennial Celebration of Bosque County, Texas, May 4, 5, 6, 7. N.p.: privately printed, 1954.

Engel, Della Mae. "Luckenbach." *Junior Historian* 11 (March 1951): 31.

Everett, Dianna, and Philip A. Bandy. *Historical Resources of the Choke Canyon Reservoir Area in McMullen and Live Oak Counties, Texas* [and] *Historical Archaeological Resources of the Choke Canyon Reservoir Area in McMullen and Live Oak Counties, Texas.* Choke Canyon Series II. San Antonio: Center for Archaeological Research, the University of Texas at San Antonio, 1981.

Farley, Lula Mae. "Unrolls History of First Military Fort in Panhandle: Mobeetie Is First Town on High Plains." *Amarillo Sunday News and Globe* (Amarillo, Tex.), 3 March 1935, pp. 11, 14.

Farmer, Jo Ann. "Sandstone Sentinels." *West Texas Historical Association Year Book* 34 (1958): 112–27.

Farson, Duke M., and Edwin L. Harvey, eds. *The Joy-Bells of Canan, or Burning Bush Songs, No. 2.* Waukesha, Wis.: Metropolitan Church Association, 1905.

————, ————, Wm. T. Pattengill, and Louis F. Mitchell, eds. *The Highway and the Way, or Burning Bush Songs No. 3.* Waukesha, Wis.: Metropolitan Church Association, 1907.

————. *The New and Living Way, or Burning Bush Songs No. 5.* Waukesha, Wis.: Metropolitan Church Association, 1913.

Finney, Robert B. Letter, Phillips Petroleum Company, Bartlesville, Oklahoma, to T. Lindsay Baker, Canyon, Texas, 13 February 1985. Typescript. Research Center, Panhandle-Plains Historical Museum, Canyon, Texas.

"500 Reunite to Bid Goodbye to Doomed Area." *Dallas Morning News* (Dallas, Tex.), 11 July 1978, sec. A, p. 9.

Floyd, Willie M. "Thurber, Texas: An Abandoned Coal Field Town." Master's thesis, Southern Methodist University, 1939.

————. "Thurber, Texas, an Abandoned Coal Field Town." *Texas Geographic Magazine* 3 (Autumn 1939): 1–20.

Fohn, Joe. "Zella Open to Invited Guests and 7 Residents." *San Antonio Express-News* (San Antonio, Tex.), 29 November 1981, sec. C, p. 2.

Ford, Fred Hugo, and J. L. Brown. *Larissa.* N.p.: privately printed, [ca. 1919].

Forrest, Clint. "Two Ghosts Along the Brazos." *Junior Historian* 28 (December 1967): 7–10.

Francis, Otis. "Money Didn't Bring WASPs." *Sweetwater Reporter* (Sweetwater, Tex.), 5 August 1984, pp. 1, 7.

Freestone County Historical Commission. *History of Freestone County, Texas.* N.p.: Freestone County Texas Historical Commission, 1978.

Friend, Llerena. "Old Spanish Fort." *West Texas Historical Association Year Book* 16 (1940): 3–27.

Gaut, H. L. "Tells of Old Fort Griffin." *Frontier Times* 5 (1928): 485.

Gay, Beatrice Grady. *"Into the Setting Sun": A History of Coleman County.* N.p.: privately printed, n.d.

Geiser, Samuel Wood. "Ghost-Towns and Lost-Towns of Texas, 1840–1880." *Texas Geographic Magazine* 8 (Spring 1944): 9–20.

Gentry, Mary Jane. "Thurber, Texas: The Life and Death of a Texas Coal Town." Master's thesis, University of Texas, 1947.

"Geo. A. Kelly: Well-Known Plow Man Passes Away." *Implement and Vehicle Journal* (Dallas, Tex.) 14 (8 October 1909): 32.

George, Eugene. "Ghost Town: A Bit of History and Legend along a Byway of the Brazos." *Texas Architect* 11 (July 1960): 4–6.

"Ghosts of Panhandle Towns." *Shamrock* (Amarillo, Tex.), Spring 1962, pp. 2–5.

Ghost Towns Scrapbooks. Barker Texas History Center, University of Texas at Austin.

Gibbs, Alta Holland. "Burnet County's Forgotten Mormons: Old Mormon Mill." *Burnet Bulletin* (Burnet, Tex.), 30 June 1938, pp. 4, 5, 6.

Gilliam, Linda. "Lajitas on the River." *Texas Highways* 30 (February 1983): 30–34.

"Girl Pilots: Air Force Trains Them at Avenger Field, Texas." *Life* 15 (19 July 1943): 73–81.

Gonzales, John. "Houston Firm Colonizes Dusty Calvary [*sic*] Outpost as Resort." *Dallas Morning News* (Dallas, Tex.), 27 September 1981, sec. AA, p. 7.

Gracy, David B., II. "Selling the Future: A Biography of William Pulver Soash." *Panhandle-Plains Historical Review* 50 (1977): 1–75.

Grayson County Frontier Village. *The History of Grayson County, Texas.* 2 vols. N.p.: Grayson County Frontier Village and Hunter Publishing Company, 1979–81.

Greene, A. C. *A Personal Country.* College Station: Texas A&M University Press, 1969.

Greer, Thomas R. "Kelsey: A Southern Place of Gathering." *Liahona the Elder's Journal* (Independence, Mo.), 26 February 1910, p. 570.

Grimm, Agnes G. *Llanos Mestenas: Mustang Plains.* N.p.: privately printed, 1968.

Grothe, Randy Eli. "Silver Fever: Revival of Explorations Breathes Life into Ghost Town." *Dallas Morning News* (Dallas, Tex.), 11 February 1980, sec. A, pp. 1, 5.

Hammack, Ed. Interview with T. Lindsay Baker at Salt Flat, Texas, 18 December 1984. Typescript. Research Center, Panhandle-Plains Historical Museum, Canyon, Texas.

Hammond, W. J. "La Reunion, a French Colony in Texas." *Southwestern Social Science Quarterly* 17 (1936): 197–206.

Hamner, Laura V. *Light 'n Hitch: A Collection of Historic Writing Depicting Life on the High Plains.* Dallas, Tex.: American Guild Press, 1958.

Hardeman County Agricultural and Industrial Edition. Quanah, Tex.: Quanah Tribune-Chief, [ca. 1928].

Harlow, C. E., Jr. Letter, Van Horn, Texas, to T. Lindsay Baker, Canyon, Texas, 12 June 1985. Typescript and manuscript. "Lobo" file, Texas ghost town research files of T. Lindsay Baker.

Harris, Sallie B. *Hide Town in the Texas Panhandle: 100 Years in Wheeler County and Panhandle of Texas.* Hereford, Tex.: Pioneer Book Publishers, 1968.

Hatchett, Bill G. Interview at Hatchett Ranch, near the site of Callahan City, Texas, 27 December 1984. Typescript. Research Center, Panhandle-Plains Historical Museum, Canyon, Texas.

Havins, Thomas Robert. *Belle Plain, Texas: Ghost Town in Callahan.* Brownwood, Tex.: Brown Press, 1972.

———. *Something about Brown: A History of Brown County, Texas.* Brownwood, Tex.: Banner Printing Company, 1958.

Hayes, Robert M. "Boom Didn't Last: East Texas Town Died Because of Bad Choice." *Dallas Morning News* (Dallas, Tex.), 4 April 1951, sec. I, p. 11.

———. "Old Larissa, Once Erudite, Now Desolate." *Dallas Morning News* (Dallas, Tex.), 5 April 1936, sec. II, p. 9.

Hayes, Emma R. "The History of Polk County."

Mimeographed. 1937. Special Collections, Ralph W. Steen Library, Stephen F. Austin State University, Nacogdoches, Texas.

Heard, Robert. "Did a Texan Fly the First Airplane: In Gillespie Co." *Radio Post*, 6 May 1971, sec. 2, p. 1.

Henderson, Jeff S., ed. *100 Years in Montague County, Texas.* Saint Jo, Tex.: IPTA Printers, [1958].

Henderson, Nat. "Praha's Finest Jewel." *Austin American-Statesman* (Austin, Tex.), 3 February 1975, p. 13.

Heritage Committee of the Polk County Bicentennial Commission and the Polk County Historical Survey Committee. *A Pictorial History of Polk County, Texas (1846–1910).* N.p.: The Heritage Committee of the Polk County Bicentennial Commission and the Polk County Historical Survey Committee, 1976.

Heritage Division Committee. *Patchwork Memories: Historical Sketches of Comanche County, Texas.* Comanche, Tex.: Heritage Division of Comanche County Bicentennial Committee, 1976.

Hill, Robert T. "End of Taovaya: The Oldest Known Texas Community." *Dallas Morning News* (Dallas, Tex.), 13 February 1938, sec. II, pp. 5–6.

———. "Where Was Taovaya?" *Dallas Morning News*, 9 October 1938, sec. III, p. 11.

———. "Where was Taovaya? Article No. 2." *Dallas Morning News*, 25 September 1938, sec. II, p. 7.

———. "Where Was Taovaya? Article No. 4." *Dallas Morning News*, 27 November 1938, sec. III, p. 13.

———. "Where Was Taovaya? The Second Ravine." *Dallas Morning News*, 20 November 1938, sec. I, p. 9.

"Historic Glen Eden, Plantation Home, Rich with Romance of Pioneer Texas." *Denison Daily Herald* (Denison, Tex.), 11 June 1936, p. 5.

History of Crosby County, 1876–1977. [Crosbyton, Tex.]: Crosby County Historical Commission, 1978.

History of Polk County. Livingston, Tex.: privately printed, 1968.

Hofsommer, Don L. Letter, Plainview, Texas, to T. Lindsay Baker, Canyon, Texas, 21 January 1984. Typescript. "Longfellow" file, Texas ghost town research files of T. Lindsay Baker.

Holden, Frances Mayhugh. *Lambshead Before Interwoven: A Texas Ranch Chronicle, 1848–1878.* College Station: Texas A&M University Press, 1982.

Hughes, Eddie S. "Ghost Town Comes Alive Again." *Dallas Morning News* (Dallas, Tex.), 13 June 1965, sec. A, p. 17.

Hunter, J. Marvin. "The Glory That Was Belle Plain." *Frontier Times* 22 (1945): 271–75.

———. *The Lyman Wight Colony in Texas: Came to Bandera in 1854.* Bandera, Tex.: Frontier Times Museum, n.d.

Hutcheson, Nita Fran. "Ghost Towns of Texas." *Junior Historian* 20 (January 1960): 9–12, 20.

Indianola Scrap Book: Fiftieth Anniversary of the

Storm of August 20, 1886. Victoria, Tex.: Victoria Advocate, 1936. Reprint. Port Lavaca, Tex.: Calhoun County Historical Survey Committee, 1974.

"Industry of Vanished Town May Return to East Texas." *Houston Chronicle* (Houston, Tex.), 28 December 1941, Art Gravure sec., p. 1.

"In the Beginning: Indians, Spaniards and Bowie: Alamo Hero Survived Fight at Calf Creek." *Brady Standard* (Brady, Tex.), 14 May 1976, sec. IV, p. 1.

Irion County Historical Society. *A History of Irion County, Texas*. Mertzon, Tex.: Irion County Museum and Historical Society, 1978.

"It's Not Just the Same Old Tune for Residents of Luckenbach." *Dallas Morning News* (Dallas, Tex.), 2 December 1977, sec. A, p. 13.

Jeffreys, R. A. "Mission La Lomita (The Mission on the Little Hill): The Story of Porcion 55 and Mission, Old and New." *Mission Times* (Mission, Tex.), 7 December 1934, Silver Anniversary edition, sec. 2, pp. 1, 6, 8.

[Johnson, Andrew.] "Adobe Walls Survivor Tells about Fight: Andrew Johnson Relates Details of Indian Battle." *Amarillo Daily News* (Amarillo, Tex.), 29 June 1924, p. 10.

Johnson, Vance. "Story of How Plains Were Populated Told in Saga of Soash: 'New Eldorado' for Farmer Provided by Land Companies." *Amarillo Sunday News and Globe* (Amarillo, Tex.), 14 August 1938, sec. F, pp. 17–18.

Jones, Ernest. "Green Grow Memories of Ghost Town Fastrill." *Palestine Herald Press* (Palestine, Tex.), 2 March 1969, pp. 3, 5.

Kantor, Seth. "Ghost Town: Once-Thriving Belcherville Now Has Population of 35." *Dallas Times Herald* (Dallas, Tex.), 9 April 1961, magazine sec., pp. 6, 8, 10.

Kaufman County Historical Commission, comps. *A History of Kaufman County*. Terrell, Tex.: Kaufman County Historical Commission, 1978.

Keeler, D. B. Letter, Quanah, [Texas], to George Findlay, Chicago, Illinois, 14 December 1905. Manuscript. Findlay Land 1905 Wallet (E. 6, D. 19), Capitol Freehold Land and Investment Company Papers, Research Center, Panhandle-Plains Historical Museum, Canyon, Texas.

Keill, Sally Van Wagenen. *Those Wonderful Women in Their Flying Machines: The Unknown Heroines of World War II*. New York: Rawson, Wade Publishers, 1979.

Kemp, Mrs. Jeff T. "Bryant Station." *Frontier Times* 8 (1931): 561–70.

Kerbow, Blewett Barnes. "The Early History of Red River County, 1817–1865." Master's thesis, University of Texas, 1936.

Kinch, Sam, Jr. "Silver Mine's Future Shines." *Dallas Morning News* (Dallas, Tex.), 6 September 1981, sec. AA, p. 22.

King, Dick. "Ghost Town." *Texas Parade* 15 (September 1954): 44–46.

———. *Ghost Towns of Texas*. San Antonio, Tex.: Naylor Company, 1953.

Kirk, Wylene. "Early Post Offices and Towns in the Permian Basin Area." *Texas Permian Historical Annual* 1 (1961): 11–21.

Kowert, Nancy. "Morris Ranch: Its Place in History." *Junior Historian* 21 (March 1961): 1–6.

Kyvig, David E. "Policing the Panhandle: Fort Elliott, Texas, 1875–1890." *Red River Valley Historical Review* 1 (1974): 222–32.

Laiche, Jean. "Shafter Lake Ghost Town of Far West Texas." *Junior Historian* 9 (September 1948): 9–10.

Langford, J. O., and Fred Gipson. *Big Bend: A Homesteader's Story*. Austin: University of Texas Press, 1952.

Larson, Henrietta M., and Kenneth Wiggins Porter. *History of Humble Oil & Refining Company: A Study in Industrial Growth*. New York: Harper & Brothers, Publishers, 1959.

Lashbrook, Lash. "Praha Pauses to Remember U.S. Veterans." *Austin American-Statesman*, 14 November 1975, p. 21.

Lawrence, John. "Boom Days at Samfordyce Saw Post Office Handling Mail for Over One Hundred Thousand Souls, Pioneer Recalls; Development Thrice Halted." *McAllen Press* (McAllen, Tex.), 30 October 1934, pp. 1, 6.

Layne and Bowler Company, Houston, Texas. *Layne Water Facts*. Houston, Tex.: Layne & Bowler Co., 1914.

Ledbetter, Barbara A. Neal. *Fort Belknap Frontier Saga: Indians, Negroes and Anglo-Americans on the Texas Frontier*. Burnet, Tex.: Eakin Press, 1982.

———. *The Fort Belknap of Yesterday and Today, 1851–1963*. Newcastle, Tex.: privately printed, 1963.

———. "Negro Frontiersman Britt Johnson Carved His Niche in Young County History." *Graham News* (Graham, Tex.), 16 April 1972, sec. 4, p. 2.

———, comp. *Scrapbook of Young County*. Graham, Tex.: Graham News, 1966.

Lee, Mary Antoine. "A Historical Survey of the American Smelting and Refining Company at El Paso, 1887–1950." Master's thesis, Texas Western College, 1950.

"Legend Says Calf Creek Was Hideout of Rustlers." *Brady Standard* (Brady, Tex.), 14 May 1976, sec. V, p. 8.

Lengert, Margaret Eleanor. "The History of Milam County." Master's thesis, University of Texas, 1949.

Lewis, Willie Newbury. "The Store at Doan's Crossing." *Amarillo Sunday News and Globe* (Amarillo, Tex.), 14 August 1938, sec. F, pp. 10–11.

"Life in Panhandle Country: E. G. Hill Station." *Transmission Lines Personnel News* (Michigan-Wisconsin Pipe Line Company, Detroit, Mich.) 12 (April 1972): 8–11.

Lindig, Anne Marie. "Gillespie County's Bird-Man." *Junior Historian* 9 (March 1949): 1, 28.

Linn, John J. *Reminiscences of Fifty Years in Texas*. New York: D. & J. Sadlier & Co., 1883.

Littlejohn, Margaret. *Hot Springs: The Fountain Ponce de Leon Failed to Find*. N.p.: Big Bend Natural History Association, [ca. 1980].

"Lobo Is Making a County Seat Fight." *El Paso Herald* (El Paso, Tex.), 15 April 1911, p. 7.

Loenthal, M. L. "Map of Doans City." 1888. Photocopy. Grover C. Ramsey Papers, University of Texas Archives.

Lofton, Monk. "Mentone Center of Least Densely Populated County in Entire State." *El Paso Times* (El Paso, Tex.), 4 July 1965, magazine sec., p. 2.

"Los Ojuelos: This Ghost Town, Though Located on Private Property, Is Easy to See." *Laredo Times* (Laredo, Tex.), 8 November 1981, sec. HH, p. 2.

Lotto, F. *Fayette County: Her History and Her People*. Schulenberg, Tex.: privately printed, 1902.

"Loyal Valley Has Its Ups and Downs." *Mason County News* (Mason, Tex.), 19 June 1958, unpaged.

"Luckenbach, Texas: Where They Say the Livin' Is Easy." *Fredericksburg Standard* (Fredericksburg, Tex.), 7 April 1982, p. 39.

Lutz, Eusibia. "Almost Utopia." *Southwest Review* 14 (1929): 321–30.

McCarty, John L. *Maverick Town: The Story of Old Tascosa*. Norman: University of Oklahoma Press, 1946.

McConal, Jon. "Chalk Mountain: If You Blink Your Eyes, You'll Miss Lodge No. 894. But, Even If You See It, You'll Probably Think It's Not Used Anymore." *Fort Worth Star-Telegram* (Fort Worth, Tex.), 25 March 1978, sec. C, p. 1.

McConnell, H. H. *Five Years a Cavalryman; or, Sketches of Regular Army Life on the Texas Frontier, Twenty Odd Years Ago*. Jacksboro, Tex.: J. N. Rogers & Co., Printers, 1889.

McCormick, Robert V., and William Hinds. "Three Frontiers." *Venture, American Natural Resources System* (Detroit, Mich.) 5 (Summer 1979): 2–7.

McCoy, Patricia R. "Pickering Lumber Company Harvested Shelby's Piney Woods." *East Texas Light* (Tenaha, Tex.), 25 July 1979, sec. C, pp. 1–2.

———. *Shelby County Sampler*. Lufkin, Tex.: Lufkin Printing Company, 1982.

McDearmon, Ray. *Without the Shedding of Blood: The Story of Dr. U. D. Ezell and of Pioneer Life at Old Kimball*. San Antonio, Tex.: Naylor Company, 1953.

[McGregor, Stuart.] "Texas Towns of Historic Interest That Have Been Abandoned or Remain Small Towns Today: 'Ghost' Towns and 'Lost' Towns." In *The Texas Almanac and State Industrial Guide*, pp. 119–24. Dallas, Tex.: A. H. Belo Corporation, 1936.

McGuffin, Ray. "Range Canning Labels." *Relics* (Austin, Tex.) 3 (August 1969): 8–10.

McKenzie, H. J. Letter, Tyler, Texas, to T. Lindsay Baker, Canyon, Texas, 2 January 1984. Typescript. "Pecos River Bridge" file, Texas historic engineering sites research files of T. Lindsay Baker.

McLemore, David. "Army Fort Restorers Focus on Authenticity." *Dallas Morning News* (Dallas, Tex.), 26 June 1983, sec. A, pp. 41–42.

McMillon, Randall. "Vanished Towns of the Rio Grande Valley." *Junior Historian* 15 (May 1955): 3, 21.

Madison, Virginia, and Hallie Stilwell. *How Come It's Called That? Place Names in the Big Bend Country*. Albuquerque: University of New Mexico Press, 1958.

Malsch, Brownson. *Indianola: The Mother of Western Texas*. Austin, Tex.: Shoal Creek Publishers, 1977.

Martin, Douglas. "Texas Hamlet to Be, and Not to Be, Site of a 'World's Fair.'" *Wall Street Journal*, 5 June 1975, pp. 1, 23.

Martucci, J. S. Letter, American Natural Resources Company, Detroit, Michigan, to T. Lindsay Baker, Canyon, Texas, 1 March 1985. Typescript. Research Center, Panhandle-Plains Historical Museum, Canyon, Texas.

Mason County Historical Commission and Mason County Historical Society, comps. *Mason County Historical Book*. Mason, Tex.: Mason County Historical Commission and Mason County Historical Society, 1976.

Mauldin, William David. "History of Dallam County, Texas." Master's thesis, University of Texas, 1938.

"The Max Hirsch Story." *Radio Post*, 26 August 1976, sec. B, p. 6; sec. C, pp. 4, 5, 8, 10.

The Members of Mt. Horeb Baptist Church. N.p.: Mt. Horeb Baptist Church, 1974.

Memories: Brown County 1856–1956 Official Centennial Program. Brownwood, Tex.: Brown County Centennial Association, 1956.

"Mission Built in 1845 Restored by Hidalgo Catholics: La Lomita Scene of Early Struggles on Rio Grande." *Mission Times*, 4 December 1936, sec. 4, p. 5.

Monde, Bennet B. "A History of Avenger Field, Texas." Master's thesis, Hardin-Simmons University, Abilene, Texas, 1980.

Montgomery, Cora. *Eagle Pass; or, Life on the Border*. New York: George P. Putnam & Co., 1852.

"Monument Erected to Trail Drivers: Doan's Store Was Important Trading Post in Heyday of Trail Driving." *Cattleman* 18 (December 1931): 9, 11.

Moore, Francis, Jr. *Map and Description of Texas, Containing Sketches of Its History, Geology, Geography and Statistics*. Philadelphia, Pa.: H. Tanner, Jr.; New York: Tanner & Disturnell, 1840. Reprint. Waco, Tex.: Texian Press, 1965.

Morgan, Ruth Edwards. "A History of Cuthbert, Mitchell County, Texas." In *Lore and Legend: A Compilation of Documents Depicting the History of Colorado City and Mitchell County*, pp. 213–15. Colorado City, Tex.: privately printed, 1976.

"Morris Ranch Holds Unique Place in History of Texas and Gillespie County." *Fredericksburg Standard* (Fredericksburg, Tex.), 28 April 1971, sec. 5, pp. 1, 8.

Moss, Mrs. J. S. "The City of Kent." *Frontier Times* 4 (May 1927): 33–35.

Neal, Bill. *The Last Frontier: The Story of Hardeman County*. Quanah, Tex.: Quanah Tribune-Chief, 1966.

Nelson, Anne. "Preston Bend, Once the Heart of Grayson County." *Junior Historian* 26 (May 1966): 30–31.

Neville, Maude. "A Texas Ghost City." *Texas Parade* 3 (June 1938): 8–9, 24–25.

"Oil History in Lower Rio Grande Valley Began with Fordyce Discovery Well Completed near Mission in October, 1934: Fordyce Celebrates Fourth Anniversary in October of 1938." *Mission Times* (Mission, Tex.), 13 January 1938, sec. 3, p. 6.

Panorama of Nocona's Trade Area. Saint Jo, Tex.: Nocona's Bicentennial '76 Committee, 1976.

Parker, Richard Denny. *Historical Recollections of Robertson County, Texas, with Biographical & Genealogical Notes on the Pioneers & Their Families*. Edited by Nona Clement Parker. Salado, Tex.: Anson Jones Press, 1955.

Pate, J'Nell. "The Battles of Adobe Walls." *Great Plains Journal* 16 (1976): 2–44.

Patterson, Becky Crouch. *Hondo: My Father*. Austin, Tex.: Shoal Creek Publishers, 1979.

Peavey, John R. *Echoes from the Rio Grande 1905 to Now*. N.p.: privately printed, 1963.

"Perico Is Wonderful Farming and Cattle Raising Territory." *Dalhart Texan* (Dalhart, Tex.), September 1931, Special Dallam and Hartley Counties edition, unpaged.

Perkins, William Coy. "A History of Wheeler County, Texas." Master's thesis, University of Texas, 1938.

Picquet, Jimmie Ruth. "Some Ghost Towns in South Texas." Master's thesis, Texas A&I University, 1972.

Pirtle, Caleb, III. "Ghost Town Visit: Treasure Hunt Disturbs Kimball." *Fort Worth Star-Telegram* (Fort Worth, Tex.), 11 February 1965, sec. 2, p. 3.

————. "Time Hasn't Found Lajitas." *Dallas Times Herald* (Dallas, Tex.), 30 May 1982, Westward Supplement, p. 20.

Polk, Stella Gipson. *Mason and Mason County: A History*. Austin, Tex.: Pemberton Press, 1966.

Pool, William C. *Bosque County, Texas*. San Marcos, Tex.: San Marcos Record Press, 1954.

Posey, James Bennett. "A History of Cherokee County." Master's thesis, University of Texas, 1928.

Price, T. A. "Busy Thurber's Career Ends as Ghost City: Homes Crumbling after Coal, Oil Firm Moves Headquarters." *Dallas Morning News* (Dallas, Tex.), 28 May 1939, sec. I, p. 6.

Pritchett, Jewell G. *A Narrative History of Coke County: From the Top of Old Hayrick*. N.p.: privately printed, 1979.

Program Sixty-Second Doans Annual May Picnic May 4th, 1946, Watts Grove on Red River, Founded May 1, 1884, by Residents of Doans Crossing. N.p.: privately printed, 1946. Folder.

"Progress of the Iron Industry in Texas." *Engineering and Mining Journal* 25 (1878): 135.

Ragsdale, Kenneth Baxter. *Quicksilver: Terlingua and the Chisos Mining Company*. College Station: Texas A&M University Press, 1976.

Ramsey, Grover Cleveland. Papers. University of Texas Archives.

The Reagan County Story: A History of Reagan County, Texas. Seagraves, Tex.: Pioneer Book Publishers, 1974.

Rister, Carl Coke. *Fort Griffin on the Texas Frontier*. Norman: University of Oklahoma Press, 1956.

Roach, Hattie Joplin. *The Hills of Cherokee*. N.p.: privately printed, 1952.

Roberts, Dick. "Beautiful Belle Plain." *Texas Highways* 24 (November 1977): 26–29.

Roberts, Wilma. "Sherwood's Homecoming Draws About 250 Persons." *San Angelo Standard-Times* (San Angelo, Tex.), 12 June 1973, sec. A, pp. 5, 8.

Rogers, John William. *The Lusty Texans of Dallas*. New York: E. P. Dutton and Company, 1951.

Roots in Young County. N.p.: Young County Historical Commission, 1978.

Rutherford, Alline, and Tom Rutherford. Interview with T. Lindsay Baker at Whon, Texas, 24 May 1984. Typescript. Research Center, Panhandle-Plains Historical Museum, Canyon, Texas.

St. Clair, Gladys Annelle. "A History of Hopkins County, Texas." Master's thesis, University of Texas, 1940.

Schmidt, Charles F. *History of Washington County*. San Antonio, Tex.: Naylor Company, 1949.

Scobee, Barry. "Silver Decline Turns Shafter, Texas, into Ghost City." *San Antonio Express* (San Antonio, Tex.), 18 October 1931, sec. 1, p. 10.

Scott, Zelma. *A History of Coryell County, Texas*. Austin: Texas State Historical Association, 1965.

Seelingson, Lelia. *A History of Indianola*. Cuero, Tex.: Cuero Record, [ca. 1931].

Sheffy, L. F. "Old Mobeetie: The Capital of the Panhandle." *West Texas Historical Association Year Book* 6 (1930): 3–16.

Simmons, Frank E. *History of Coryell County*. N.p.: Coryell County News, 1936.

"Smeltertown" vertical file. Southwest Collection, El Paso Public Library, El Paso, Texas.

Smith, Cynthia Ann. "Old Larissa." *Junior Historian* 6 (December 1945): 13–14, 16.

Smith, T. C., Jr. *From the Memories of Men*. Brownwood, Tex.: privately printed, n.d.

Smith, Tevis Clyde. *Frontier's Generation: The Pioneer History of Brown County with Sidelights on the Surrounding Territory*. Brownwood, Tex.: privately printed, 1931.

Smithwick, Noah. *The Evolution of a State; or, Recollections of Old Texas Days*. Compiled by Nanna Smithwick Donaldson. Austin, Tex.: Gammel Book Company, 1900.

Smyer, Joe Pate. "A History of McMullen County, Texas." Master's thesis, University of Texas, 1952.

Spikes, Nellie Witt, and Temple Ann Ellis. *Through the Years: A History of Crosby County, Texas*. San Antonio, Tex.: Naylor Company, 1952.

Spiller, Wayne, comp. *Handbook of McCulloch County, Volume I*. Seagraves, Tex.: Pioneer Book Publishers, 1976.

Spoede, Robert William. "William Whipple Johnson: An Enterprising Man." Master's thesis, Hardin-Simmons University, 1968.

Stambaugh, J. Lee, and Lillian J. Stambaugh. *The Lower Rio Grande Valley of Texas*. San Antonio, Tex.: Naylor Company, 1954.

Steely, Skipper. *Six Months from Tennessee*. Wolfe City, Tex.: Henington Publishing Co., 1982.

Stephenson, Malvina. "America's WASPS: Unsung Heroes of Our Air War." *Service Woman*, 14 April 1944, p. 16.

Stewards Mill Store, Freestone County, Texas, Owned and Operated by Mr. and Mrs. Frank Bragg, Route 1, Fairfield, Texas. N.p.: privately printed, [ca. 1965]. Folder.

Stewart, Charles. "The Killough Massacre." *Junior Historian* 11 (September 1950): 17–18.

Stowers, Carlton. "Hondo Crouch and His Backwoods Camelot." *Dallas Morning News* (Dallas, Tex.), 15 December 1974, magazine sec., pp. 6–8, 10, 12, 14.

Strickland, Rex W. "Establishment of 'Old' Miller County, Arkansas Territory." *Chronicles of Oklahoma* 18 (1940): 154–70.

———. "Miller County, Arkansas Territory, the Frontier That Men Forgot." *Chronicles of Oklahoma* 18 (1940): 12–34.

Sullivan, Jerry Melton. "Fort McKavett, Texas, 1852–1883." Master's thesis, Texas Tech University, 1972.

Syers, William Edward. *Off the Beaten Trail*. Waco, Tex.: Texian Press, 1971.

Taylor, I. T. *The Cavalcade of Jackson County*. San Antonio, Tex.: Naylor Company, 1938.

Taylor, Sheila. "Home, Sweet Home: Kelsey Remains Faithful to Freedom." *Dallas Morning News* (Dallas, Tex.), 4 January 1981, sec. E, pp. 1, 4.

Texas, New Birmingham as It Is, October, 1891. [New Birmingham, Tex.]: n.p., 1891.

"Texas Tech Leaves 1910 Church in West Texas Town of Mentone." *Medallion* (Austin, Tex.) 21 (September 1984): 1.

Thonhoff, Robert A. "A History of Karnes County." Master's thesis, Southwest Texas State College, 1963.

Thurman, Violet Bierman. *"Old Town" Indianola: Cattle Folks in Texas*. San Antonio, Tex.: Standard Printing Company, 1952.

Tolbert, Frank X. "A 'Lost City' on the Brazos." *Dallas Morning News* (Dallas, Tex.), 25 November 1967, sec. D, p. 1.

———. "New Birmingham: Not Even Ghost of Former Self." *Dallas Morning News*, 16 July 1962, sec. 1, p. 10.

———. "Old Fort Griffin Town Sinful Place in 1870's." *Dallas Morning News*, 25 April 1954, sec. 4, p. 1.

———. "Their Happy Home Was a Courthouse." *Dallas Morning News*, 29 May 1957, sec. III, p. 1.

———. "Tolbert's Texas: Elm Creek Raid Had Movie Climax." *Dallas Morning News*, 24 October 1964, sec. 4, p. 1.

———. "Tolbert's Texas: 40 Mexican Troops Liven up Tiny Lajitas." *Dallas Morning News*, 26 September 1982, sec. AA, p. 2.

———. "Tolbert's Texas: Steaming Temple 'Melts' out Cash." *Dallas Morning News*, 8 September 1965, sec. D, p. 1.

———. "Tolbert's Texas: Story of the City of Burning Bush." *Dallas Morning News*, 24 June 1964, sec. 4, p. 1.

Toole, Joe, and Don Gregg. "Graveyard of a Dream." *Junior Historian* 12 (December 1951): 23, 28.

"Town Being Restored as Replica of Old West." *Amarillo Sunday News-Globe* (Amarillo, Tex.), 30 November 1980, sec. B, p. 11.

"Towns Fade in West Texas, Scientists Told." *El Paso Herald Post* (El Paso, Tex.), 14 September 1956, p. 7.

Turner, Allan. "Fredericksburg or Kitty Hawk?" *Radio Post* (Fredericksburg, Tex.), 26 October 1972, sec. C, p. 10.

Turner, Thomas E. "Old Store Awarded Historical Marker." *Dallas Morning News* (Dallas, Tex.), 26 March 1965, sec. 1, p. 12.

Tyler, Ronnie C. *The Big Bend: A History of the Last Texas Frontier*. Washington, D.C.: National Park Service, 1975.

U.S. Department of Commerce. Bureau of the Census. *The Eighteenth Decennial Census of the United States: Census of Population, 1960*. Washington, D.C.: Government Printing Office, 1961.

———. *Fifteenth Census of the United States: 1930: Population*. Washington, D.C.: Government Printing Office, 1931.

———. *Fourteenth Census of the United States Taken in the Year 1920: Population*. Washington, D.C.: Government Printing Office, 1921.

———. *A Report of the Seventeenth Decennial Census of the United States: Census of Population, 1950*. Washington, D.C.: Government Printing Office, 1952.

———. *Sixteenth Census of the United States: 1940: Population*. Washington, D.C.: Government Printing Office, 1942.

———. *Thirteenth Census of the United States Taken in the Year 1910: Population*. Washington, D.C.: Government Printing Office, 1913.

U.S. Department of the Interior. Census Office. *Ninth Census of the United States: Statistics of Population*. Washington, D.C.: Government Printing Office, 1872.

———. *Population of the United States in 1860; Compiled from the Original Returns of the Eighth Census*. Washington, D.C.: Government Printing Office, 1864.

———. *Report on Population of the United States at*

the Eleventh Census: 1890. Washington, D.C.: Government Printing Office, 1895.

————. *Statistics of the Population of the United States at the Tenth Census (June 1, 1880).* Washington, D.C.: Government Printing Office, 1883.

————. *Twelfth Census of the United States Taken in the Year 1900: Population.* Washington, D.C.: Government Printing Office, 1901.

Upshaw, Larry. "Everybody's Somebody in Luckenbach." *Texas Highways* 19 (December 1972): 18–22.

Vail, Richard H. "El Paso Smelting Works." *Engineering and Mining Journal* 98 (1914): 465–68, 515–18.

Valley By-Liners. *Gift of the Rio: Story of Texas' Tropical Borderland.* Mission, Tex.: Border Kingdom Press, 1975.

————. *Rio Grande Roundup: Story of Texas Tropical Borderland.* Mission, Tex.: Border Kingdom Press, 1980.

————. *Roots by the River: A Story of Texas Tropical Borderland.* Mission, Tex.: Border Kingdom Press, 1978.

Vandygriff, James Clyde. "Kelsey, Texas: The Founding and Development of a Latter-Day Saint Gathering Place in Texas." Master's thesis, Brigham Young University, 1974.

Von Netzer, Garet. "Engel's Store Has Seen Over 100 Years of Business: Pioneer Days of Luckenbach Recounted." *Radio Post,* 29 July 1965, p. 2.

Walsh, Terry. "Church and Cemetery: College Mound Not on Map, but in the Hearts of Many." *Dallas Morning News* (Dallas, Tex.), 29 April 1957, sec. I, p. 13.

Walter, Clyde. "His Favorite Haunt." *Houston Chronicle* (Houston, Tex.), 15 February 1959, magazine sec., p. 26.

Webb, Walter Prescott, ed. *The Handbook of Texas.* 2 vols. Austin: Texas State Historical Association, 1952.

Weddle, Robert S. *The San Saba Mission: Spanish Pivot in Texas.* Austin: University of Texas Press, 1964.

Welch, Charles. "'Jumping off Place': Doan's Crossing Once Was a Teeming Gathering Place for Cattle Drives; Now It's Obscure." *Cattleman* 36 (May 1950): 18–19.

Werner, George C. Letter, Houston, Texas, to T. Lindsay Baker, Canyon, Texas, 27 December 1983. Typescript. "Pumpville" file, Texas ghost town research files of T. Lindsay Baker.

Wheat, Jim. *More Ghost Towns of Texas.* Garland, Tex.: Lost & Found, 1971.

"Where First Settlers Started County: Doans First

Community in Wilbarger County." *Vernon Daily Record* (Vernon, Tex.), 30 August 1949, sec. III, p. 4.

White, Dabney. "Oil Discovery Brings New Boom to New Birmingham." *Frontier Times* 11 (1934): 497–99.

White, James C. *The Promised Land: A History of Brown County, Texas.* Brownwood, Tex.: Brownwood Banner, 1941.

Whitmire, Jerome R. "The History of Stonewall County, Texas." Master's thesis, Texas Technological College, 1936.

Wilbarger, J. W. *Indian Depredations in Texas.* Austin, Tex.: Hutchings Printing House, 1889.

Wilkins, Charles S. "Thurber, Texas: A Sociological Study of a Company Owned Town." Master's thesis, University of Texas, 1929.

Williams, Pete. "A Capital of Yesterday: A Ghost Town Today." *Junior Historian* 6 (May 1946): 33–34.

Willis, Roysten E. "Ghost Towns of the South Plains." Master's thesis, Texas Technological College, 1941.

Wilson, Torrence Bement, Jr. "A History of Wilbarger County, Texas." Master's thesis, University of Texas, 1938.

Winfrey, Dorman H. *A History of Rusk County, Texas.* Waco, Tex.: Texian Press, 1961.

————. "New Birmingham, Texas." *Junior Historian* 3 (January 1943): 1–5.

————. "New Birmingham, Texas: Iron Queen of the Southwest." Mimeographed. Thursday Study Club, Alto, Texas, Collection, Special Collections, Ralph W. Steen Library, Stephen F. Austin State University, Nacogdoches, Texas.

Winn, W. P. Interview with T. Lindsay Baker at Sher-Han, Texas, 1 December 1984. Typescript. Research Center, Panhandle-Plains Historical Museum, Canyon, Texas.

Witte, Adolph Henry. "Spanish Fort, an Historic Wichita Site." *Bulletin of the Texas Archeological and Paleontological Society* 10 (1938): 234–44.

Woods, Otto. "Oil in the Valley, 1910." *Daily Review* (Edinburg, Tex.), 7 December 1952, unpaged.

"Work on the Brazos River." *Implement and Vehicle Journal* (Dallas, Tex.) 14 (8 August 1909): 11.

Wylie, Rosa Lee. *History of Van Horn and Culberson County, Texas.* Hereford, Tex.: Pioneer Book Publishers, 1973.

Yoakum, H. *History of Texas from Its First Settlement in 1685 to Its Annexation to the United States in 1846.* 2 vols. New York: Redfield, 1855.

Zavisch, Florine. "Historical Tour Revives Colorful Days of Past." *Pleasanton Express* (Pleasanton, Tex.), 26 October 1966, p. 8.

Index

191

196